ISIS

MANAGEMENT OF SAVAGERY

by Ambassador Abdullahi Alazreg

Translated by Bahereldeen Abdallah

DORRANCE
PUBLISHING CO
EST. 1920
PITTSBURGH, PENNSYLVANIA 15236

The contents of this work, including, but not limited to, the accuracy of events, people, and places depicted; opinions expressed; permission to use previously published materials included; and any advice given or actions advocated are solely the responsibility of the author, who assumes all liability for said work and indemnifies the publisher against any claims stemming from publication of the work.

Dorrance Publishing Co
585 Alpha Drive
Suite 103
Pittsburgh, PA 15238
Visit our website at www.dorrancebookstore.com

ISBN: 978-1-4809-3583-9
eISBN: 978-1-4809-3560-0

TABLE OF CONTENTS

INTRODUCTION

In January 1984, I began my post-graduate studies in New York through a student exchange program funded by the American government, through which students from friendly countries were offered grants. Obviously, this was a one-sided "exchange" and the name given to this program served diplomatic purposes, so as not to hurt "friendly countries' feelings" towards the United States.

I will put a charitable spin on it and say that the program was for good and humanitarian purposes, because, even though as Americans say, "There is no free lunch," since at that time the Cold War was at its tensest and the struggle between the two sides, America and Russia, was at the height of its frenzy. Nevertheless, I continue to express my gratitude to the American people, whose tax dollars funded my studies. This gratitude has left behind a certain appreciation in my heart for the American people, who are, in truth, a people overflowing with humanity and not lacking in feeling for those like us, the poor and destitute of the world. This is evidenced by the billions they spend on humanitarian causes, even though humanitarian aid organizations "eat up" most of it, as shown by Graham Hancock in his book, *Lords of Poverty*.

Thus, we must differentiate between the various administrations' practices of implementing their foreign policies and the American people themselves, who are good-hearted and know very little about the world outside of their own country. The typical American might believe that Sudan is a state in the U.S., or a part of one.

As I said, in 1984, the Cold War was at its most tense and the most obvious manifestation of this was what was occurring in Afghanistan. At that time, the United States threw its weight behind the mujahideen, supporting them with money and by facilitating the departure of volunteers from within America to fight in Afghanistan.

I remember, when I was in New York, the Maktab al-Khidamat (Afghan Services Bureau) sat facing the Al Farooq Mosque—where we used to pray—on Atlantic Avenue in Brooklyn. Muslims flocked to the Maktab al-Khidamat, filled with religious enthusiasm and zeal against what they considered the "atheistic and infidel communism" violating Muslim land in Afghanistan. They poured forth like a thundering deluge, filling Afghanistan's valleys, plains and mountains, fighting with slogans of victory or martyrdom. They were spurred on by verses from the Quran that promise a paradise as wide as the heavens and the earth to those that attain martyrdom. They were further incited by good news, more like prophecies, eloquently expressed by Abdullah Yusuf Azzam, one of their leaders, about the inevitability of not only the defeat of the Soviet Union, but also its collapse, the disintegration of its republics and rebellion by the Muslim republics against the Moscow government. In their minds, as well, was Sayyid Qutub's prophecy that foretold the end of Communism. Later, they were motivated by the strength of their belief in the miracles that they witnessed on battlefield of jihad, like the scent of musk emanating from the blood of martyrs.

Young Muslims from all Muslim countries flocked to Afghanistan, but Saudi Arabia provided the lion's share; 25,000 young men from Saudi Arabia participated in the jihad in Afghanistan. Hundreds even went from my own country, including some of my friends.

The war against the Soviet Union came to an end in 1989 with the withdrawal of Soviet troops from Afghanistan and the flight of the Afghani communist president to the United Nations building in Kabul for refuge. In 1996, however, Taliban forces were able to extract him from the building. It is said that they castrated him, dragged him through the streets and killed him.

Later, Abdullah Yusuf Azzam and Sayyid Qutub's prophecies about the Soviet Union came true. Its republics came apart helter-skelter. Analysts attribute some of the reasons for its dissolution to the exhaustion of its economy as a result of its expenditures during the war in Afghanistan.

The influx of mujahideen to Afghanistan resulted in the creation of a robust foundation for global jihad, made up of young people from all over the world. Even for those that did not go to fight, they grew to feel in their hearts a sympathy and yearning for jihad, nourished by the literature published on jihad and the stories told by their returning brothers. It was further fueled by Western adventurism in certain Muslim countries in the period following the Soviet invasion of Afghanistan, leading to a growing feeling of injustice towards the West and, from there, an overwhelming desire for rebellion against these perceived injustices.

Time passed and I was sent as a diplomat to Washington, D.C. in 1994. It was the year after the explosion at the World Trade Center in New York City, which had led to the arrest of five Sudanese men and the Blind Sheikh, the Egyptian Omar Abdel-Rahman, among others, and their being charged with the crime.

I remember that I requested permission from the ambassador, the late Ahmed Suleiman, to meet those five Sudanese men that had been arrested in their prison in New York, and he allowed me to do so. I requested a meeting with them through an official note from the embassy to the US Department of State. After some days, the latter provided us with their approval and informed us that we would meet them in prison in private. And so, my esteemed diplomat colleague, Mahmoud Youssef El-Haseen, and I travelled to New York and met them in a heavily guarded prison, a maximum, maximum security prison (note the repetition of the words). I remember that among their security measures, they put a stamp on the back of our hands. However, we could not see anything of the nature of the stamp until placing our hands in a device that shone ultraviolet light on it. At that time, I saw that the stamp was the word "Miami" written on my hand. When we exited the prison, we again placed our hands in the device, and the word "Miami" appeared on my hand. All of this, just so that the prison authorities could be sure that the person that enters "Miami" is the same one who exits "Miami". This was in spite of my purposefully trying to erase the stamp while inside the prison, to find out whether my attempts would remove it. However, it was no use; the word stayed on my hand without me being able to see it with my own eyes, except with those rays of ultraviolet light.

We met with our oppressed brothers and our visit had a positive effect on them. They were gentle young men, religious, patient and steadfast, except for one of them! His name was Siddig Ibrahim.

The four of them informed us that the fifth had betrayed them and that he would become the "state's evidence" at the trial. They offered as proof that he was separated from them and placed in the section for "rats" in the prison. When we asked what the section for "rats" was, they told us it was the section for those arrested that were "cooperating" with the government. Unfortunately, time proved them right. I still remember my discomfort with the fifth and telling my colleague how I felt that those young men were honest and that the fifth was a liar. Of course, as diplomats, among ourselves, we do not use that forbidden word—liar—in diplomacy. Diplomacy prescribes you to describe a liar as someone who "economizes in telling the truth"!

Interestingly, in its letter, the Department of State had promised us that we would meet those young men in private. Instead, we met them in a room whose four walls were glass and, on one of those walls, was a large camera that transmitted our images and voices throughout the whole meeting! This forced me to intervene during the meeting to warn them against revealing some of the details of their case and to postpone that until the trial, mentioning to them that my diplomatic immunity would protect me, but that I feared for them. This is because the most that a government can do to a diplomat, even if he committed a crime, is to declare him "persona non grata."

The time of the trial arrived and I attended some of the proceedings. It resulted in sentences of dozens of years for the four with a reduced prison sentence for the fifth, according to the reports I received, and the predictions of those prisoners came true.

In America, it is not surprising for someone who is Muslim and black to receive harsher sentences. Our black American brothers have shown the oppressive nature of the American courts towards them, even for misdemeanors. This is despite the fact that their crimes are, in general, conventional ones and that, in contrast, crimes committed by whites are typically "white-collar crimes," that cost the American economy eight times more than black crimes (see the book: *The Myth of the American Justice System*). Thus, those young men faced flagrant oppression despite their innocence, and suffered injustice even more than the Prophet Joseph, at the hand of the Pharaoh. However, the shared commonality between them and Joseph is that "then it occurred to them after they had seen the signs that they should imprison him for a time." Yes, signs that would exonerate them appeared to them, but they were not interested in anything like that. Proof of their innocence appeared to the American authorities after they arrested Ramzi Yousef, tried him and threw him in prison, but those poor young men were left in prison.

Ramzi Yousef was the mastermind and the executor of the explosion at the World Trade Center. He admitted this in prison to someone I know. This man—whom I met in Damascus in September 2001, two days after the attacks carried out by al-Qaeda—told me that Ramzi Yousef was in a cell next to his and that they would both stand in the doorways of their cells and converse with one another. He informed me that Ramzi Yousef admitted to him that he was the one behind the operation. The person who told me this was a famous Palestinian. Do not think that, in revealing this, I have divulged a secret: the Americans, themselves, revealed this and published it some years later. However, American law forbids re-trying a person for whom a verdict has already been handed down, or what is called "double jeopardy."

I said that what happened to those young men was harsher than what happened to Joseph because Joseph's innocence was proven when the plotters admitted their guilt. Then, God granted him power in the land, and he was placed over its store-houses. He was released from prison and God brought his family from the desert, placing his parents on the throne. God gave him the two gifts of being released from prison and his family coming from the desert, as the discord and hardship of the desert is similar to the discord and hardship of prison. For those friends of ours, however, their outcome was for them to remain in prison. God forgive me if my comparison of them with Joseph was out of place.

I remember that the American lawyer that volunteered to defend them was a leftist. I have always enjoyed American communists and leftists because they are people filled with chivalry and a desire to help those in the world that have been beaten down, always standing up to the arrogance of savage capitalism. I remember that he informed me by phone that the FBI had prevented him from pleading in their defense. He added that he was sure of their innocence, but that proving it in court would require hiring a lawyer with expertise, which would cost about $500,000 for each one of them. Unfortunately, at that time, the Sudanese government did not have that kind of money.

It became known that the person who got those young men entangled in this was an Arab man named Emad Salem. It became known that he was a double agent, working both for an Arab intelligence agency and the American intelligence agency and that both of these bodies wanted to implicate Sudan in a terrorism case.

As I heard, Emad Salem used to frequently visit our mission in the United Nations, claiming that he was an Islamist hostile to his country's government, that he was despised by them and kicked out of his country by its intelligence services, that he was an admirer of the Sudanese Islamist experiment and the Islamist regime in Sudan. One of these times, my colleague, Siraj al-Din Hamed, who was a diplomat in our mission there, met with him. Salem repeated these same phrases, after cursing his country's regime, and asked Siraj al-Din Hamed for a visa to enter Sudan. However, Ambassador Siraj doubted Salem's intentions, this being a characteristic of a prudent, experienced diplomat. He told Salem that the requirements for obtaining a visa for Sudan did not include feelings of love and admiration or hatred and loathing towards one side or another. He informed Salem that he would need to fill out the necessary forms, indicating all of his data, and that the consul would be the one to make the decision. He was not given a visa.

The double agent continued to frequent the mosque in New Jersey where Sheikh Omar Abdel-Rahman served as imam after he emigrated to America. This attracted a number of Muslims, especially Arabs. The double agent continued to get close and to endear himself to Sheikh Omar, until the sheikh came to trust him and Salem became his companion, guiding the blind man. The sheikh was bright, intelligent and humorous, but perhaps he ruled out that the intelligence services agencies could catch him in a New Jersey mosque. Or, perhaps, he did not care about the bad things that could befall him, like one so deeply involved in his faith that he does not care about the vicissitudes of time, repeating, "Whoever deceives us with respect to God, we are deceived for God."

I have been told that those five Sudanese men were among those that frequented Sheikh Omar's mosque. Most of them were truly and honestly religious, thus the double agent was able to use them to achieve the two intelligence agencies' goal of involving the Sudanese government in an act of terrorism. For their part, those five men were just regular young Sudanese men that did not listen to security instructions and did not serve any security offices. They were Sudanese like all of us in their kindness and, sometimes, in their naiveté, thinking well of all people. This kindness and naiveté makes us see precaution and wariness, especially if the other person is an Arab Muslim, as a form of mistrust not suitable for a Sudanese person.

We do not know gemstones. I, for example, despite my wanderings in both Eastern and Western countries, do not know how to differentiate between a diamond and a piece of glass. That is what the double agent claimed: that he worked in the diamond trade. No doubt, his country's intelligence agency advised him to claim to the Sudanese that he worked in this kind of trade. I say this because, at an earlier time, another agent for that same intelligence agency used to visit us at the embassy in Nairobi and claimed that he worked in the diamond trade. One time, he pulled a pouch from his pocket and told me that it contained an unrefined diamond. However, I could not differentiate between it and a piece of a smashed bottle. The recurrence of the claim to working in the diamond trade in two different countries, by two different agents for the same country, makes me certain that the orders to do so came from the same source.

In the beginning of March 1992, the Bosnian War broke out. As happened in Afghanistan, mujahideen from all over the world flowed in to assist their Muslim brothers. A similar experience occurred as when they went to Afghanistan and returned after the jihad to America; Muslims in America became excited about the jihad in Bosnia. However, the majority did not take into consideration that the world had changed and that the Russian Bear that America so hated and feared no longer existed as it had. The double agent used the religious feelings of those young Muslim men and began to speak to them of the arrogance of the West and America, their tyranny and oppression of the Muslims and their exploitation of Muslim wealth. He began to speak at length about jihad and the blessed trial that the mujahideen underwent in Afghanistan. Those kind young men heard him, even listened with interest. Why would they not when he was a man that frequented mosques and enjoyed the friendship and trust of Sheikh Omar? Then, the agent began to speak to them about the tragedy of "our Muslim brothers" in Bosnia and their need for assistance and to teach them the difference between "offensive jihad" and "defensive jihad," in which the Muslim defends his honor or his Muslim brother's honor against any attacker.

The agent had close ties, through his routine reports, with the FBI. He informed the FBI of everything Sheikh Omar said and everything that happened around him, just as he informed them of what those Muslims, including our kindly brothers, around Sheikh Omar said. Little by little, he began to focus in his relations specifically on those young men. He recorded all of his conversations with them on a little recorder, given to him by the FBI, that he kept in his pocket. One time, when he was taking Siddig Ibrahim to New York City via the Holland Tunnel, he secretly started the recorder and began to work him up about the tyranny of Americans and their oppression of Muslims. He asked Ibrahim his opinion on blowing up the Holland Tunnel at rush hour, when the tunnel would be crowded with cars. Our friend became excited and took the matter further, expressing his elation, welcoming and excitement at the wonderful idea, where thousands of "dirty infidels" would meet their death by burning and choking, all while the recorder was rolling.

That same day, they passed by the United Nations building and the agent proposed the same idea of blowing up the UN building, a symbol of the "tyrants" that controlled the Security Council, and the recorder was rolling.

The double agent proposed to the young men the idea of going to fight jihad in Bosnia "in assistance of God's religion and against the infidels." They approved of the idea and were even delighted with it. He then took them a step further, more practical this time, suggesting to them that he teach them how to make a bomb with local materials, as a kind of early training for them, so that they would be more prepared and advanced than other volunteer mujahideen. When they accepted the idea, he quickly distributed tasks among them. One was tasked with preparing urea, the fertilizer, another with supplying the barrels to make the explosive paste and another was asked to buy gasoline and other raw materials. The agent tasked himself with renting a large empty warehouse that would be suitable as a place for practicing making bombs out of materials available on the market.

In reality, the FBI was tasked with preparing the warehouse. They installed cameras and bugs so as to follow what was happening very closely. At the arranged time, the young men brought all the necessary materials. After a theoretical demonstration of how to make explosives, he asked them to make a "mixture." They complied and began to work, all while the FBI was following a live transmission of the proceedings within the large warehouse. At the very moment that the young men began to mix the materials, counterterrorism officers stormed the building, pointing their weapons. The rest of the story is known, as was previously stated.

At the Al Farooq mosque in Brooklyn, where we used to pray, occasionally an Egyptian man named El Sayyid Nosair would come to pray, as well. El Sayyid Nosair used to frequent the Maktab al-Khidamat, located across the street from the mosque that would send mujahideen to Afghanistan. He wanted to join the mujahideen and brought his brother from Egypt to take his family there. However, his goal was not achieved because of his father's strong opposition: his father insisted that he not go and that he make his family his primary concern.

When the Blind Sheikh, Omar Abdel-Rahman, came and settled in New Jersey, El Sayyid Nosair began to frequent his mosque and to listen to his sermons. His desire to fight jihad increased as did his love for the mujahideen's battles. However, the war in Afghanistan had already come to an end.

One day, El Sayyid Nosair was present in a hall where the radical rabbi, Meir Kahane, was giving a speech in which he spoke about the need to expel the rest of the Palestinians that remained in the Promised Land that God had given to Abraham and his sons! A man fired at the rabbi, killing him in a pool of blood. El Sayyid Nosair was arrested, but the prosecution was unable to prove that he was the one that pulled the trigger, so they released him. This was in 1990 and was considered the first terrorist attempt in America for which Muslims were accused.

On the afternoon of 26 February 1993, a yellow Ford van and, with it, a red Chevrolet, entered the parking lot of the World Trade Center in New York, and parked on the underground B-2 level. The two men parked the car amid the many other cars and the Chevrolet waited for them. One of the two men in the van gathered four bottles filled with nitroglycerine and put the bottles in the trunk next to boxes containing 1,200 pounds of explosive materials made by hand from a mixture of urea and nitric and sulfuric acid. Among the boxes were three tanks containing compressed hydrogen to strengthen the blast. The man put a detonator and a fuse on each of the bottles, lit the fuses and closed the back door of the van.

The two men knew that they had only twelve minutes to safely exit from the World Trade Center building, so they jumped into the Chevrolet and started up towards the exit. Near the ground-floor exit, a truck blocked their way, so they began to yell at the truck's driver. It took three precious minutes to convince the driver to move, but they came out from under the building and set out on the main road. A massive explosion occurred in the parking lot of the building, killing six people and wounding 1,024 others. The building itself, however, was only damaged lightly, and cost no more than 500 million dollars to repair!

In the summer of 1992, Emad Salem, the double agent, informed the FBI that the Muslims around Sheikh Omar Abdel-Rahman had gathered 8,500 dollars and were discussing weapons and explosives. He told them that the group doing so was headed by Palestinian named Mohammed Salameh, who had knowledge of techniques for manufacturing explosives.

According to American sources, (The National Interest, Winter 1995/ 1996 , and other American sources), that summer, Sheikh Abdel-Rahman called the number 810614 in Pakistan. Those sources believe that that event was related to the arrival of two men in New York from Pakistan via JFK Airport a few weeks following that phone call. One of the two men was named Ahmed Ajaj. Ajaj was arrested in the airport following the authorities' discovery that he carried a false Swedish passport. However, the authorities did not discover the manual for the manufacture of explosives that was in Ajaj's suitcase. There was more than one manual and on one of them, the words "the foundation of jihad" were written in Arabic, noting that the Arabic word for foundation is "al-qaeda"!

The other man who came from Pakistan presented the airport authorities with an Iraqi passport with the name of Mohammed Azan. However, he told the airport authorities that it was not his real name, adding that his real name was "Ramzi Yousef." After an investigation that was not that long, the airport authorities released Ramzi Yousef, ordering him to submit an application for political asylum. All of these events occurred in August and the beginning of September of 1992. By these events, I mean Sheikh Omar's conversation and the arrival of the two men from Pakistan. The two men trained in al-Qaeda camps in Afghanistan some time before their arrival in America; Ajaj trained in Khalden camp and Yousef in Sada al-Malahim. From the airport, Ramzi Yousef got into a taxi and went directly to the Al Farooq Mosque and the Maktab al-Khidamat, across Atlantic Avenue from the mosque in Brooklyn. There, he met the Palestinian, Mohammed Salameh and, together, they went to Salameh's apartment in New Jersey.

Ramzi did not waste much time. He began to gather the chemical materials used to manufacture bombs. For this purpose, he appointed Nidal Ayyad and used the money that Salameh's group had gathered, which the double agent had informed the FBI of. This money was not enough, so Ramzi Yousef sent a message to his uncle, Khalid Sheikh Mohammed, (the mastermind behind the September 11 attacks who is now imprisoned in the American prison at Guantanamo). In this communication, he informed his uncle that he needed 660 dollars to supplement the previous amount, without revealing the plan to him. Khalid Sheikh Mohammed sent the money from Pakistan.

On 23 February 1993, Salameh rented a van from a company specializing in truck rentals in New Jersey and paid 400 dollars in cash. However, he returned to the company a day before the 26 February 1993 explosions and informed them that the van had been stolen.

After the explosion on 26 February 1993, Ramzi Yousef used a passport different from the one that he had entered with and flew to Pakistan. Two other accomplices in the bombing left the US a few days following this.

The Palestinian, Salameh, did not know that American car manufacturing companies hide encoded symbols within the structure of the cars in order to prevent theft and to discover car thieves. When the American police found a part of these symbols, they were able to find out the rest of the symbols by calling the manufacturing company and investigated the car, until their investigation led them to the truck rental company in New Jersey.

When Salameh returned to the truck rental company with the police report informing them of the theft of the van, he found FBI agents awaiting him. After that, all the strands of the plot were revealed to the Americans and Salameh, Ajaj, Ayyad and four others ended up in prison, each sentenced to 240 years.

Before the bombing, the FBI reinforced their relationship with Emad Salem, who gathered what remained of the cell that El Sayyid Nosair, who longed to fight jihad after missing his chance in Afghanistan, had joined, as well as our five Sudanese friends. The rest of the story is known. What is important is that the American authorities arrested them on 23 June 1993 and, eight days later, Sheikh Omar Abdel-Rahman joined them.

The American authorities began to search for Ramzi Yousef, putting two million dollars on his head as a reward for whoever directed them to him. After his arrival in Pakistan, Ramzi Yousef became a roving jihadist. He seemed to be present everywhere. He tried to assassinate Benazir Bhutto and participated in explosions in Iran and Thailand. In 1994, Ramzi traveled to the Philippines to train armed militants on Basilan Island. In September of the same year, he settled in an apartment in Manila, the capital. It is said that Bin Laden's brother-in-law rented the apartment for him. However, Ramzi himself was not a committed member of al-Qaeda, although al-Qaeda and other jihadists knew that he was behind the 1993 explosion. He was perhaps receiving support from Bin Laden without them knowing one another, as Bin Laden financed many jihadist groups, as recommended by those he trusted. Bin Laden himself denied having any link to the 1993 explosions at the World Trade Center.

On 6 January 1995, Ramzi and his confederate, Abdul Hakim Murad (Pakistani), were manufacturing a bomb in their apartment in Manila and, because of some mistake, a fire broke out in the apartment, forcing them to flee. After a short period of time, Murad returned to the scene of the crime, as does any plotter or criminal, and was arrested by the police. Ramzi, however, quickly left the country for Pakistan.

Another time, confirmed information reached the FBI that Ramzi was present in a country in the Arabian Peninsula, so the FBI sent a team to arrest him. However, the information reached Ramzi, who then left the country. When the American delegation reached the country, they found no trace of the man. The FBI and CIA's hunt for Ramzi Yousef did not last much longer, though, after the fire in his Manila apartment; one of the jihadists could not resist the temptation of the money and informed the Americans of Ramzi's location. The Pakistani authorities, in coordination with the Americans, arrested Ramzi Yousef in Islamabad on 6 February 1995. He was extradited to America and sentenced to 240 years for the bombing and another sentence of life imprisonment. Two sentences of this sort are laughable and ridiculous.

At the trial, Ramzi admitted what he did and said, "Yes, I am a terrorist and I am proud of being a terrorist. I would like to add that I did what I did not for motivations of personal revenge, but out of my conviction that bombing targets within America is the only way to make America change its policies."

Before the trial, when he was in a prison cell neighboring one of the leaders of Hamas at a maximum security prison in New York, Ramzi admitted to this man that he was the mastermind of the 1993 World Trade Center bombing. As I said before, I heard this two days after the September 11 attacks from that leader within Hamas when we met in Damascus. At that time, Ramzi had been residing in the American prison that he was moved to for six years. In that year – his sixth year of imprisonment – his uncle Khalid Sheikh Mohammed achieved his goal for him.

Neither Ramzi Yousef nor El Sayyid Nosair were committed members of al-Qaeda. However, the Americans tend towards easy explanations, so they attributed each operation to al-Qaeda and categorized each actor as a member of al-Qaeda. In reality, Bin Laden was not directly behind any of these operations. What Bin Laden *did* do directly, though, was to let the genie out of the bottle. And that is the most dangerous. 100,000 mujahideen trained in Afghanistan and eastern Pakistan—the Tribal Areas. When they spread around the world, they increased in number and jihadist groups were born that were organizationally independent from al-Qaeda, although they agreed with al-Qaeda's ideology.

The five Sudanese men that were arrested and that I met in the maximum security prison in New York were not members of al-Qaeda, they did not even form a jihadist organization. They shared, however, with hundreds of millions of Muslims in empathizing with their oppressed brothers and desired to assist them.

Although when I was studying in New York, I was immersed in the situation that I was in, I was not oblivious to the desires of the world's Muslims for a league (Caliphate) to organize, unite and assist them against their enemies. However, I did not discern the depths of what Bin Laden had done or of the experience of jihad in Afghanistan and the effect this would have on international and geo-political relations in the Middle East and other countries.

CHAPTER ONE

SECURITY STRATEGY AND STRUCTURE

Security Strategy and Structure

Christoph Reuter informs that people had different opinions on how to evaluate and to describe Samir and tried in many ways to learn about him. After meeting him in the small town where he lived for many months, they concluded that they could not figure out his essence and truth – thus indicating that he was a skilled intelligence agent. Some of his neighbors said he was polite, but cautious and discreet. Some people said that he was a smarmy flatterer, while others described him as courteous and a good listener and even others thought he was sneaky, cunning and sly. They were unable to gather any information about him, so for many months they ignored him. They did not know or realize the truth of his business until the day he was killed. All of these characteristics make an intelligence agent a successful spy. Samir Abd Muhammad al-Khlifawi, though, was more than this: he was a security strategist, skilled planner and executor of his plans in the best way.

At a hearing organized by Congress, members listened to and interrogated Bud McFarlane, the National Security Advisor, about the Iran-Contra scandal. On 5 May 1987, members of Congress accused McFarlane of selling weapons to Iran, working with an Iranian businessman with a bad reputation, Manucher Ghorbanifar. McFarlane responded that there are matters that cannot be accomplished by Mother Teresa – in other words, a pious nun would fail if she had to perform a task that requires cunning and slyness. Thus, it is no shame if an intelligence agent is "accused" of cunning, deception, caution and, sometimes, flattery, if all of this is done to protect his country's project, as set by its leadership.

Even those that killed Samir Abd Muhammad al-Khlifawi in January 2014 did not know the identity of this tall man in his fifties. The name that they knew him by was Haji Bakr. As for his real name, no one in the Syrian town of Tell Rifaat was aware of it.

Samir was a colonel in Saddam Hussein's intelligence agency and worked in the Iraqi Air Defense Military Intelligence. After Bremer's decision to dissolve the Iraqi military and intelligence services, Colonel Samir found himself out of work, dependent on his family and, thus, filled with bitterness and hatred towards the invading American administration and the Iraqi politicians that supported them. In this, he was like the hundreds of thousands of Iraqis that had positions in the government, military or security services. Colonel Samir, again like many thousands of others, joined the factions of the resistance, fighting the occupation and the Baghdad government, and his name became Haji Bakr.

Those that killed Haji Bakr did not know that they had killed the strategist of the Islamic State in Iraq and Syria (ISIS), who developed the strategic vision of the security apparatus, its system of expansion and control, the organizational structure of the apparatuses entrusted with security and intelligence work and their relationship with other apparatuses, so as to achieve control over the territories into which they intended to expand. Haji Bakr was the engineer that developed the design of ISIS in this regard and he pulled many of the strings.

The German magazine, *Der Spiegel*, was the first global media outlet to receive the dangerous documents that were found hidden in an annex of the house in which Haji Bakr resided in Tell Rifaat. It was a folder containing ISIS's plans and a blueprint for its apparatuses, explaining how it could gain control over the territories it planned to expand its control into. It encompassed the structure of its apparatuses and instructions and procedures for gaining control over the territory under the control of Syrian factions, whose situation was close to chaos. These documents are the best source for explaining how, in 2014, ISIS achieved such a rapid expansion and, for the first time, they offered a clarification of how its leadership was organized and what role Haji Bakr and the "remnants" of Saddam Hussein's regime play in ISIS. Most importantly, Haji Bakr's documents clarify the plan for taking over Syria so as to allow ISIS to push towards Iraq.

Der Spiegel states that the studies that it undertook, as well as other documents that it gained access to, demonstrate that Haji Bakr's instructions were implemented meticulously according to his plans. The magazine further states that the man who was hiding Bakr's documents continues to fear to this day that ISIS will kill him if they learn his identity. Haji Bakr and a detachment of his companions arrived in Syria in late 2012.

The Astonishing Plan

Haji Bakr's plan stated that the foundation of the Islamic State required taking control over the greater part of Syrian land and, then, using this as a launching pad to push into Iraq. As soon as he arrived in Tell Rifaat, Bakr settled in a house that would not draw attention. His choice of Tell Rifaat was appropriate for implementing his project because of the number of those in the town that had adopted Salafism. In this way, the circumstances of the Syrian War led to many people having a similar attitude to settling there, inspired by ISIS supporters, until, in 2013, it became one of the regions in which there were hundreds of fighters that had taken up the religion of ISIS. In Tell Rifaat, Haji Bakr drafted his plans that encompassed the structure of the state, including the local levels, ways of infiltrating the villages and who would head and oversee them. He specified the chain of command in the security apparatus, even noting the individual responsibilities of each official he designated. In short, what Bakr developed was a precise technical plan for what *Der Spiegel* calls an "Islamic Intelligence State," saying that the caliphate that Bakr designed in his plans is managed by an organization or apparatus similar to the security service in East Germany during the communist era, commonly known as the Stasi. In the months that followed his arrival in Tell Rifaat, Haji Bakr implemented his plans in a surprisingly detailed manner.

Bakr's plans begin with establishing an Islamic Dawah office and inviting the residents of the area to listen to religious lectures and courses on the manner of life according to the Quran and the Sunnah. Then, a few people would be mobilized to gather information on the residents of the area where the Islamic Dawah office is located in order to obtain the greatest possible amount of information on them. Haji Bakr demanded that the following information be obtained: a list of the names of influential families; the names of the powerful people in those families; their sources of income; the names and manpower of the brigades fighting in the area or the town; names of the leaders of these brigades, who controls them and their political orientation; to monitor their illegal activities "in accordance with Sharia law" – which could be used to blackmail them if necessary.

He asked those new spies to record the details of the illegal activities, such as if the person were homosexual, a criminal or had some secret activity, so that they could make use of this information if necessary. Bakr wrote, "We will appoint the smartest and train them to be judges in the Sharia courts."

Furthermore, in each city, some "brothers" would be selected to marry women in the most influential families, in order to "ensure their penetration into these families without their knowledge." Those new spies were tasked with obtaining the greatest possible amount of information about the targeted cities, the people that lived in those cities, who is in charge of them, which families there are religious, which *madhhab* (Islamic school of thought) they belong to, the number of mosques and imams and how many wives and children these imams have. It included other information, such as an evaluation of the imam's sermon, if he tended towards Salafism or Sufism, if he supported the opposition factions or the ruling regime, what is his position on jihad, from where does he receive his salary and who appointed him and how many supporters of democracy there are in the city.

Bakr asked these agents to work like seismic waves, sent to learn about the social classes and their composition and to gain knowledge of the locations of the small cracks and old rifts in all of them. In *Der Spiegel*'s words, "In short, any information that could be used to divide and subjugate local residents." Those informants included veteran spies from the intelligence services and opponents of the regime that were in conflict with one of the rebel factions. Some of them were young men or teenagers in need of money, others were those that gravitated to work such as this. Most of those found on Bakr's lists and documents were between 17 and their 20s and were recruited in Tell Rifaat.

The plan included fields such as finance, education, childcare and media, but it is clear that its governing theme, carefully addressed in the records of responsibilities and necessary reports, was the issues of surveillance, spying, assassination and kidnapping.

For each provincial council, an emir or commander was assigned to be responsible for assassinations, kidnappings, snipers, communications and encryption. There would be an emir to supervise the other emirs. According to *Der Spiegel*, the "nucleus" of all this work would be a cell whose leader's work would be to spread fear. Bakr designed the organizational hierarchy and chain of command of the security apparatus so that all its apparatuses worked in parallel, with the goal that each individual would continue to monitor the other. The magazine commented on this security model, saying, "It seemed as if George Orwell had been the model for this spawn of paranoid surveillance." In fact, Bakr modified Saddam's intelligence services, in which even senior commanders could not be certain that they were not being spied on.

Der Spiegel believes that the secret of ISIS's success in controlling situations and expanding is due to the fact that it combines two opposites: the extremist doctrine of a religious group and the caution and strategic calculations of the Baathist remnants within it.

Of note is the fact that Haji Bakr, like al-Baghdadi and his deputies, graduated from Camp Bucca prison, as well as Abu Ghraib prison, in the period between 2006 and 2008. He joined al-Zarqawi's group in Anbar and he and his colleagues used their time imprisoned at Camp Bucca to create a wide network of relationships.

Of course, Haji Bakr was not originally an Islamist. According to the testimony of a relative of the Iraqi journalist, Hisham al-Hashimi, who was a colleague of his when Haji Bakr was at the Habbaniya base, he was a nationalist and an officer known for his extraordinary intelligence and his firmness in logistics. He was among those of his colleagues in the intelligence services that joined with the Islamists fighting the occupation. He shared in the 2010 decision to choose al-Baghdadi as emir; as a sheikh, al-Baghdadi would help to give an Islamist face to the resistance faction so as to attract Muslims.

In 2010, the idea of militarily defeating the Iraqi government and its forces seemed a difficult matter to achieve. Thus, Bakr's group resorted to forming a secret organization, working underground through "terrorist" operations and gaining strength by suggesting to important persons within the Sunni tribes that they could protect them if they paid a certain amount of money and, if not... When the protests in Syria became militarized, the group sensed in this a golden opportunity, especially after 2012, when the Syrian government was defeated in northern Syria and withdrew from many areas.

Chaos prevailed in many districts in northern Syria. Hundreds of local committees made up of citizens were established, as were many military brigades. In this state of weakness, this group, made up of the powerful combination of those former officers, saw an opportunity to exploit this situation through close coordination with Abu Mohammad al-Julani (leader of al-Nusra Front), whom al-Baghdadi had sent to Syria ahead of them.

Many Westerners believe that the rapid rise of ISIS was a result of the interaction of the terrorism practiced by al-Qaeda, crimes like those of the Mafia and the fiery discourse of the Islamists that glorifies martyrdom and speaks to their sacred task of eliminating the blasphemy of the "lackeys of colonialism." However, a deeper analysis of the reasons for the group's rise, according to

Christoph Rueter, informs us that the existence of an apocalyptic religious vision alone, without other factors that interact with it, is not sufficient to control a large swath of territory over two countries, that terrorism alone does not establish a country and that the Mafia does not create such excitement nor worldwide devotion among its members, making them ready to give up their lives and travel to the "Caliphate" from all around the globe, a journey whose results are not guaranteed for those that prefer life over death.

Westerners struggled to explain the phenomenon of ISIS's rapid rise because they project their understanding of religion onto any phenomenon dominated by religious discourse. They should be pardoned for this because of their inability to differentiate between Islam and Christianity. Christianity calls for the separation of church and state because "Render to Caesar the things that are Caesar's, and to God the things that are God's": there is no connection between the things that are Caesar's and the things that are God's. It is difficult for Westerners to understand that a group that states that its approach and objectives are religious could be capable of strategic planning, political trickery and the making of alliances. They believe that it is difficult for a religious group to design a precise media and propaganda message, to implement this through media apparatuses and outlets and to excel in the use of digital technology.

Expansion

ISIS's expansion began in a hidden way, without noise or clamor, so that only about a year later did Syrians become aware of a noticeable presence of jihadists in their land. Christoph Reuter continues to inform that ISIS's presence began with the opening of Dawah offices in numerous Syrian cities in the spring of 2013. Their presence was seemingly innocent, like any religious charity organization in any part of the world. These Dawah offices did not arouse suspicions upon their opening in Raqqah, Manbij, Al-Bab, Atarib or Azaz. Their presence was not even noticed in some of the towns and did not arouse any interest. However, some noticed that a jihadist group had rented a number of apartments in Manbij, when fighting broke out there in January, and that this group was storing weapons in these apartments, in which some men were quietly residing. This same process occurred in the other towns, but very quietly and cautiously. When ISIS had mobilized a sufficient number of followers, under the pretext that they were students of Sharia, their expansion began. Gradually, they began to raise their black flag in the areas in which they were sure they had a comfortable number of supporters and rented more houses. They withdrew from or did not announce their presence in the areas that resisted their obvious presence or in which they were not sure of having a sufficient number of supporters. In ISIS's modus operandi, the first order of business was expansion without any dangers facing the resistance movement. They would, however, liquidate or kidnap the elements they categorized as "anti-Islamic," but did so secretly, washing their hands of it and denying any link to such heinous acts. These acts were met with wide denouncement from the local community: killing just on mere suspicion of the person's views can only be seen by society as a criminal act that cannot be justified.

In the beginning, the fighters hid themselves as best as they could. Nor did Bakr and his vanguard invite men from Iraq. Instead, at this stage, they banned the arrival of Iraqis and only recruited a small number of Syrians, mostly for the purposes of gathering information. They resorted to a more complicated choice: gathering together all of the Salafi mujahideen and those that had religious fervor that had begun to arrive in the area in the summer of 2012. Their cover was that they were Saudi students of Sharia, relief workers or employees, humanitarian workers with the Dawah offices that came from North Africa and volunteers from Tunisia and Europe. Except for the Chechens, most of those that came had no military background. Many of them were gathered in Syria under Iraqi auspices and leadership. All of this is according to Christoph Rueter.

However, at the end of 2012, the establishment of military training camps began in many areas. No one knew to what group these camps belonged, because organization within them was precise and disciplined, banned from talking to the media and very few were from Iraq. In the camps, the new arrivals were submitted, for two months, to a military course and a course in indoctrination, in which they were trained to be absolutely obedient to the leadership. This resulted in absolutely loyal forces. Those foreign fighters knew no one except for their compatriots in the camps. In the second stage, they proved that they would fight fiercely and that they had no mercy, since they had no reason to be merciful towards those they saw as opposing Islam. Furthermore, they could be quickly deployed to any place that the leadership designated. This was unlike the forces of the Syrian factions, who were mostly concerned with protecting their towns and who had responsibilities to take care of their families – for example, assisting with the harvest.

Haji Bakr's documents reveal that, in the fall of 2013, ISIS recruited 2,650 foreign fighters in the Aleppo Governorate alone. A third of them were Tunisians, followed by Saudis, Turks, then Egyptians and a smaller number of Chechens, Europeans and Indonesians. In truth, to this day, Tunisians are the largest group of Arab fighters in ISIS, despite the processes of Westernization and secularization that occurred during the eras of Bourguiba and Ben Ali. As for Europe, the largest groups later came from France, Belgium and Britain. However, in proportion to population, among Western countries, the most fighters came from Australia (yes, Australia is classified as a Western country despite its geographical location).

Even later, the Syrian fighters in other brigades outnumbered those jihadists. Although the Syrian brigades did not trust the jihadists, they did not unite to fight them, as they did not want to open another front. Instead, during that stage, they wanted to focus their efforts on fighting the ruling regime in Syria. For its part, ISIS increased the appearance of its strength with a simple trick (according to Reuter): all of its forces wore black clothing and black masks. On the one hand, this made their appearance frightening and, on the other, no one could know their exact numbers. When 200 fighters in black clothing and masks appear in five different locations in a town, this causes a kind of confusion about their numbers. At the same time, the spies secretly disseminated by ISIS, through the Dawah offices, kept the leadership informed of the areas of weakness or division among the residents and of where there was a kind of local struggle, allowing ISIS to present itself as protective force and to empower itself.

The Capture of Raqqah

Der Spiegel relates in detail how ISIS captured Raqqah, saying that the operation began with subtle skill, gradually developed into a brutal attack and ended, in March 2013, with ISIS forces defeating their opponents without much struggle. A city council was quickly formed, as were unions for lawyers, doctors, journalists and women. Youth associations and the movement "For Our Rights" were founded, as well as many other initiatives. ISIS began to eliminate those who had previously been classified as an enemy or who might represent a threat in the future. The first to be killed was the head of the city council, who was kidnapped in mid-May by masked men. He was followed by the brother of a well-known novelist in the city. Two days later, the man who led a group that painted the revolutionary flag on the walls of the city disappeared. Terror began to do its work in silencing any voices of protest. The disappearances and killings increased, affecting many. Sometimes the corpses would be found and sometimes there would be no trace of them. In August, the military leadership of ISIS sent a number of cars driven by suicide bombers to the headquarters of the Free Syrian Army brigade, Ahfad al-Rasul, killing dozens of them while the rest of the brigade's forces fled. Then, ISIS wove a network of secret deals with other brigades, all of whom were gripped by the fear that they were on ISIS's list of targets.

On 17 October 2013, ISIS called the notables of Raqqah to a large-scale meeting. Some thought that this was a reconciliation initiative. Among the 300 people that attended the meeting, only two spoke up against ISIS's capture of the city and against the kidnapping and the killing practiced by the group.

One of those that spoke up and protested was a well-known human rights activist and journalist, Muhannad Habayebna. He was found five days later tied up and killed with a gunshot to the head. A picture of his body was then sent via email to some of his friends, under which was written, "Are you sad about your friend now?" A few hours later, 20 members of opposition groups fled the city for Turkey. With extreme cruelty, any opposition in Raqqah had been finished off.

A short while later, 14 tribal leaders from the largest tribes in the area of Raqqah swore their allegiance to Emir Abu Bakr al-Baghdadi and ISIS recorded a video of the ceremony. Ironically, these were the same tribal leaders that had sworn their absolute allegiance to President Bashar al-Assad two years earlier.

The Killing of Haji Bakr

According to the *Der Spiegel* article, until the end of 2013, everything was moving according to what Haji Bakr had planned. The Caliphate, which had not yet been announced, was expanding into village after village, without facing any resistance from the Syrian rebels. It seemed that the tyrannical force of ISIS had terrified them. However, after ISIS's men viciously killed a well-loved leader of one of the opposition factions in December 2013, a surprise occurred. After his death, secular and Islamist brigades—including members of al-Nusra Front, loyal to al-Qaeda—joined forces to fight ISIS. After attacking ISIS in all places at the same time, they robbed ISIS of its technical advantage: its ability to quickly move their forces to any place in which they were urgently needed.

In only a few weeks, the forces of the Syrian brigades were able to push ISIS forces out of large areas of northern Syria. Even Raqqah, which ISIS had adopted as its capital, almost fell at the hands of those brigades. It would have fallen were it not for a trick used by ISIS: they dressed in the military uniform of the brigades, allowing them to infiltrate among those fighters, and suddenly began to fire on them. There was nothing for those fighters to do except to flee. In this way, a simple masquerade aided ISIS forces, leading them to victory – they just changed out of their black uniform into American jeans and vests. They did the same thing in the town of Jarabulus. Thus, the elements of ISIS have shown that they have no lack of flexibility in their thinking and are not above playing tricks when they want, as the hardline jurisprudential position is open to reconsideration in certain circumstances. They perhaps justify this as being one of the necessities of war. However, the question is, will this *fiqh* of necessity be expanded to include the scope of politics? This question will remain unanswered until we see what occurs in the management of the state that is continuing to expand day after day.

During the shift in the factions' loyalties against ISIS, Haji Bakr remained in the town of Tell Rifaat, as ISIS forces had the upper hand there. However, In January 2014, with the beginning of the brigades' attack, the city was divided within hours. Half of the city remained loyal to ISIS, while brigades captured the other half. Unfortunately for Haji Bakr, he was stuck in the wrong half. He stayed there, hidden, and refrained from moving to the well-guarded section controlled by ISIS. That was the wrong decision, as one of his neighbors snitched on the godfather of snitching! This neighbor told the fighters of the opposing brigade that an ISIS sheikh lived in a house near his. The leader of this brigade, Abdelmalik Hadbe, and his men advanced towards the house. A trembling woman opened the door and told them, "My husband isn't here!" The rebels replied, "How is he not when his car is parked outside?" At that moment, Haji Bakr appeared at the door in his pajamas. Hadbe ordered Bakr to accompany him, but he protested that he needed to put on his clothing. Hadbe insisted that Bakr accompany him in what he was wearing. With that, Bakr jumped with an agility unexpected at his age and slammed the door behind himself. He then hid behind the stairs and yelled, "I have a suicide belt and I'll blow all of you up, including myself!" Then, he came out, holding a Kalashnikov, and began to fire. Hadbe responded with fire, killing Bakr.

When the men later realized the identity of the man that they had killed, they searched the house, gathering computers, mobile phone SIM cards, a GPS and papers. They said that nowhere in the house did they find a copy of the Quran! Haji Bakr died and the rebels took his wife as hostage. However, at the request of Ankara, she was later exchanged for a Turkish hostage. Bakr's papers remained hidden in a room in the house for a few months.

Other Documents

In January 2014, after ISIS leadership was forced to evacuate a part of Aleppo, the brigades that fought ISIS found another set of documents that confirmed that Haji Bakr's plan had been implemented in its entirety. ISIS was forced to evacuate its headquarters quickly and thus was unable to take all of its folders or to eliminate them, because of how many of them there were. Some of these folders remained as they were when the al-Tawhid Brigade, the largest of the opposition brigades in Aleppo, took over the headquarters. The al-Tawhid Brigade allowed *Der Spiegel* access to all of the documents, except for a list of ISIS spies within the brigade itself.

Examination of these documents shows a highly developed, complex system followed by ISIS, including the infiltration and surveillance of all Syrian factions and groups, including the members of ISIS itself. The documents include long lists of the names of their agents that they planted in each brigade fighting in Syria, even within militias loyal to the regime. ISIS's information was so developed that they even knew who the Syrian intelligence agency spies were within the opposition brigades.

The man who holds these documents in his possession said to *Der Spiegel*, "They knew more than we did, much more." Among the documents, personal dossiers for the fighters were found, including detailed letters of application from foreign fighters. The folder for the Jordanian Nidal Abu Eysch, for example, includes all those that have taken up jihad in his region, their telephone numbers and the file number of a misdemeanor case against him in his country. He writes his hobbies as: hunting, boxing and bomb making.

Looking at these documents, one feels that ISIS wants to know everything, but that they want to deceive everybody about the truth of their aspirations. One of the reports, for example, notes justifications that ISIS could announce for seizing the largest flour mill in Syria. Among these justifications were allegations of embezzlement in the mills and un-Islamic behavior among the workers.

The documents found in Aleppo reveal the direct results of Haji Bakr's plan to establish the Islamic State. They include and encompass details of requests of normal life. For example, 34 fighters want to get married, as Bakr recommended in his plan. The documents include requests for personal needs. Abu Luqman and Abu Yahya al-Tunisi need an apartment, Abu Suheib and Abu Ahmed Osama request bedroom furniture, Abu al-Baraa al Dimashqi requests financial assistance, in addition to a complete set of furniture, while Abu Azmi needs an automatic washing machine.

Shifting Alliances

In the early months of 2014, another aspect of Haji Bakr's legacy began to come into play. I mean by this the legacy of his decade-long ties with the Syrian intelligence agency. This is according to reports that discussed his former ties.

This intelligence relationship began in 2003, when Damascus thought that, after Bush's victory in taking control over Iraq, its turn would come next and that perhaps Bush would order his troops to march towards Syria to overthrow the regime. So as a precautionary measure against such an event, the Syrian intelligence services organized the sending of thousands of Islamist mujahideen from Libya, Saudi Arabia and Tunisia to al-Qaeda in Iraq. As a result, 90% of suicide attackers entered Iraq via Syria. In this way, a strange relationship grew between Syrian generals, international jihadists and former officers in the Iraqi military who had been loyal to Saddam Hussein, some of Haji Bakr's group among them. This was a joint project taken up by bitter enemies, whose parties repeatedly met in a location to the west of Damascus. At that time, the goal was to make life hell for the Americans in Iraq. No one doubted that this was a noble goal.

In this regard, it is worthwhile to mention that Paul Bremer, who governed Iraq after the occupation, Donald Rumsfeld, the Secretary of Defense, and President Bush had previously accused Syria of establishing relationships with the jihadists that were fighting the invading American forces. They also accused Syria of easing passage of jihadists to Iraq, turning a blind eye to training camps established by jihadists in Syria, supplying, in coordination with the remnants of the Iraqi military, those jihadists with Iraqi passports and treating their wounded in the Al Nour Hospital in Damascus. In a dispatch sent to the State Department on 11 July 2008, the American Embassy in Baghdad accused the Syrian government of also turning a blind eye to jihadist networks in Syria.

In September 2007, the American forces in Iraq arrested a group of jihadists in the area of Sinjar, finding in their possession documents that, according to America, implicated Syria in working with the jihadists. They called these documents the "Sinjar records."

Some of those that have observed what I have previously related say that, beginning in 2014, the relationship between the former Iraqi officers and the Syrian intelligence services led to Syrian regime jets targeting the locations of the leadership and headquarters of the brigades that had entered into battles with ISIS, reviving the pact between them. Those observers say that this arrangement caused confusion among the foreign fighters, because they believed that jihad would be different.

These observers believe that ISIS gained back the territory that it had lost to the brigades because they increased the number of car bombs that they sent to their bases and because of Syrian Air Force strikes on these bases.

They try to adopt this opinion, that there is a new pact between ISIS and the Syrian government, offering as proof that Division 17 of the Syrian Army had been besieged by brigades for over a year, until ISIS attacked these brigades. ISIS drove them off and Syrian forces recommenced using Division 17 Air Base to supply its troops. Observers say that the Syrian forces there no longer feared any attacks. However, if this alliance were real, it quickly ended. About six months later, specifically after they took control of Mosul and seized many weapons there, ISIS attacked and captured the base. Or, perhaps, the plan to capture the base had been awaiting some logistical preparations that were not ready until after the seizure of Mosul. ISIS invaded the base and slaughtered the soldiers that they captured (Atwan).

Thus, it is clear that the security system established by Haji Bakr and the other former Iraq security and intelligence officers, the remnants of Saddam Hussein's regime, is a strong and disciplined system. It is capable of gathering information that, to this day, enables the survival and protection of ISIS. This security apparatus was able to recognize the danger of internal rebellion and to eliminate anyone who would be able to organize or to lead such a rebellion. At the same time, the precise surveillance system implemented by ISIS's security apparatus gives it access to information and data on people from banks, property and land registers and money transfer offices. ISIS knows much about its citizens. They know who owns what houses and fields and how many sheep the sheepherders own!

The American Role

The American general, head of Camp Bucca in Iraq, told the Washington Post on 4 November 2014 that, by November 2011, al-Qaeda had begun to carry out specific suicide attacks in Damascus and Aleppo. This same general also said that, since the end of 2011, the Obama administration had become a part of the proxy war to change the Assad regime.

This fact is corroborated by the Senate Intelligence Committee report on Benghazi, which revealed a secret operation by the CIA, with the cooperation of some Arab states, to arm Syrian fighters, sanctioned by CIA Director David Petraeus. Through this operation, weapons were moved from Gaddafi's stockpiles. In order to carry out this operation, the CIA was required to establish companies in Libya whose publicly stated aims were completely unrelated to their real goal: moving Gaddafi's stored weapons. The CIA resorted to the use of these companies so as not to reveal its role in the operation. However, in October 2012, a Defense Intelligence Agency report describing the operation leaked. This report stated that the weapons had been moved from Benghazi by boat to two Syrian ports that, at the time, were controlled by the Syrian opposition. The report further said that the operations to move Libyan weapons continued until August 2012.

At the time, CIA officers were secretly and very discreetly undertaking this operation from what superficially appeared to be business office in Istanbul, in coordination with a number of countries. The operation ceased after the killing of the American ambassador in Benghazi in September 2012. Despite the announcement made after the revelation of the secret operation, that the United States was cooperating with the "moderate" Syrian rebels, all in Washington were aware of the fact that the weapons were eventually ending up either in the hands of al-Nusra Front—loyal to al-Qaeda—or with ISIS.

Although Obama rejected Petraeus's plan in 2012 to arm the Syrian opposition, in April 2013, he agreed to an operation to train the "moderates" among the Syrian opposition. This operation has recently been recognized by the Pentagon as a failure, even a scandal. With the first group of 500 graduates from the units set to be trained, either groups of them joined al-Nusra, or al-Nusra attacked their camps and scattered or captured their troops. Of the 500, only 50 fighters were left, of whom 34 were later captured by al-Nusra. Through this, the United States lost tens of millions of dollars.

In October 2014, the American Vice President acknowledged that some countries had taken on a role in arming the Syrian opposition, naming them;

however, those countries responded by denying these allegations. He stated, "They poured [into Syria] hundreds of millions of dollars and thousands of tons of weapons" that ended up in the hands of the jihadists. However, Vice President Joe Biden's admission and complaint came too late. By this time, both al-Nusra and ISIS had become the two most powerful brigades in Iraq and Syria. The number of foreign mujahideen in those groups had reached 15,000, among them 2,000 Westerners. At the recommendation of some of the countries supporting the opposition, the Army of Conquest was formed, which perhaps was not approved of by Western countries because of al-Nusra's participation.

The CIA called the operation to secretly transport weapons to Syria from Libya "the rat line," which began in 2012 with the participation of the British intelligence services agency. Reports inform us that some of the imaginary companies that were established for the purpose of transporting weapons were working under the cover of being Australian. The CIA did not have to reveal this operation to Congress because they intentionally included British intelligence as a cover and a way to circumvent the law. In American law, the CIA is allowed to withhold information about operations in which foreign intelligence agencies participate. In cases where the CIA is not working with other intelligence agencies, it is obligated to inform the senior leadership of Congress of all of its operations by writing a document called a "finding" for Congress's approval. It should be noted that the American consulate in Benghazi was opened only for the purpose of transporting weapons to Syria and had no political responsibilities, as is usually the case in the absence of an embassy. Consulates are typically not authorized to perform political tasks; however, in the absence of an embassy, consulates of major countries perform political tasks, relying on their power rather than on the Vienna Convention.

CHAPTER TWO

"WHERE DID THEY COME FROM?"

A Child of Zarqa

In 1966, a child was born to Fadel Nazal al-Khalayleh and his wife, Omm Sayel, in the al-Masoum neighborhood in the Jordanian city of Zarqa, whom they named Ahmad.

In 1985, Fadel Nazal al-Khalayleh—who had belonged to the Jordanian Bedouin Beni Hassan tribe, loyal to the ruling Hashemite family, and who had been a mukhtar (a village Mayor) in his village neighboring the city of Zarqa—died. Ahmad was much affected by the loss of his father and took refuge in a life of transgressing his conservative Bedouin tribe's traditions: he drank alcohol and smuggled it, among other things that upset his family. After he reached the point of publicly demonstrating his debauchery by getting a tattoo on his arm, he was enrolled in a series of religious classes at a Zarqa mosque, in hopes that it would return him to the right path. The religious classes were an experience of real change in the life of this young man. He became influenced by the Salafi school, which calls for cleansing Islam of impurities, emulating *al-salaf al-salih* [the pious predecessors] and the Sunnah and rejecting the features and manifestations of Western life, which have dominated all aspects of Muslims' lives and which, it believes, have contaminated Muslims' lives with democracy and other ideas.

Aspects of righteousness began to appear in the life of the young man and he married his cousin, with whom he had two sons and two daughters.

At that time, at a distance of 1,000 miles from Amman, in Afghanistan, a war was raging between the mujahideen and the Soviet Union. Another young man from Saudi Arabia named Osama Bin Laden, along with a Palestinian sheikh named Abdullah Azzam, established the Maktab al-Khidamat in Hayatabad, a Pakistani city neighboring Peshawar. Through the Maktab al-Khidamat, they made a call to all Muslims throughout the world to come to the rescue of their Muslim brothers in Afghanistan and to fight the "infidel" Soviets. This office helped to offer travel, food, housing and training coordination services to the incoming mujahideen.

Peshawar became the destination for those that were later known as the "Afghan Arabs," those that flocked to the jihad in Afghanistan. They came in the thousands: Western bureaus have estimated that 100,000 Muslims from all over the world trained in Afghanistan in the period between 1979 and the time that Russia withdrew defeated from Afghanistan. Among those that came to Pakistan was the Egyptian surgeon Ayman al-Zawahiri, who worked with the Red Crescent and visited Afghanistan. Al-Zawahiri was a commander of Islamic Jihad, the group accused of killing Anwar Sadat. After his release in 1986, al-Zawahiri returned to Peshawar and resumed his work with the Red Crescent as a doctor in the Red Crescent Hospital, as well as engaging in work with the mujahideen. During this period, his relationship with Bin Laden became closer; however, it is said that his relationship with Abdullah Azzam was not strong. Azzam rejected al-Zawahiri's talk about the permissibility of killing Muslims, arguing instead that the targets that should be focused on were the infidel West and its followers, such as Israel.

In November 1989, Azzam and two of his children were killed by the explosion of a bomb buried on the side of the road. It blew up the car that they were riding in on their way to pray in the mosque. My friend Fath al-Rahman Ali has told me that he was only a short distance away from the explosion, since, at the time, he was working with a relief organization among Afghani refugees. A month following this event, Huthaifa, the son of Abdullah Azzam, went to the airport in Peshawar to welcome incoming mujahideen. One of these arrivals was Ahmad Fadel al-Khalayleh with a new name: Abu Musab al-Zarqawi. Huthaifa has said that al-Zarqawi was the only one among the new arrivals that drew his attention.

Al-Zarqawi moved from Hayatabad to the Afghan city of Khost, where he trained in Sadah, a camp loyal to the martyr Abdullah Azzam, only to witness the defeat of the Red Army. Thus, he missed the jihad against "the infidels" because, at that time, Russia had begun to withdraw! He remained there, however, until 1993. During this time, al-Zarqawi enlisted in the Sada al-Malahim military training camp along the Afghani-Pakistan border and joined the Taliban forces in their 1992 attack on Kabul. He worked, as well, as a correspondent for *al-Bunyan al-Marsous*, a newspaper for the mujahideen. However, it was noted that his skills in writing and his religious knowledge were clearly weak. Sada al-Malahim was the same camp that Ramzi Yousef—the mastermind behind the 1993 explosion at the World Trade Center in New York—graduated from, as well as Khalid Sheikh Mohammed—the mastermind behind the September 11 attacks that reduced the two towers to dust in 2001.

In 1993, al-Zarqawi returned to Jordan and the Jordanian intelligence services put him under surveillance, fearing that the Afghan Arabs would direct their weapons at their countries' governments. The Jordanian intelligence services' hunch was proven correct when they discovered, in 1993, that the mujahideen returning from Afghanistan were forming jihadist cells. At that time, Jordan was conducting peace talks with Israel, which resulted in the Wadi Arabah Treaty. In Jordan, the relationship that al-Zarqawi had established with Abu Muhammad al-Maqdisi (Issam Muhammad Tahir al-Barqawi), a scholar of Salafi jihadism of Palestinian origins, grew stronger. Al-Maqdisi is among those that hate the West and its allies. At that time, he published his book *Millat Ibrahim*, in which he drew clear dividing lines between the Western system and Islam. Together, al-Zarqawi and al-Maqdisi began to preach these ideas and to attack the Jordanian government and its relationship to Israel and America. According to Atwan in *The Digital Caliphate*, though al-Zarqawi enjoyed a kind of charisma, in the estimation of his lawyer Mohammed al-Dweik, he lacked intellectual depth. Al-Maqdisi established his jihadist cell, which he called Bayat al-Imam, and al-Zarqawi joined. Shortly thereafter, the security authorities arrested them. They accused al-Maqdisi of smuggling weapons and found grenades in al-Zarqawi's house. At the trial, al-Maqdisi attempted to turn the court's prisoners' dock into a pulpit for his preaching: he attacked the government and even accused the late King Hussein of violating the sanctities of God. The court sentenced them to 15 years in prison. However, in 1999, after they had spent five years in a maximum-security prison in the Jordanian desert, the new king, Abdullah bin al-Hussein, pardoned them.

My source in al-Qaeda rejects the above narration, which is mainly Atwan's, and informed me that Bin Laden never gave money to Al-Zarqawi.

He told me that Al-Zarqawi secured some funds from supporters of Jihad in Saudi Arabia through a Palestinian friend of his. He also challenges the allegations that Al-Zarqawi recruited Mujahidin from refugee camps in Lebanon, or that he was the first man of the camp in Herat. This source claimed that the first man in the Herat camp was an Afghan from Herat itself. He also claims that Saif al-Adel never intervened in order for Bin Laden to change his opinion about al-Zarqawi. He believes that al-Zarqawi was well versed in Arabic, well self-educated and good a writer. Furthermore, he opposes the point that the Jordanian security found weapons in al-Zarqawi house. Additionally, regarding the indecent in which Mohammed Baqir al-Hakim was killed, my source claims that al-Zarqawi was only two hundred meters away from the site of the bombing, he confirmed the point that his father in law was the man who carried out the operation.

Yet, this source confirms what was written in one American report I once read, which said al-Zarqawi attended the funeral of his mother when he sneaked in to Jordan from Iraq; and that he sneaked to Iraq through Iran. He said the Iranians didn't detain him because he was not known to them as an important person among the jihadist, as they did with famous ones like Saif al-Adel

According to this al-Qaeda source, al-Zarqawi's hatred of the West, particularly of America has no parallel. He wished to wake in the morning to find the "leader of the infidels" wiped from the surface of the earth!! . The source believes that Gamaat al-Tableegh is the Muslim group that led al-Zarqawi to the Mosque in Zarqaa for the first time after his early chaotic life. He is not sure about al-Zarqawi's marital status and his first marriage before his trip to Afghanistan. But agrees that presentation of the picture of the man in the Security Council by Collin Powell is the incident that brought fame to him among the "World jihadists ", after which he became second to Bin Laden.

As prison often does to those with political views, prison made al-Zarqawi more fanatic and extremist. In prison, he and al-Maqdisi formed a jihadist cell. According to Mary Anne Weaver in the July/August 2006 issue of *The Atlantic*, al-Zarqawi was the one who truly controlled the cell's members, to the extent that he could order them to move with his eyes alone. She further states that, while in prison, he focused on building his muscles and reading the Quran. Those who were in prison with him have said that he would cry fiercely while reading the Quran. After his release in 1999, he left for Pakistan, smuggling himself into Afghanistan after the Pakistani authorities arrested him in Peshawar for not having obtained a visa to enter the country. During this trip to Afghanistan, for the first time, al-Zarqawi met Bin Laden in Kandahar, which the Taliban had adopted as its capital. Those that tell the story (like the authors of *ISIS: Inside the Army of Terror*) say that the meeting between the two was not a warm one. Bin Laden was not comfortable with the presence of a tattoo on al-Zarqawi's arm and thought, at first, that he was a Jordanian intelligence agent. Bin Laden was bothered by al-Zarqawi's pride and arrogance, as well as his extremist views and his fanaticism towards the Shiites, whom he said must be annihilated, which did not please Bin Laden, as his mother was a Syrian Shiite.

Despite that, on the recommendation of Saif al-Adel, a former colonel in the Egyptian Special Forces and an al-Qaeda's security official, Bin Laden agreed to make al-Zarqawi head of a training camp in Herat, the third largest Afghan city, close to the border with Iran. When this occurred, al-Zarqawi encouraged a number of recruits from Palestine and Jordan to join his camp, which he called al-Tawhid wal-Jihad, the same name that he would use for his group in the period after he went to Iraq. During this time, bin Laden saw al-Zarqawi as rebellious and al-Zarqawi did not pledge allegiance to al-Qaeda, continuing to enjoy some autonomy, despite the fact that bin Laden provided the 5,000 dollars of initial capital to fund the training operations at his camp. Al-Zarqawi focused on suicide operations (according to his enemies) or on martyrdom operations (as he saw it).

In December 2001, after the Americans bombed his camp in Herat, al-Zarqawi left Afghanistan, reaching Iraq by slipping through Iran. There, he joined members of al-Qaeda who had gone to northern Iraq ahead of him.

Those coming to Iraq from al-Qaeda—who had snuck through Iran—formed an alliance with the Kurdish Mullah Krekar's group, Ansar al-Islam. In that isolated part of the mountains of Iraqi Kurdistan, the two groups worked to ban drinking alcohol, listening to music and watching satellite channels. Many researchers, among them Abdel Bari Atwan, say that Saddam Hussein did not know about the presence of elements of al-Qaeda hidden among the Kurdish jihadists. At that time, information on developments in Kurdistan would not have been easily available as the area was under a no-fly zone and American protection. On the other hand, Saddam himself had changed his Baathist approach, announced the "Return to Faith Campaign" and written "Allahu Akbar" on the Iraqi flag.

On 3 February 2003, Secretary of State Colin Powell announced to the Security Council that Saddam had links to al-Qaeda. This was based on information leaked by Jalal Talabani's group to the Americans, which said that al-Qaeda groups were conspiring with Saddam to produce chemical weapons. Later, it was clarified that this information had no basis, but it was too late. A few weeks after Colin Powell's speech to the Security Council, America began its obliterating strike on Iraq.

It should be noted that Colin Powell showed a picture of al-Zarqawi in the Security Council, claiming that he was the link between al-Qaeda and Saddam Hussein. However, al-Zarqawi had not yet pledged allegiance to al-Qaeda and was located in the Kurdistan region, which was subjected to a no-fly zone and was no longer completely under Saddam Hussein's control. According to Mary Anne Weaver, as a result of his picture being shown in the Security Council, his status and fame among jihadists grew.

The Kurdish opposition were not the only ones to leak misleading information to the Americans. Ahmed Chalabi's group also participated in this. He was often mentioned by top Americans during the war against Saddam and for a period after, until they turned against him, just as they had turned against many before him that collaborated with them. The matter of Chalabi's deception of the Americans came to light, as did the matter of his embezzlement of banks' money, leading to a Jordanian bank prosecuting him in court. His star fell and he became insignificant, according to reports published at the time.

During his time in Iraqi Kurdistan, al-Zarqawi snuck into the Ain al-Hilweh camp in southern Lebanon to recruit jihadists for the network that he planned to form. We should note here that, in 2006, a top official in the Jordanian intelligence services declared to the American periodical, *The Atlantic*, that the Jordanian intelligence services are entirely sure that al-Zarqawi had no links to Saddam Hussein.

Following the American invasion of Iraq in 2003, al-Zarqawi moved his group, al-Tawhid wal-Jihad to fight in the Sunni region of Iraq. He became famous for carrying out two large operations. The first was on 7 August 2003 when his group exploded a car bomb at the Jordanian embassy in Baghdad. The second was the explosion of the UN headquarters in Baghdad twelve days following the first operation, in which 22 people were killed, including the UN envoy to Iraq, Sergio de Mello. Al-Zarqawi's men also murdered the prominent Shiite leader Abdul Majid al-Khoei in Najaf in April of 2003. And on February 1st 2004, 100 people were killed in Erbil.

On 29 August of the same year, al-Zarqawi's group killed more than 100 people, among them the senior Shiite leader Mohammad Baqir al-Hakim in an explosion carried out by Yassin Jarrad, al-Zarqawi's father-in-law. These operations led to further fame for al-Zarqawi among the Sunni tribes and the remnants of Saddam's forces, to whom he appeared as a symbol of resistance, and caused mujahideen to flock to him from outside of Iraq.

Al-Zarqawi spread an atmosphere of instability in the Sunni region and caused so much damage to the invading forces that the Americans put a ransom of 25 million dollars on his head!

Al-Zarqawi was harshly and unwisely excessive in his killing of Shiites, just as he was excessive in killing any Sunnis that showed sympathy with the invading forces. This caused his sheikh, Abu Muhammad al-Maqdisi, to criticize him. In November 2005, after al-Zarqawi bombed a hotel in Amman, Jordan, killing 60 people, al-Maqdisi attacked al-Zarqawi's methods of jihad in a program on the Al-Jazeera network, also criticizing the al-Qaeda leadership.

The extremist path followed by al-Zarqawi helped him to maintain the cohesiveness of his group, as it was composed of elements that shared in his same approach. However, this path was weaker in its ability to mobilize and recruit among Iraqis. In fact, it made the Americans' task of inciting and mobilizing the leaders of the Sunni tribes against him easy and helped them to form the Sunni Awakening.

My al-Qaeda source tells me that when al-Zarqawi started operations in 2003 his followers were around 1500 men, but by 2006 the number of his men was close to 15,000.

Brian Fishman believes that the disagreement between al-Zarqawi and al-Qaeda was old, as al-Zarqawi opposed al-Qaeda's plan to target and defeat the distant enemy before turning to the close enemy. This has been confirmed by the Egyptian al-Qaeda security official known by the name of Saif al-Adel, who remains imprisoned in Iran. Despite the fact that their goal was one and the same—establishing the Islamic caliphate—their disagreements as to approach, style and timing has been clear from al-Zarqawi's days in Afghanistan. This disagreement between them lasted until after 2004, when al-Zarqawi swore allegiance to al-Qaeda. His severity eased with the arrival of the "distant enemy" in Iraq itself. However, al-Zarqawi's gratuitous bloodshed and his extremism in targeting all Shiites did not please Bin Laden. It seems, though, that maintaining their relationship publicly in the last periods of al-Zarqawi's life benefited both al-Qaeda and al-Zarqawi. Al-Zarqawi took advantage of al-Qaeda's legitimacy among those seeking to fight jihad and recruited from among that pool. Al-Qaeda was able to keep their name alive through al-Zarqawi's actions after having been weakened by American strikes in Afghanistan. In his last days, al-Qaeda ordered him to stop targeting civilians and Shiite targets, but he disobeyed these orders and paid them no attention.

Al-Zarqawi was proud of his approach, which al-Qaeda considered a deviant jihadist approach, incompatible with the system and teachings of Islam. That being al-Qaeda's opinion of him, what do you think the opinion of the average moderate scholars of the Islamic world was on him? Al-Zarqawi became known among the mujahideen as "the Stranger." This was a nickname that pleased him, as it was allusion to the hadith, "Islam began as a something strange and it will return to being strange, so blessed are the strangers." Thus, he considered that his jihadist path, though it seemed strange, was pleasing to God because it was consistent with the strangeness used to describe the prophets in the early periods of their prophethood. Al-Zarqawi did not care much about the repulsion that this extremist approach was met with by Sunni society around him because he maintained the cohesion of his group relative to what was around it.

Al-Zarqawi believed that continuing to slaughter the Shiites would cause them to take revenge on the Sunnis. These attacks of revenge by the Shiites would, in turn, unite the Sunnis against the Shiites, adding them to his ranks, and bring Sunnis from outside of Iraq to fight the Shiite aggressors, further strengthening his ranks. The idea of provoking a sectarian war was deeply rooted in his mind. He publicly stated its benefits in alerting the Sunnis that the Shiites want to eradicate them. Al-Zarqawi not only targeted Shiites because of his religious conviction that they were infidels. He did so also for the purpose of punishing them for their alleged cooperation with the invading forces. However, how can all Shiites be categorized as cooperating with the occupation when some of them fought the occupation and some of those attained martyrdom while doing so?

Al-Zarqawi, though, was extremist in his position on all Shiites and would describe them as the "scum of humanity," calling them "poisonous snakes" or "deadly poison." Al-Zawahiri took notice of the harmful effects of al-Zarqawi's strategy of targeting Shiites: it was distorting the image of the movement of the mujahideen. He warned al-Zarqawi of this in the summer of

2005. Al-Zawahiri also saw that this indiscriminate targeting was distracting the movement from its greater goal—fighting the American forces—and that al-Zarqawi's attacks were random, not differentiating between religious institutions, cultural institutions or residences. His November 2005 attacks on three hotels in the Jordanian capital of Amman, which were met with wide condemnation throughout the Arab world, were an example of this. These attacks also further alerted the Jordanian authorities to the danger that al-Qaeda posed, causing them to increase their activities and surveillance, which led to their observation of 300 jihadists sneaking into Jordan, perhaps awaiting instructions from al-Zarqawi to carry out operations.

On advice from the Jordanian intelligence services, the American intelligence services observed a link between an Iraqi Sunni cleric and al-Zarqawi. In June 2006, they followed this cleric to the house in which al-Zarqawi was hiding in the area of Baqubah. This later allowed American forces to bomb the residence, an attack in which al-Zarqawi was heavily injured. When the American forces extracted him from the debris, they found him alive, staring at them with a gaze overflowing with rage. However, as a result of his injuries, he soon breathed his last.

The killing of al-Zarqawi meant that al-Qaeda in Iraq had been infiltrated and that spies sent by intelligence apparatuses were among their ranks. Thus, they undertook greater precautionary measures to protect the new emir who followed al-Zarqawi, known by the name of Abu Hamza al-Muhajir. According to the American General William Gladwell, he was an Egyptian whose real name was Abu Ayyub al-Masri.

The writer of *Black Flags: The Rise of ISIS*, Joby Warrick, believes that the mistakes made by the United States and the Arab leadership facilitated the rise of al-Zarqawi and, following him, ISIS, who make al-Qaeda look, in comparison, small and moderate.

Recruitment and Joining ISIS

In an interview by the Al Jazeera network with the former Iraqi National Security Advisor Mowaffak al-Rubaie, the latter stated that Twitter and Facebook were the reason that 30,000 Iraqi soldiers in Mosul lay down their weapons, removed their military uniforms and fled from the city when ISIS attacked them. This was a reference to the power and efficiency of the movement's messages on social networking channels in provoking fear and panic due to the scenes they show of throat-cutting.

Before targeting Mosul, ISIS began a massive propaganda campaign, among whose films was "Saleel al-Sawarim" [The Clanging of the Swords], which the writers of *ISIS: Inside the Army of Terror* described as "jihad porn." The film shows scenes of the killing of ISIS enemies with silencers, most of whom are security, military and police officers. The jihadists come up to them at their positions, both during the day and at night, filming the entire operation. It contains scenes of one the leaders of the Sons of Iraq—the Sunni forces, formed by the Americans, which fought the armed opposition to the Americans. ISIS fighters enter his house and invite him to dig his own grave with the help of two of his sons, who admit, in front of the camera, that their father was the one who convinced them to work with the Iraqi government. The scene ends with this leader recommending that all those that belong to the Sons of Iraq repent, saying, "Here I am, digging my own grave," before being shot and buried. There is another scene in which an official is questioned on what he knows about counter-terrorism in the city of Samarra in his own bedroom. He is asked to remove his military uniform from the wardrobe, then is blindfolded and his head is cut off. There are other scenes, as well, of sniping soldiers, blowing up security and military installations and suicide or martyrdom operations, the locations of which are filmed from afar, but are incredibly bloody and violent in a truly terrifying way. Thus, this film and others like it provoked fear and dread in the soldiers.

However, the effects of this film and other ISIS's media and propaganda materials are not limited to the soldiers and security forces. It has been proven that they have an effect on enlistment and recruitment. Young people that love the action films marketed by Hollywood are seduced by these scenes of terror, especially those among them who are activists, who are religious and follow the developments of world politics or those that empathize with the West's oppression of Muslims, Western transgressions in

Iraq and Afghanistan or what happened to the Palestinians in the West Bank and the Gaza Strip and in Srebrenica, among other things. These people are not opposed to seeing scenes of violence against the major Western countries or those that they consider to be collaborating with the West. Thus, ISIS's killing of those that side with or that are loyal to the West is seen by those young people as a heroic act. In this way, the films affect their decision to immigrate to ISIS's territory.

The authors of *ISIS: Inside the Army of Terror* state that even those that fell victim to or were brutalized by ISIS attest to ISIS's power of persuasion. Thus, many believe that it is ISIS's power of persuasion that attracted supporters from different backgrounds. This process of persuasion is carried out via the Internet and social networking channels, as well as through real-life examples, such as its success in operations of expansion, its military victories and its seizure of cities and military garrisons. Furthermore, ISIS's system of administrating the areas that it controls and its ability to make security prevail in these areas represents another element of attraction. The authors of the abovementioned book cite many examples that explain how people from different sectors of society in Syria, for example, came to join ISIS.

Hamza Mahmoud is from a Syrian family from the city of Al-Qamishli. He began to communicate with the nearby ISIS camp, provoking his wealthy family's anger, who warned him against joining the group. When all of their efforts ended in failure, his father broke his leg! However, as soon as he was healed, he disappeared and cut off communication with all of his family, except for his brother, who was shocked by the ideas that his mujahid brother began to expound upon and his defiant defense of ISIS's men and their devotion to their religion. They also cite an examples of a Kurdish man joining ISIS. Though the Baathists that form a part of the ISIS leadership are those that killed his family in Halabja with poison gas during the days of Saddam Hussein, he believes that a gradual change has occurred within them since the "Return to Faith Campaign" and that the shock of the invasion and the growth of their friendship with Islamists in American prisons bettered their faith. This Kurdish man joined ISIS after he heard the group's spokesman, Abu Mohammad al-Adnani, say, "Our war with Kurds is a religious war. It is not a nationalistic war—we seek the refuge of Allah. We do not fight Kurds because they are Kurds. Rather, we fight the disbelievers amongst them, the allies of the crusaders and Jews in their war against the Muslims…The Muslim Kurds in the ranks of the Islamic State are many." In October 2014, one of the ISIS military leaders that headed the attack on the Kurdish-majority Kobanî was the Kurdish Abu Khattab al-Kurdi.

Some people join ISIS because of their hatred of the Shiites in Iraq or in protest of what they consider the Nusayri government (Sunnis often do not classify the Nusayris—the Alawites—as Muslims because some Nusayris say, "There is no god but Ali"! Whereas the Shiites treat them as Shiites.)

In Syria and particularly in Iraq, these people saw ISIS actions as an antidote to the Shiites and their transgressions against the Sunnis. The London-based newspaper *The Telegraph* has published an interview that they conducted with Sheikh Ahmed al-Dabash, one of the leaders of the Sunni rebellion in Iraq and the head of a brigade called the Islamic Army. In this interview, which took place in June 2014 in New York, Sheikh al-Dabash stated, "I want to say to America and the world, this is not an ISIS revolution. This is a Sunni revolution. We ask the EU and America to support the Sunni people. We are not terrorists." Another Sunni fighter said to the BBC that same month, "ISIS [is] so far the best thing that has happened to many Sunni tribes since 2008."

Many young men, especially from the Arab world and particularly those that have Baathist backgrounds, joined ISIS because of their conviction that the nationalist project had failed. For them, severity and brutality in assistance of their ideology was not strange. The campaign of the Baathist message failed to achieve its goals of unification, just as it failed to bring the country into an era of civilization, culture and modernization. Furthermore, the power of this nationalist project, in addition to its chauvinism, does not harmonize with the spirit of today's tyrannical globalization. So, they aborted this option. These people and others do not see a real example of Islam in many of the Islamic countries, though they may be called "Islamic." Rather, they accuse these countries of subordination to the West, which they see as the manifestation of oppression. Thus, they find or think that ISIS represents courageous Islam that has come to protect their honor in countries whose culture venerates "honor."

ISIS has also enlisted many of those who were imprisoned in Iraq or Syria into its ranks. In the depths of prison, the factors of isolation, loneliness and complaints of grievances coalesce, giving rise to a special type of link. The religious among them took advantage of this climate and spirit, beginning to say to them, {O my two companions of the prison, are many lords differing among themselves better or Allah, the One, the Most Supreme?} Numbers of prisoners returned to God, but they became more obstinate and adamant towards their jailers, loaded with the bitterness of oppression and the conviction that the ruling jailers had deviated from the true path, turned away from justice and sold the causes of the homeland to its enemies. Thus, prison became an incubator of bitterness and future insurgents in Iraq and Syria, just as it is in any place where prisoners of conscience are arrested.

For example, the man nicknamed al-Athir al-Abbasi founded the armed group called the Lions of Sunna Brigade after his release from Sednaya Prison then, soon after, joined ISIS. Al-Baghdadi, his deputies and a number of his companions in prison founded armed organizations.

Others joined ISIS in admiration of its power, discipline and military abilities in its campaigns against other armed groups and its invasion of the lands where they reside, finding it to be the group worthiest of joining. Others joined because brigades, like the Free Syrian Army, have turned into gangs, which some writers have described as groups of bandits that have exhausted the citizens and some of whose leaders have become war profiteers. Elements of some of the Islamist brigades have aligned themselves with ISIS, believing them to be the most militarily capable and enjoying their clear perspective and lack of compromise in confronting the "infidels, secularists and apostates." These people either do not perceive or ignore ISIS's excesses in designating all those that disagree in opinion with them, even on secondary matters and even if they were their former brothers in jihad from al-Qaeda, as "infidels."

That many were splitting off from various brigades and joining ISIS was seen clearly in September 2014. In this month, 11 brigades, including al-Nusra Front, released a statement announcing their disavowal of the Western-backed Syrian National Coalition (the political arm of the Free Syrian Army and the like) and called for unity within an Islamic framework. In October, seven groups founded the "Islamic Front," releasing a statement in which they rejected democracy and advocated a system based on an Islamic Shura council. Despite the certain amount of extremism in this position, it did not lead those who hold it to become members of ISIS. This is according to the author of *The Digital Caliphate*.

However, ISIS took advantage of the disunity among the various brigades and, especially after ISIS's expansions in Syria and Iraq, many of these brigades' members flocked to join ISIS. The nature of extremism is that it leads to further extremism.

As for the the most deep-rooted Islamist groups in Syria, such as the Muslim Brotherhood, they distanced themselves from the loud extremist jihadi discourse, announcing that they are among mainstream supporters of advancing democracy. Even al-Nusra Front has positioned itself—to a certain extent—within a national program that has no international ambitions.

There is a faction of Sunnis in Iraq that grieve over the loss of the status that they used to enjoy and that have suffered atrocities after its loss. This faction has found that its only choice is to support ISIS and believe that that struggle has become one between Sunnis and Iran and its associates. In response to accusations against them, they justify the excessive violence as a manner of deterring Shiite supremacy. The authors of *ISIS: Inside the Army of Terror* cite the example of the secular lawyer Saleh al-Awad, who resides in the city of Jarabulus. He had been extreme in his criticism of ISIS before announcing his support of them because, in his view, they are the only antidote against the Kurdish expansion! Many people in the area of Al-Hasakah share in this opinion, while others in the areas of Baqubah, Homs and Hama have the same convictions. All of these people became captives of the theory of fighting fire with fire and evil with evil. This is a theory that is unwholesomely distant from the teachings of the true religion.

Of course, there are many that have not joined ISIS, but support it for the protection that they believe ISIS offers to the Sunni community, even though some of them do not have religious commitment and perhaps some of them are are even agnostic. Sunnis, particularly in Iraq and Syria, express their sense of being targeted and complain about the hardship, torture, violence and murder that they have suffered, circulating films of the torture and massacres in Houla, al-Bayda and Fallujah. For this reason, they do not oppose ISIS's violence, not because of religious justifications, but because of the political conviction that all states are founded by violence and bloodshed.

Their intellectuals discuss the European Hundred Years' War between England and France that occurred between 1337 and 1453 (despite its name, it lasted 116 years), the world wars, the wars of founding empires and countries, the violence that marred these wars and the amount of blood that was shed during them. For this reason, they do not oppose ISIS's bloodshed.

However, whoever repeats the claim that all those who join ISIS are people of intellectual principle and conviction talks nonsense. There is no doubt that among those that have joined ISIS are a number of opportunists and, perhaps, some who were previously criminals, who exploited ISIS's announcement that they would pardon all those that had perpetrated crimes if they repent before they fall into their power, as stated in the Quranic verse.

Production of Mujahideen in Prison

Just as Camp Bucca and other Iraqi prisons produced mujahideen, such as al-Baghdadi, much of the leadership of ISIS and the leadership of other jihadist and non-jihadist armed brigades, Syria's prisons produced jihadists. Many of these jihadists formed their own jihadist organizations, either alone or in co-operation with others.

For example, we find that three of the most important leaders of Syrian jihadist groups spent time in the Sednaya military prison outside of Damascus. These are: Zahran Alloush, leader of the Battalion of Islam, later becoming the leader of the Army of Islam; Alloush's companion in prison, Hassan Aboud, nicknamed Abu Abdallah al-Hamawi, leader of Harakat Ahrar ash-Sham; and, thirdly, Issa al-Sheikh, leader of the Suqour al-Sham Brigade. All three of them were arrested in 2004 and were released from Sednaya Prison in 2011, after the amnesty declared by the Syrian leadership, which the leader of the al-Nusra Front, Abu Mohammad al-Julani, benefitted from.

While the first three remained in Syria and founded their jihadist organizations, Abu Mohammad al-Julani set out for Iraq, joining al-Qaeda. He remained in Iraq until al-Qaeda in Iraq sent him to Syria to establish a branch there. The truth of his identity was revealed when the dispute between al-Julani and al-Baghdadi widened and al-Julani announced his loyalty and affiliation with al-Qaeda under the leadership of Ayman al-Zawahiri.

My al-Qaeda source, a Syrian, has informed me that he joined these four Syrians in their prison for some time and added that they were always talking about forming a fighting group if the regime released them. He believes they were real pious Muslims, and described Alloush as a Salafi close to the Wahhabis in his thinking. Another Syrian residing in Sudan who supports humanitarian activities in his country, and used to know Alloush, told me that he was a moderate and against ISIS.

According to an article published in *The Guardian* on 16 June 2014 on al-Qaeda's repudiation of ISIS, one of al-Qaeda's leaders, Adam Gadahn, previously wrote to Bin Laden in January, calling upon him to announce his displeasure with the Islamic State in Iraq's actions, even before the announcement of ISIS. This communication was found in what is known as the Abbottabad papers—the documents that were found in Bin Laden's house after his assassination.

Observers of the jihadist phenomenon in Syria estimate that those who were previously imprisoned in Sednaya, at some point before the announcement of ISIS, led more than 60% of the opposition fighters in Syria. However, their numbers gradually decreased after the announcement of the caliphate in 2014, as many of their fighters joined with al-Baghdadi.

These four organizations gained a good reputation among civilians in Syria because they were more respectful of citizens' private property than the fighters of the Free Syrian Army and quickly founded Sharia boards to restore people's rights, in addition to their bravery in combat. Some have gone so far as to say that most of the territory controlled by the opposition in Syria was gained by these jihadist brigades.

The prison commander at Camp Bucca, where al-Baghdadi and others were imprisoned, confirmed the impact of prisons in creating extremism. He told the *Washington Post* on 4 November 2014 that 24,000 people were imprisoned at Camp Bucca, among them leaders of al-Qaeda, Baathist officers and innocent civilians and that it was like a "pressure cooker for extremism." He further stated that, during their period of imprisonment at Camp Bucca, nine of the leaders of al-Qaeda planned and developed the details of the Islamic State's foundation.

Ayman al-Sudani and His Companions

There is no doubt that you, I and all of us are the biological fathers of our children, but perhaps we are only biological fathers and nothing else. We are the ones that obtained them through God's will and ability in this existence at this time in human history. However, fatherhood almost ends at this point! In the aspects of education and the formation of thoughts, convictions and culture we are no longer alone. There is a partner that shares with us in the education of our children and the construction of their culture, convictions, thoughts and way of life. This partner is stronger than you or I and is appreciated by your children and my own more than you or I. Thus, this partner becomes the one with a greater influence on our children than us. No doubt, our children respect us. In their hearts, however, there is a kind of [*sic*] even about many of the aspects of our culture, our way of life, the style that we follow in the administration of our country and ways of confronting the challenges of our age. In these aspects, our children have opinions and convictions that differ from our own. These are the thoughts and convictions most often formed by the "greater partner" in the education of our children: the Internet in all of its contemporary manifestations. This greater partner is the one with the stronger influence on our children, even the closest to them. This partner makes few demands of our children. For them, this partner is, perhaps, the easiest to deal with: it does not criticize their performance in university, does not weigh them down with responsibilities, does not frown in protest of something that they have done and does not scold them for their mistakes. Furthermore, it is entertaining, offers them factors of pleasure, taking them around the world in seconds. It makes them laugh, pleases them and entertains them. It informs them about factors and patterns of life and culture in a way that is beyond my power or your own and beyond our abilities. I am almost certain that any one of our children say to themselves, {By Allah, you are most surely in your old error} when we make a statement about any aspect of contemporary life.

I remember, one time, my friend and I were conversing with his daughter, a university student in Great Britain. In truth, she is polite and well-mannered. When we asked her about her opinion on her father and my generation, she replied in two words: "low IQ." This is the new version of "By Allah, you are most surely in your old error" There is no one that thinks you are surrounded by the challenges of your era and informed of its scientific and cultural developments and then accuses you of error and lack of intelligence.

This greater partner, who has seized our children and flipped their world-view, is the one that brought Ayman to ISIS territory. Ayman used to spend long hours with this partner shut up in his bedroom, while we ignored him. Ayman surfed the worlds of Twitter, Facebook, YouTube, WhatsApp, submerging himself in these worlds, while we ignored him. It came to the point where he almost no longer felt our presence because he was in his more welcoming and pleasurable world and did not need us much. Gradually, the greater partner came to widen the rift between us and Ayman, as Ayman's virtual world was wide, interesting, diverse and stimulating. In it were thoughts, views and cultures much greater than those of his father. Ayman continued to maintain a relationship with his father in which there was much respect and esteem, but he no longer found his father's guidance and knowledge to be the wisest, as he used to think when he was young.

I remember, when I was Ayman's age, I was not always skeptical of my father's visions and experiences. I would listen to his experiences, as well as those of my uncles, my father's friends and their whole generation, with pleasure and enjoyment. However, Ayman came to have another authority in his life, which he would turn to anytime he heard something from his father. The greater partner's authority is called Google!

In the seclusion of his room, Ayman began to learn things about the world and to compare his life with the lives of the people of his country. Through the Internet, he saw and he heard, despairing at the state of the country. He began to form a political opinion critical of the leadership of his country, accusing this leadership of curtailing the rights of the country and its people. His companions in their final year of the college of medicine also began to share in his convictions and he found that they all had the same school of thought. The ties between them became even closer through trips in which they spent the day at a farm in Alkadroo or Soba and through trips in which they listened to the talks on religion that Dr. Yasser would present. Dr. Yasser was a young religious man who spoke to them about the deterioration of the situation of Muslims due to Western control over their rulers, the West that is "openly dissolute, immoral apostates from God's true religion," according to him. Yasser spoke to them of the "pinnacle of Islam...jihad" and that "whoever did not attack or did not make up his mind to do so died an ignorant death." He told them that the the most virtuous jihad is a word of truth before a tyrannical ruler and that the best of martyrs is the man who stands before an Imam and enjoins the good and forbids the wrong and is killed as a result. This was in

May 2014. There were 17 young men and women, whose ages ranged from 19 to 21, that used to go on these trips. They were pure adolescents, but they were not inexperienced or naïve in their knowledge of the state of the world and the developments of its political conditions. They were overflowing with excitement and desire to fix the state of their country and the Muslim world. With the passing of time, six of them—four boys and two girls—found that they were more closely linked than the others.

The six met in Ayman's house in Al-Manshia. After his mother and father, both doctors, emigrated to the United Arab Emirates, Ayman lived with his sister and a servant in a house there. Ayman invited Dr. Yasser, whom he called Sheikh Yasser. At that meeting, a long discussion took place between Yasser and the six young men and women about how to fix the state of Muslims. Yasser began to tell them that the humiliation that Muslims suffer is the inevitable consequence of the neglect of jihad and that as soon as a people neglect jihad, they are dishonored. The discussion touched upon "Jewish and Christian conspiracies" against Muslims and Yasser riled the young men and women up, telling them that they were qualified to do something, that circumstances would not be fixed by sitting around and that negative attitudes are what destroyed the Muslims. The young men and women burned with enthusiasm. Yasser was well-spoken, adroit and cultured. He also spoke to them about what he called the "disgraces of Western civilization" and its moral decay as exemplified by permitting homosexuals to marry, the dissolution of the family, throwing the elderly in homes and not forbidding illicit sex. He spoke to them about the tyranny of the West, its desecration of Muslim blood in Iraq and Afghanistan, its oppression of Muslims and its violation of their honor in Abu Ghraib, Guantanamo and Bagram prison. He analyzed the political situation in Sudan and accused the so-called Muslim Brotherhood government of neglect, servility and weakness, further stating that there is no hope in Sadiq al-Mahdi or al-Mirghani, let alone the infidel communists or the agents of the Darfur movements and Malik Agar, ignorant racists and lackeys of the Crusaders. The young men and women's excitement flared up further and, in their following meetings and gatherings, most of their talk revolved around what Yasser said and the truth of his views and approaches. Of course, their perusal of jihadist websites on the Internet further strengthened and reinforced their convictions. They began to spend hours listening to and watching what these websites broadcast, amazed by the mujahideen's courage, sacrifice, love of their religion and faithfulness.

In June 2014, al-Baghdadi announced the Islamic Caliphate from the pulpit of the Great Mosque of al-Nuri in Mosul. In their first meeting following that, Sheikh Yasser began to speak to them about the model state, "the state of purity"! A state where the women are conservative, unlike those women that are clothed yet naked who fill the streets of Khartoum! A state where sharia law is implemented, zakat is levied, jizya is imposed on the Christians and the honor of Muslims is protected. A state where Muslims are blessed with their honor without the oppression of tyrannical rulers, but where the noses of the tyrants and the devil are rubbed in the dirt. At that moment, Yasser revealed to the young men and women the truth of his affiliation with ISIS, saying that al-Baghdadi, the true scholar of God's religion, was his leader and commander. He advised them to peruse ISIS's websites and to watch "Saleel al-Sawarim."

Those young men and women truly were pure and they all lived in close-knit, successful and conservative families that met all of their needs. All of them were either in their last or next-to-last year of university. Yasser succeeded in stroking their ambitions and increasing their commitment to their religion. They began to organize weekly Quranic recitation groups in Ayman's home in Al-Manshia. Yasser would also attend and had begun to encourage them to join ISIS, to sacrifice themselves for "God's true religion" and to renounce this world, as there is no life except for the afterlife. Little by little, the group began to increase their perusal of jihadist websites. One time, Yasser gave them the Kik website, as well as other secret websites through which they could communicate with young people like themselves within al-Baghdadi's state and Skype numbers so that they could speak to them face to face. The group became addicted to communicating with their companions in Iraq and Syria. Yasser assured them that websites like Kik and JustPaste.it cannot be traced, even by the Americans, because they hide the sender's location and identity. There is truth to this claim. As Yasser's mentorship of the group continued, their ties were consolidated and the group's trust in him increased to the point where they swore their obedience to him to assist the "state of truth and to join the community of truth." Through social networking channels and safe websites, their companions within the Islamic State encouraged them to "immigrate" to aid in building the state. In March 2015, the six young men and women pledged to one another that they would immigrate to the Islamic State. At that time, four of them had graduated from the university and they convinced the other two that they could finish their fourth year of study within the Islamic State.

Some of the families of these young men and women noticed that they had become more isolated from the rest of the members of their families and that had begun to spend more time shut up in their rooms talking on Skype or sending messages through social networking channels. Their families noticed that signs of worry had begun to appear on the faces of their children. However, when their families enquired about what they had noticed, they did not open up about what was preoccupying them, instead, they reassured their families and changed the topic of the conversation. Their families convinced themselves that these were perhaps some of the mood swings, changes and fluctuations that young people their age are afflicted by, as they were, indeed, at that age of transformation. Not one of them imagined that their son or daughter was planning an incredibly dangerous matter.

The group began to meet Yasser at Ayman's residence to plan for their immigration to the Islamic Promised Land! They set a date for their departure and Yasser assured them that, for whoever could not pay it, he could arrange for the costs of the tickets and something for the costs of the road. In truth, at the end of May 2015, Yasser supplied them with six tickets and handed one of them 300 dollars. He gave them directions, saying that, when they arrived at the Istanbul airport, they should accompany one another in groups of two. Then, after they completed the procedures to enter Turkey, he told them that they should stand separately at a specific point in the airport, where a person, whose features he described to them, would come to take them to a bus and a taxi that would transport them to another bus stop. There, they would take a bus to Gaziantep, a city on the Turkish-Syrian border. He warned them, as well, not to speak much about their purpose to whoever sat near them on the plane and for each one of them to claim to be simply passing through Istanbul towards a different country.

On the day that had been set for their travels, each one of the six invented an excuse that would keep them away from the house that day. They agreed to meet a few hours before traveling near the airport, in front of Amwaj Restaurant.

The young men and women arrived at the Istanbul airport and were met by a Syrian man in his late 30s. He was elegant, dressed in a navy blue suit and red tie and carrying a Palestinian keffiyeh, this being one of the most important signs for them to recognize him by. He spoke with a Levantine accent and was friendly and courteous. The man took them outside of the airport, directing the four young men to take the bus to the specific bus stop inside of the city and asked to two girls to take a taxi. Before that, the six of them had changed the 300 dollars into Turkish liras at a currency exchange in the airport. In different vehicles, the six arrived at the bus stop to the border city of Gaziantep, where, in groups of three, they took a bus to that city. When they arrived in Gaziantep, another man, who had been described to them by the Syrian in Istanbul, met them. He took the boys to one house in the city and the girls to another. He assured them that the houses were "safe" and that they should not be afraid. They spent the day in Gaziantep and, in the morning of the following day, the man came to them and smuggled them across the border, where they found a van that took them to Raqqah, Syria. There, the girls were dropped off at the "maqarr," the hostel for women, and the boys were dropped off at the hostel for bachelors. They were all welcomed with greetings and congratulations. Someone made a stirring speech to them and they became excited and overcome with emotion so much so that some of them tore up and burned their Sudanese passports!

In Khartoum, the families felt the loss of their children when they did not return home, even at a late hour, and became worried. Each family asked those of their sons or daughters' friends that they knew, but did not find a trace of their children. In the morning of the following day, the families informed the authorities and went to the airport to ask there. In the airport, the families of the four boys identified their children in images from the airport's cameras, but the girls were not identified because they were wearing veils that hid their facial features. They returned to their homes all filled with grief and drowned in sorrows.

A few days later, the families of the six young men and women arrived in Istanbul to continue tracking their children. Ambassador Assem Tatay and his Deputy Chief of Mission, Ali Hamida, received them and, along with councilor Abdel Haq, Security Chief at the embassy, strove to inform the Turkish security authorities in the hopes that they would help them find their children. However, it was too late. At that time, the six young men and women had been moved to Al-Akirshi camp, near the Syrian city of Raqqah.

In Al-Akirshi, the women were separated from the men and all underwent a course in brainwashing that took 12 days. The program includes a series of lectures on the Tawhid, in which they study *Al-Aqidah Al-Wasitiyah*, the principles of Islamic jurisprudence and the rules of interpretation of the Quran. Books are distributed to them, such as *Mukhtasar al-Aqida* [A Summary of the Doctrine], written by Abu Bilal al-Harbi, who appears from his name to be Saudi; *An Explanation of Imperative Obligations*, published by ISIS's Bureau of Da'wah, Endowments and Mosques in the State of Raqqah, the northern sector; *The Captive*, by ISIS's El-Hemma Library, published by ISIS's Bureau of Legal Counsel and Research; *Clarification of Doubts* by Imam Muhammad ibn Abd al-Wahhab; and *The Jihad Trade*, by Sheikh Omar Abdel-Rahman (the Blind Sheikh now imprisoned in America).

After completion of this course, each mujahid meets with ISIS security officials, who enquire if he has any previous military experience. If he informs them that he has no military knowledge, he is sent to al-Manakher military camp. This is for men only: women are not subject to military training. However, husbands can train their wives to shoot. In this camp, the mujahid learns the basics of using personal weapons and, later, trains in the art of combat, engagement, camouflage and military planning. Booklets on the Katyusha rocket launcher and methods of firing rockets with it and another about military maps and how to read and apply them are distributed to the trainees. They also give them the book, *Field Philosophy*, written by the Palestinian Yusuf Hassan Hijazi in Gaza in 2011.

After completing both the ideological and military courses, the mujahideen are sorted into positions according to their abilities. Some are sent to the front of the fighting and others are sent to cities, where they are assigned civilian jobs. After selection and examination, a segment of them, who have been carefully chosen, are asked to return to their countries to work secretly for the Caliphate on missions assigned to them. This group is selected because of their unique abilities in speaking and communication, camouflage and their ability to make difficult decisions.

After the security examination has finished, each mujahid is given a form on which he writes his will and which includes information on his job and assignment in the Islamic State, number of wives and children and number of "slaves" and children with these slaves, if there are any. There is another form called the "martyrdom operations" form, issued by the Mujahideen Affairs Department. It explains the reasons for the operation and the will of the future martyr. ISIS also has a special form for keeping inventory of the spoils of battle. The mujahid can present a request for a female slave to the emir of his military unit, whose job it is to make a decision in this regard! In light of all these forms, *Al-Monitor* states that ISIS is the most organized and disciplined in documentation and recording information.

In Istanbul, I met the father of a Sudanese man who joined ISIS. He is a respected and religious Sudanese businessman and a man of piety, benevolence and charity. This man had searched for his son for almost two months. Ambassador Assem told me that all the families that have come to Istanbul tracking their children who have joined ISIS are very respected families: they are specialist doctors, successful businessmen and distinguished professionals. However, a shock has befallen them and broken their hearts and they return to Sudan filled with grief, sadness and pain.

It remains for me to note that those that have joined ISIS have come from many countries—almost 90—and that there are no less than 90 Sudanese among them. They came from all social classes and many of them had attained a distinguished profession in their country. Furthermore, as our ambassador in Iraq informed me, the chief justice of Mosul under ISIS is now a Sudanese man who graduated from Omdurman Islamic University.

One of my diplomat colleagues at the consulate in Istanbul, whom I trust entirely, informed me that a father of one of the Sudanese men that joined ISIS came to them in Istanbul, hoping, through a mediator or someone who had ties to developments within ISIS territory, to find his son and to bring him back. The man who spoke to me said that the father mentioned to them that his son used to tell him that he would not die a shameful death in his bed, but that he did not take his son seriously. He said that his son used to tell him that, if he wanted to join ISIS, he could ease the matter of travel for him. However, he thought that this was just "childish talk"! When communication was facilitated by his son initiating a call from inside ISIS territory, with all his feelings of compassionate fatherhood, the father began to exhort him to return and tried to interest him in life in Europe. The son laughed and asked what does all that mean to him after God has blessed him and adopted him as a mujahid fighting for God to uphold his word and to participate in building the Islamic State? He asked his father to pardon him, even tried to interest his father in joining ISIS, as ISIS needs specialized doctors like him. His father said that he was convinced that his son would become a martyr.

One of the young men who joined ISIS returned because his mother came to Istanbul with his father to search for him, bringing his infant brother who was born less than three weeks earlier, and this moved his heart. However, when he met him in Istanbul, he told his father that he came so that they did not return to Sudan empty-handed and filled with grief and so that he did not embarrass them. He told them that he would go with them to Sudan but that he would return again to fight jihad with ISIS.

The security officer that I met has a record of estimates of the number of those from Arab countries who have joined ISIS's cadres. He told me that most of the returnees are members of al-Nusra Front and not ISIS. He claimed that ISIS takes the cellphones away from each new arrival and that they do not return them until after they are assured of the sincerity of the arrival's affiliation and dedication in supporting them. This verification could take months, but they allow him a means of calling his family if he wants. The confiscation of cellphones is a precautionary security measure taken by ISIS for fear that their headquarters or camps would be targeted for bombing. He told me that there are different types of people who return. There are those return due to their conviction that they have completed their duty of jihad and that their obligation has been concluded: those will not go back to fight jihad with ISIS once again. There are those sent by ISIS to undertake missions outside of their territory and who might go back. A very few do not like one aspect or another of ISIS's approach and will not go back. This security officer also says that there are those that savor life with ISIS and that those will never return.

Those children of ours are sincerely religious and truly loyal to their faith. However, their knowledge of religion and their study of *fiqh* is highly questionable.

Foreign Fighters

ISIS has proven that it has a great ability to recruit and attract foreign fighters, whose numbers are estimated to be 30,000 or even, in some estimates, 40,000 fighters. It has also proven its ability to compensate for its human losses, which are estimated to be 6,000 fighters or, according to estimates by the American authorities, more than 10,000 killed in one year.

However, Orrin Schwab informs us that the phenomenon of drawing in foreign fighters by the thousands to participate in a war is not a new invention unique to ISIS. As an example of this, he mentions what was know as the Abraham Lincoln Brigade, which included 40,000 volunteer fighters, both men and women, who, due to their attraction to the cause, came from 52 countries to participate in the Spanish Civil War, alongside the Spanish Republicans. This war took place between 1936 and 1939 between the Nationalists and the Republicans and was won by the Nationalists. Schwab notes that 2,800 Americans joined the Abraham Lincoln Brigade.

Schwab further adds that the Third Reich also recruited volunteers during World War II, whose numbers were estimated to be between 300,000-500,000 foreign volunteer fighters from throughout Europe and even some that came from the Middle East to participate in the Waffen-SS. In the Waffen-SS there were 400 fighters that came from Ireland and were called the Irish Brigade.

As for ISIS, Tina Kaidanow from the Bureau of Counterterrorism within the US Department of State noted in September 2015, "The stream of foreign fighters volunteering to join ISIS is still flowing and even rising. And this flow will continue due to ISIS's unprecedented ability to attract and mobilize extremist followers through its use of the Internet and social networking platforms."

Estimating the number of foreign mujahideen that have joined ISIS cannot be undertaken by counting heads directly. Instead, it relies on reports of estimates performed by states about the number of their citizens that have traveled to join ISIS and recent intelligence reports have noted that the number of Western fighters in ISIS rose from 4,000 to at least 4,500. The American Bureau of Counterterrorism that this accumulation being carried out by ISIS occurs through what they call the "network effect." This is where friends recruit one another and families recruit other families.

It should be noted that not all of the foreigners that have arrived in ISIS's territory have been employed in ISIS's army. Some of them have been employed in civilian jobs. For example, Doctor Sameh Dhu al-Kurnain, a German of Egyptian descent who obtained his doctorate in Germany, has been appointed Dean of the College of Education at Mosul University. Doctor Dhu al-Kurnain has said that he left Germany and his wife and wed himself to jihad!

Women Mujahideen

It had been the general impression that women, in general, do not play a fundamental role in armed struggles and that those that did participate in operations of armed violence were individuals and exceptions that proved this "ancient" rule. However, the increase in the number of girls that have joined ISIS has completely overturned this rule. The percentage of women among the 4,000 foreign fighters has reached more than 10% (550 girls) and a similar number of girls play roles in supporting and assisting the activities of the state and society in ISIS.

From another perspective, investigative journalism research, studies and reports inform us that an overwhelming proportion of these girls that joined ISIS actually made this decision in full awareness of its consequences. This is particularly true as all of them are educated and no small number of them were exceptional in their studies and exemplary in their behavior and observance of the rules of social propriety (from the report, "Women and Extremism," published by the Institute for Strategic Dialogue).

Studies also show us that most of the girls that have joined ISIS actually came from comfortable social and economic backgrounds. Furthermore, the family ties within their families were strong and close-knit, causing their families to experience shock and defeat upon discovering that their daughters had joined ISIS. They also tell us that their mothers and fathers did not recognize early enough that their daughters were adopting jihadist thoughts.

Studies also inform us that these girls come from various ethnic backgrounds, varying locations, and different family backgrounds as regards the religious commitment of their mothers and fathers.

They also prove to me the falseness of the widespread belief that these girls have gone with the purpose of getting married or that whoever recruited them promised that they would become wives of mujahideen. Rather, the concept of "jihad al-nikah" [sexual jihad] is one circulated by intelligence apparatuses. Furthermore, it is a naïve idea as shown by the fact that it did not have an effect on motivating the girls to join ISIS. In fact the reasons that motivated them are varied. However, this does not negate the fact that many of them actually did marry mujahideen, were pleased to become housewives and aspire to give birth to the new generation of mujahideen.

These girls play other important roles for ISIS. Many reports have stated that they are better at recruiting Muslim girls in the West, for ISIS propaganda and at publishing their views and invitations to live under ISIS protection, particularly through social media platforms. Their positive comments on the life that they lead within ISIS is even used by ISIS's bodies specialized in propaganda and marketing. This is another indirect role that they play in recruitment ("Till Martyrdom Do Us Part," published by the Institute for Strategic Dialogue).

We can summarize the factors that motivates those girls to join ISIS as the following:

The feeling of social and/or cultural isolation from the Western society that they live in. This includes the question of identity and uncertainty towards belonging to Western culture

The feeling that Muslims throughout the world are experiencing violent oppression.

The sense of anger, sadness and frustration towards the lack of a positive response to confront the oppression that Muslims are experiencing.

Details of these three factors are the following:

Throughout their lives in Western societies, as most of them came from ethnic minorities that immigrated two or three generations earlier, they have experienced verbal insults or physical disrespect and innuendos about their ethnic affiliation. The girls who wear hijab or niqab have experienced insults and racist comments. These verbal and physical insults increase every time there is a "terrorist" operation undertaken by a Muslim. Unfortunately, press and media agencies feed this behavior that is insulting to Muslims and exaggerate in depicting Muslims as terrorists and killers. This is despite the fact that studies have proven that Muslims have killed fewer people than Christians in the West have.

I know a Sudanese woman (who has a Sudanese father and an English mother) who removed her hijab in the days following the killing of a soldier of the Queen's Guard in a London public street by two African Muslims. She removed it because of the insults that she experienced, which caused her to fear for her own safety and that Muslim women would be killed in the heart of London (a Saudi university student was, in fact, killed). In addition, new media outlets have accelerated the flow of images of corpses of women, children and the elderly and the destruction of houses and displacement of residents in Palestine, Iraq, Afghanistan and Burma, etc.

This generation alternates all of this with the accompanying comments that all of this has been done by the "infidels" against us, creating an estrangement between them and Western societies and a vision of "us versus them." This has been further exacerbated by the continuation of this for years without an adequate response or by the fact that the international community, at the head of which are the great Western powers, does not protect those oppressed Muslims. Of course, all the jihadist movements worked to further fan the flames of these ideas, growing and spreading them through new media. Thus, the West became the evil, murderous enemy or, at least, a participant in these crimes. So, these women ask themselves, "Why should I live in a society like this? Why should we not travel to aid the oppressed and persecuted? For this is a just cause, even humanitarian heroism."

The above were push factors that led to women joining. As for the pull factors, they are:

Achieving idealistic goals in performing a religious obligation and building an honorable city in the Islamic Caliphate.

Living in and belonging to a community that achieves brotherhood (or, in the case of women, sisterhood).

To enter into an experience with a certain amount of romanticism as regards its newness, idealism and strangeness.

Of course, social networking media, through the effective propaganda that ISIS broadcasts, play a large role in these pull factors.

Western Women Mujahideen

It should be noted that the first person to recruit women for jihad in the modern jihadist movement was Abu Musab al-Zarqawi. He used them in martyrdom bombings or, as some call them, suicide bombings. It is also important to note that ISIS does not use women in fighting. However, it is obvious that ISIS has succeeded in attracting women to join its ranks in an unprecedented manner. Thousands of women from all over the world have travelled—or "migrated" in the language of the jihadists—to support the "Caliphate" over the course of almost a year and a half. However, the influx of this number of women was not noticed early on. While the Westerners have suitable estimates for the number of Western women and girls that have joined ISIS, the number of women that have joined from Arab and Islamic countries is not known exactly.

The available information tells us that ISIS settles those Western women— and all other women—that have joined in groups that speak the same language. It also informs us that the ages of the Western women range from 14 to 46, excepting one German girl in ISIS territory who is 13. Thus, we can see that the Western women in ISIS territory are generally younger than the Western men who join.

We should add that those who have joined—both men and women—come from different ethnic and family backgrounds. Though the large majority of them are from Muslim families, some of them are recent converts to Islam. Furthermore, their levels of education range from high school to post-graduate study. All of these factors and variation in backgrounds demonstrate ISIS's ability to lure and attract Westerners, among others, and the success of its highly-developed recruitment strategies, on top of the continuing lack of a coherent Western or global strategy to confront the challenge of ISIS's ability to recruit.

It should be indicated that Western governments continue to view the issue of the influx of Muslim Westerners to ISIS from a socio-economic perspective or from the perspective of the issue of assimilation and equality. If it were true that the issue of economic equality and marginalization was the reason for this rebellion and the primary motivation for Muslim Westerners to join ISIS, the first to rebel and to become extremist would have been the European Gypsies (there they are called the Roma community). Because of their numbers and what they have suffered, they could have formed the largest terrorist group in Europe. Furthermore, the variation in social and economic backgrounds shows that this is not a complete explanation for the reasons that these women have joined ISIS.

Those Western women who have joined ISIS look with contempt at the Western project to emancipate women. They see it as a deception and a lie, like the sexualization of women and their exploitation as sexual objects. Furthermore, ISIS is an opportunity to free themselves from this tyranny and to enjoy solidarity, sisterhood, a real sense of belonging and self-respect. It is portrayed to them, as well, as a "true" project of empowerment and liberation, as Sasha Havlicek stated to the Foreign Affairs Committee of the UK Parliament on 28 July 2015.

In accordance with ISIS's propaganda machine as it appears on social networking sites, it has been reported that a specific secondary culture has emerged among Western Muslim women. Although, on the one hand, it is rooted in general Western culture, it also rejects Western culture.

What established this specific culture is, first, the presence of the capacity to reject because of the push and pull factors that I noted earlier. It was further reinforced by ISIS's message through social media that addresses these young women, saying, "You are not objects as you are treated according to Western culture. We give you great consideration and value." ISIS further bolstered this message during its negotiations with the Jordanians for the release of the pilot al-Kasasbeh, when they made the release of Sajida al-Rishawi, a woman accused of terrorism—who was, at that time, imprisoned in Jordan—a prerequisite for al-Kasasbeh's release. Despite all that I have mentioned above about the various reasons that motivated women to join ISIS, we cannot ignore the factor of adventure, especially at the age of these girls. Furthermore, we cannot ignore that ISIS took on a concrete form, thus differing from al-Qaeda, for example, in that it controls territory. This creates a stimulus for immigration to this territory, which becomes the focus point for their desires. Thus, ISIS's control over its territory is a matter of credibility for them as regards their message and thought.

The information available shows that the majority of the girls are educated and that most of them even excelled in their studies. Thus, the assumption that they are naïve or ignorant of ISIS's practices, which are described as brutal, is a shameful simplification, as ISIS's practices are well-known, including the marriage of ISIS fighters to a number of the female arrivals.

All the Westerners that have joined ISIS know the consequences of this choice: they may be killed, or suffer what that consider martyrdom. They also know the consequences of this choice in the Western countries. Austria, for example, forbids anyone who has joined a terrorist organization from returning to the country. In America, even communication over the Internet or preparing to join ISIS can lead to a sentence of 20 years in prison. They know all of this, just as they know of some of the difficulties of living in ISIS's territory as compared to the easy life that they lead in the West.

It is evident that the ISIS propaganda and the process of indoctrination that they are subject to, in addition to the push factors have made these women honestly committed to ISIS's ideological ideas and doctrine. Just look at their tweets on Twitter, such as Umm Ubaydah's on 20 November 2014, Umm Khattab's on 10 October 2014 or Umm Shaheed's on 28 November 2014, which sing the praises of cutting off heads and cheer, "Allahu Akbar," boast of their suicide belts or American grenades or ask permission from the "Commander of the Faithful" to fight or to blow themselves up.

How Did Khadiza and Her Friends Join ISIS?!

In the following, I tell the stories of some of the Western girls that joined ISIS, how they were recruited and what paths they took to settle down in ISIS territory.

I begin with the story of Khadiza and her friends, published in the *New York Times* on 17 August 2015. Khadiza was known for being sociable, cheerful and kind and for having a tendency towards humor. She was also known as being intelligent and excellent in her studies. She lived with her family in Bethnal Green, London.

One morning, Khadiza woke up early and informed her mother that she was going to school to spend some time reading in the library there. She took her backpack and promised her mother to be back before 5 p.m. When she did not return, her sister sent her a message, but received no response. Her sister went to the school, but did not find her. Looking into Khadiza's wardrobe, her family found that it was empty. The next day, after they had informed the police, an officer from the counterterrorism squad came to inform them that their daughter had travelled to Turkey accompanied by other girls. At a later date, the police showed them a tape of Khadiza and her friends, Shamima and Amira passing through the security checkpoint at Gatwick airport, on their way to flight number 1699 headed to Istanbul, and another tape of them in Turkey that shows the three girls riding a bus from Istanbul to the Syrian border.

Teachers at Bethnal Green Academy praised the three girls' good manners and behavior and the other students with whom they studied expressed their admiration of them. Khadiza, for example, was at the height of academic excellence: in her room, a letter of praise was found, written by one of her teachers. She even used to tutor her other peers. Amira was a good public speaker, well respected by all. One thing that came to mind was the one time that she defended the right of Muslim women to wear the hijab. One of their classmates said, "They were the girls you wanted to be like."

Members of the three girls' families said that they noticed a change in the girls, but that they attributed it to the changes and outbursts that young people their age experience. Their families have said that, after the girls' arrival in Syria, when they asked them the reasons for what they did, they girls responded that they left a society that lacks morality in search of one full of the virtues of religion, so as to give their lives meaning! In one of Amira's tweets, days before she left, she wrote, "I feel like I don't belong in this society." The *New York Times* adds that these girls wore the hijab in a society whose streets are hostile to this type of clothing. Furthermore, going to Syria allowed them the ability to decide their destinies.

On 17 August 2015, the *Daily Mail* wrote, "All three of the Bethnal Green girls are now married off to ISIS fighters." Khadiza married a Canadian, Shamima a European and Amira married an Australian called Abdullah Elmir. The girls were married in the third month following their arrival in ISIS territory, leaving those living in the hostel for unmarried women to accompany their husbands. The lawyer for the three families states that that the families have said that they are no longer the girls that they knew, that they have changed a lot. For example, Khadiza married even though, in her first communication with her sister in London, she stressed that she did not "migrate" to ISIS territory in order to get married, but she intimated—to the shock of her sister—that she was thinking about this idea!

ISIS has a "Marriage Bureau" that coordinates and organizes the meetings of those who want to get married. In the first meeting, they meet for five minutes. If they like one another, the length of the second meeting is extended. This is all done under the surveillance and supervision of the Al Khansaa Brigade, the all-female morality police specifically for women in ISIS territory.

From the perspective of propaganda, Western women joining ISIS is considered a great gain. This is because ISIS can point to them with pride, saying that these Western women abandoned the West and chose "the land of the Caliphate."

Khadiza's family states that her friend, who joined ISIS about two months before Khadiza, would send Khadiza messages through social networking sites encouraging her to migrate and goading her to leave "the land of the infidels" to be blessed with life under the banners of the Caliphate, in a "clean" and cooperative society, where life has meaning, so as to share in building the Islamic State and the victory of the oppressed.

Investigations carried out by the police have proven that four other girls planned on traveling to Syria. Three of them were from the same neighborhood as the girls who left and the fourth was from a nearby neighborhood. The judge made the decision to take away their passports.

A surprising element in the story of these three girls is that they excelled academically and that, despite this, they went to join ISIS in a year when they were supposed to take the exam to pass into the next stage of their education.

In the past months, despite their previous excellence, it was noticed that they had begun to neglect to finish their schoolwork. This is an indication that their focus had moved to another issue that they considered to have greater importance and priority. Furthermore, it has been proven that, for many who have joined ISIS, the influence of their peers or friends who preceded them was important in attracting them and motivating them to migrate. It has also been proven that young people shutting themselves up in the privacy of their rooms with social media is an issue that necessitates close observation by parents. This is especially true if they have been noticed to be quieter or more tense and rebellious. From observation of the three girls' accounts on social networking sites, we can see that they exchanged messages about the situation of Muslims in Syria and Myanmar, images of victims of killing and torture in those places and videos of this type from different places around the world where Muslims live that are experiencing instability. In Western society, where Islamophobia is propagated, these local and global factors cause pressures that made Khadiza and her generation feel that they do not belong and that they are oppressed. Thus, they search for an alternative to their societies. When I was an ambassador in London, I noticed that many young Muslims do not trust some of the Islamic centers and organizations that have links to the British government. Often these were founded somewhat secretly and indirectly by the British government to influence British Muslims and to distance them from foreign influences, in order to create a "British Islam." These young people mentioned examples, among which was the Quilliam Foundation, which they described as an arm of MI5 (the British internal security agency).

On 15 February 2015, two days before their travels, one of the girls sent a tweet to a British Muslim named Aqsa Mahmood, an ISIS recruiter who works through social networking sites. She lives in the British city of Glasgow. However, all this was known too late.

Khadiza's family has stated that it is unlikely that Khadiza had access to the 1,000 pounds sterling to buy the ticket to Istanbul. They have estimated that she would have needed almost 4,700 dollars to cover all of the expenses of the trip with some incidental expenses. The police have confirmed that investigations have proven that the ticket cost more than 1,000 pounds sterling and that it was paid for in cash at a travel agency in London! It has further been proven that the three girls had no source of money, leading to questions about an outside party that covered their expenses! With the assistance of the Turkish police, a hidden camera on the Syrian-Turkish border observed the three girls along with a bearded man as he led them in crossing the border. Dogan News Agency has stated that the police have arrested this man, who admitted that he demands 1,500 for each operation of smuggling a person across the border.

In a communication between Khadiza and her sister, she informed her sister that they were eating French fries, pizza and chicken. This led the family to come to the conclusion that they were residing in the city of Raqqah, the capital of the Caliphate. In the communications that the three girls had with their families in London, they did not seem to regret having left their families and their past lives in London. One time, the line of communication was cut off between Khadiza and her sister because of an air strike on the city.

Recently, an editor of a British tabloid paper pretended to be a young girl who wanted to join ISIS and communicated with Khadiza through Twitter and Kik. Khadiza gave her information as though she were retracing her own steps. She advised her to tell her parents that she was going to attend a review session to get away from the house. Then, she should take a plane to Istanbul and a bus from Istanbul to Gaziantep, a Turkish city near the Syrian border, where it would be easy to smuggle her into Syria. She advised her to deal with a travel agency on Brick Lane in her same neighborhood, which is unique in that it allows the option of paying for the ticket in cash without being asked too many questions. As many in Britain know, using cash for large expenses always causes doubts and questions about the possibility of money laundering or ties to organized crime.

The Sons of Iraq

In 2004, the armed brigades opposing the American-British occupation of Iraq increased and proliferated. Al-Qaeda, in one of its manifestations, was among them, as were other jihadist brigades. The fighting with the invading forces continued through that year and the year that followed. None of the invading forces' strategies to quell the flames of the resistance succeeded, especially in central and northern Iraq, where the Sunni groups are centered that claimed, in particular, many American soldiers. This is because, in their intelligence and knowledge, which exceeds that of the American cowboys, the British chose to control southern Iraq, where the Shiites who were loyal to the invading forces are centered. Thus, they did not lose many from the ranks of their forces.

In 2005 Anbar province was out of control despite the presence of the Coalition Forces, not only in terms of security, but also in terms of al-Qaeda's control over the province's resources. al-Qaeda's control reached a point where each director general of any department in the government had some-one from al-Qaeda sitting beside him, according to Global Security.

In 2004, as well, some notables from Sunni tribes in Anbar Province felt that cooperating with the invading forces would serves some of their eco-nomic interests. For this reason, one of them, called Abdul Sattar al-Rishawi (known as Abu Risha) from the Dulaim tribe, began to secretly communicate with the Americans, expressing his desire to cooperate with them to fight al-Qaeda in Anbar.

Sheikh Abu Risha started low level contacts, but by mid-August 2006 these low level contacts led to a formal meeting between him and Col. Sean MacFarland, and an agreement was struck. Soon recruits sent by the Sheikh started to flood American bases in Ramadi. Middle East Forum, Fall 2010.

This was met with approval by the Americans, who had been thwarted by the Sunni resistance and by its largest faction, al-Qaeda, and they were at their wit's end about how to stop it.. The Americans approved of Abu Risha's initiative and found it to be a golden opportunity to split up the Sunni ranks, deprive al-Qaeda of its support and to drive a wedge between the two parties, so as "the water turns against the fish," as Mao Zedong said. Here, Sunni so-ciety is the water that shelters the fish of the Iraqi resistance, al-Qaeda being among this group. Abu Risha's meetings with the Americans resulted in the formation of a tribal organization to fight against al-Qaeda. It was known as the Sons of Iraq and became famous as the Awakening movement or, after it increased in number and formed in other Sunni cities, the Awakenings movement. The formation of the Sons of Iraq is seen as an important development in that it had an effect on al-Qaeda in 2007 and 2008 in particular, and the developments and manifestations of al-Qaeda in a different way, as I will show. The Americans spent millions of dollars buying the sheikhs that established the Sons of Iraq and the volunteers, whose numbers reached 80,000 members.

The amassing of the tribes under the banner of the Sons of Iraq was completed in 2005. The organization was officially announced in September 2006, under the leadership of Abdul Sattar al-Rishawi, with the name of "the Anbar Salvation Council."

Observers of the state of Iraq under the occupation say that some Sunnis were weakened after a disagreement with al-Qaeda in which the group killed hundreds of them who were accused of cooperating with the occupation. In 2005, it is said that some of the sheikhs of the Albu Mahal tribe communicated with the Americans, as well, offering to fight al-Qaeda in exchange for the benefits of money and power that they collected because of this cooperation.

Because of sympathy and personal anger or because of the enticement of money, some of those that had previously fought with al-Qaeda or other armed brigades joined the Sons of Iraq. They were encouraged and had their hopes raised by the sheikhs of their tribes, especially as the Americans promised the sheikhs to later employ all those thousands in fixed employment in the army or other security forces or in civilian jobs. They also promised to assign the matter of administrating the Sunni areas to the sheikhs and the leadership of the Sons of Iraq. Thus, the enticement of money interwove with the enticement of power, motivating all these masses to join the Sons of Iraq.

The result of this was that, by the beginning of 2007, the previously impenetrable centers, such as Ramadi and Fallujah, were cleaned up of al-Qaeda. Of course, they were assisted by additional forces sent by the Americans to Iraq that year, which brought their numbers up to 30,000.

I should note here that the Sons of Iraq and the Americans did not target al-Qaeda alone. They claimed that they were targeting all of the resistance movements. Aside from al-Qaeda, these were groups of Baathists and officers in the military and security forces in Saddam's army that were dispossessed by Bremer's decisions for de-Baathification and to dissolve the military and security apparatuses and formed armed brigades. American sources estimated their numbers of their forces at 50,000, all of whom were in opposition to the Americans. Additionally, there were seven Sunni brigades that had come together under the umbrella of the Jaish Ansar al-Sunna, which was founded by these brigades five months after the occupation. However, al-Zarqawi's group, which was called al-Tawhid wal-Jihad, did not announce its unification with al-Qaeda until December 2004, when this group was the largest of the Sunni brigades and the deadliest for the Americans, British and their supporters. Even the Shiite cleric Muqtada al-Sadr sent forth his troops, fought alongside the Sunni brigades, participated in the First Battle of Fallujah and, after the battle, even prayed a prayer of thanks with the Sunni brigades in celebration of their shared victory. It should be noted that the resistance began 1 May 2003, the same day that President Bush announced, from the warship, "Mission accomplished." That same day that the President of America thought that the mission was over, the resistance against his forces began with hand grenades, killing seven American soldiers in their base in Fallujah.

The sheikhs that formed the Sons of Iraq perhaps did so because their saw al-Qaeda as deleterious to their interests. Al-Qaeda had begun to monopolize the markets that used to be under their sole control, such as smuggling oil and petroleum products from the Baiji Refinery. Furthermore, it did not seem that al-Qaeda was flexible in cooperating with them in this regard. Al-Qaeda began to routinely smuggle oil into Ramadi in order to resell it in other Iraqi markets, which had been the trade of the tribes. The sheikhs of the Sons of Iraq took advantage of the occurrence of two kidnappings and subsequent killings by al-Qaeda of sheikhs from the Albu Aissa and the Albu Diab tribes to promote the Sons of Iraq and to incite people against al-Qaeda and other resistance groups.

Abu Risha represents those sheikhs whose interests were harmed by the growing power of the resistance in his area. He worked in smuggling and research into his biography states that he was head of a gang of highway robbers that intimidated people and collected their money. Additionally, he was an opportunist and had ambitions to expand his control by attaining administrative and political positions in his area for himself and for the other sheikhs that supported him. Abu Risha enticed the unemployed young men in his area to join the Sons of Iraq by promising that, through the Americans, 900 of them would be employed in the Iraqi police in October and November 2006. Using the recruits of the Sons of Iraq, the Americans established security checkpoints, spreading these throughout the entire area, to observe and frustrate the movements of al-Qaeda and its likes. Abu Risha's ego was inflated by the Sons of Iraq's accomplishment in severely weakening al-Qaeda and his self-confidence increased. In 2007, he said to the *New York Times*, "I swear to God, if we have good weapons, if we have good vehicles, if we have good support, I can fight Al Qaeda all the way to Afghanistan." Abu Risha met with President Bush during Bush's visit to Baghdad that year. However, Abu Risha did not achieve his goal of expelling al-Qaeda from all of Iraq as he was assassinated one day after his meeting with Bush. On its November 9th 2012 issue, the Washington Post wrote that in 2008 the US had "contracted" 103,000 fighters working for the Awakening, and signed ceasefire deals with 779 separate Iraqi militias.

The Americans succeeded in reducing the number of resistance operations. Security improved in Anbar with attacks dropping from 1350 in October 2006 to just over 200 in August of 2007, according to The Middle East Forum Journal. They say that they did so by 90%, but this percentage only includes operations in which there were casualties. It does not include any other operations, although these caused non-human damages and fear and sapped resources. The experiment worked to a certain extent, but only temporarily, for reasons I will enumerate below.

The Americans resorted to implementing the Sons of Iraq experiment after despairing of the recruits in the army or the police having any efficacy, saying that these recruits lacked the will to fight. This is what they said at the time and was repeated word for word by an American military commander after ISIS seized Mosul on 10 June 2014. In addition to lack of will and desire to fight, some of them stole military equipment, smuggling it and selling it to those same enemies of America that they were enlisted to fight. The American Government Accountability Office warned of this in a report that it published in 2007, *The Washington Post August 6th,* which stated that 190,000 machine guns and handguns had disappeared (I repeat, 190,000 firearms). This means, as well, that the American government's weapons circulated through Iraq, used to kill that same government's soldiers. The situation was at its absolute worst: the Sunnis and the Shiites exchanged repugnant, terrible killing operations that targeted people based on their identity. Based on their identity, people were kidnapped, tortured, hunted down and expelled from their homes. Operations of religious or sectarian cleansing occurred, for which the Sunnis suffered the most. The occupation forces attempted to decrease the slaughter by fencing the areas and isolating them from one another based on sectarian identity. This solution worsened the sectarian sorting, increased the isolation of the two parties and kindled tales and talk that further fanned the flames of sectarianism. At the military level, in 2007, al-Qaeda was strong before being affected by the amount of American forces and operations by the Sons of Iraq. ABC news on August 25, 2014 quoted an American military official who was monitoring ISIS's movement, and described it's withdrawal from a battle around Erbil by saying "these aren't the same guys we fought in Operation Iraq Freedom .... they are tactically withdrawing . Very professional, well trained, motivated and equipped. They operate like a state with a military." Sergeant Benjamin Hanner, part of an armored unit of Stryker combat vehicles, described an attack on one of the cities in which al-Qaeda was centered. He said that they confronted them with a storm of sniper fire and RPGs and that they fight in small groups in a deceptive manner. The sergeant told the Washington Post, "These guys know what they're doing. They're controlled, their planning is good, their human intel network and early-warning networks are effective. They are skilled in using decoys. On one mile of our road they place 27 IEDs, but they made sure that only one in three or four was primed to explode. Never in my life have I seen organization like this"! Another sergeant said to the newspaper about al-Qaeda, "They are organized and all of them are trained and are good at shooting, so that they really hit their targets. Instead of sneaking around corners, shelling then running, they target you directly then begin to maneuver around you. The scene that you see looks like American soldiers are training." This is according to *The Digital Caliphate*.

On a similar note, on 4 June 2015, Nicolas Pelham wrote that a few hundred ISIS fighters held out for two months in Tikrit against 24,000 elite forces from the Iraqi army. They did not abandon the city until American planes began to bomb them. Pelham discusses the difficulty of regaining Mosul, considering that ISIS forces are extremely vicious and their numbers in Mosul are many times more than those that held out in Tikrit. Thus, he rules out the Iraqi government achieving an imminent victory in Mosul.

In June 2010, the Pentagon announced that, over the past three months, it had killed or arrested 34 members of al-Qaeda's senior leadership out of 42. However, the developments after this demonstrated that killing the leadership of al-Qaeda does not lead to the group's death, except for those that want to deceive or reassure themselves. The Americans killed al-Awlaki and al-Qaeda in Yemen became more vicious, until it was able to occupy a part of Hadhramaut. They killed Bin Laden and ISIS appeared, even more vicious and extreme in its brutality and strength than Bin Laden's al-Qaeda. This is in addition to the fact that these jihadists work in a system whose central leadership is constantly changing its location and members. This central leadership delegates authority to the local leaders and, thus, killing the upper leadership has little effect. ISIS benefited from the experiences of jihadists that came before them, who the Americans killed as soon as they obtained their cellphone number. Each idiot jihadist that used his cellphone was killed. For this reason, ISIS worked to design a special cellphone app and a communications network particular to them. Thus, it has become difficult to kill its members, except for those who are excessive in their cellphone use, those that are ignorant of the security measures or those who have had their location identified by a spy.

From the beginning, neither the Shiite government in Baghdad that controlled them nor the Sunni politicians were content with the formation of the Sons of Iraq. However, the Americans imposed the Sons of Iraq on them. As the Americans trusted the group, Sunni politicians feared that the Sons of Iraq would produce a new Sunni leadership that would compete with them oor even take their place. Anbar province's 2009 elections proved that the Awakening were a threat to the Sunni politicians when they secured 20 percent of the popular vote. The Shiites opposed them because they feared that the Sons of Iraq would become a solid core and rebel against them. Additionally, the Americans' promises to the Sons of Iraq to enable them to control their areas would remove the Sunni areas from Baghdad's control.

Therefore, when the Americans began their partial withdrawal in 2009, al-Qaeda and other resistance groups began to increase their activity. They rushed to target those Sunnis that they considered traitors. These were, in their opinion, those who "were prominent members of the Sons of Iraq." They killed hundreds of them, while some fled from Iraq to save their skin.

From another perspective, as a way of promoting themselves, the jihadists say that, as a result of the occupation and the weakening of al-Qaeda, life became more liberal in Iraq. The bars that were closed by Saddam Hussein in the 1990s reopened in 2010 and are now crowded with drinkers. Girls now frequent Baghdad's hookah cafes. Nightclubs have opened that publicize their dancers who dance until dawn.

The Failure of the Sons of Iraq

In the spring 2011 issue of the *Middle East Policy* journal, Myriam Benraad wrote an amazing study in which she argued that economic factors and narrow personal interests were the motivations behind the sheikhs' formation of the Sons of Iraq.

After the partial withdrawal of the Americans from Iraq, the members of the Sons of Iraq began a reverse migration back to the ranks of al-Qaeda and other brigades fighting the occupation. Though their numbers were not large, the study states that some of them continued to enjoy the monetary benefits that were amply bestowed upon them as members of the Sons of Iraq while working secretly with the armed brigades. Thus, they were trying to have it both ways. The study comes to the conclusion that this breaking off from the Sons of Iraq because it was, from the beginning, not based on "tribal patriotism." Instead, economic motivations represented the most important factor in its formation. It demonstrates this by pointing to the fact that the Albu Mahal tribe made a living by smuggling goods across the Syrian border. Thus, when al-Qaeda restricted this activity, they found in forming and joining the Sons of Iraq an alternative source of money, weapons and protection. I spoke earlier, as well, about Abu Risha's interests and history.

Just like the role played by Lawrence of Arabia, who used to distribute money to the Bedouins to the extent that he was called "the man with the gold"; so was the role of the Americans and their Dollars in alluring Sheikh Abu Risha and other sheikhs. The US forces spent more than 400 million USD by January 2009 on the sheikhs and supporters in the Awakening.

With the Americans' transfer of authority to the Iraqi Shiites in November 2009, the new authorities reneged on all the Americans' promises to the sheikhs of the Sons of Iraq. Of the 94,000 real and nominal members of the Sons of Iraq, only half of them were employed by the government in temporary jobs with moderate pay. Only a very few found permanent jobs. Of the 100,000 members of the Awakening, only 9000 had been employed by Iraqi security system, 30,000 have been employed by Iraqi ministries according to *The Middle East Forum Journal*. The government, under the leadership of al-Maliki, did not allow the sheikhs to control security in their areas or enjoy administrative and political authority, as the Americans had promised them. Instead, al-Malaki began to accuse the members of the Sons of Iraq of being Baathist and al-Qaeda infiltrators, revoking their permits to carry weapons in Diyala, Iraq's most violent area. This was considered a form of disarmament despite its failure to restore security to the region. Even worse, some of the leadership of the Sons of Iraq were pursued and arrested on the charge of terrorism.

With this, the hopes behind the promises dissipated. The Sunnis considered this a result of a betrayal by the United States, who used them and then threw them in the garbage. Out of frustration in 2012 Ahmed Abu Risha and many sheikhs joined anti-government camps in Anbar and made the same demands according to a report by Global Security. In all this, al-Qaeda found a better climate for attracting young men to its ranks, especially after the completion of the American withdrawal. Al-Qaeda worked to hunt the leaders of the Sons of Iraq and to chase them away from behind. Thus, the distance between the Sunnis and Baghdad increased and it has become difficult now to use the Sunni tribes to fight ISIS, as their lack of trust deepened because of their experience in the Sons of Iraq. For their part, the Shiites still remember that the Sunnis are the ones that quelled their revolution in 1991 after Saddam was thrown out of Kuwait. Saddam used them after the army's failure to put down the revolution in southern Iraq. Thus, the lack of trust is deep-rooted and the experience of the Sons of Iraq further strengthened this in the hearts of Iraq's Sunnis.

Recovery After the Sons of Iraq

The Awakening started in al-Qaim in 2005, by the rebellion of al-Bou Mahal Tribe. Yet the movement was weakened when al-Qaeda killed those leaders who cooperated with the Americans.

The second revolt of Sunni sheiks was announced by Sheikh Abdu Sattar Abu Risha in a conference of sheikhs in his home, and called their gathering the Awakening Council. Yet the real support to this council came only after Abu Fahad joined them. In 2006 they succeeded in assisting the Americans to push al-Qaeda out of Sunni provinces. The security situation in these provinces improved significantly in 2007, but by 2008 the leaders of the Awakening Council started to compete and seek to dominate one other. At this time al-Qaeda also started targeting the leaders of the Awakening Council.

In 2009, after being weakened by the Sons of Iraq, the Islamic State of Iraq (ISI) took refuge in Mosul, where most of its leaders congregated and which became like a safe haven for them. Thus began the period of recovery. The expert Charles Lister from the Brookings Doha Center states that, a year following this, the number of attacks and bombings carried out by the group began to increase, especially in urban areas. It also began to direct itself more towards professionalization in its military operations by adding previous military professionals to its military leadership. In this stage, they began to gather information on members of the security service, the police and the military, as well as on local government officials. Its intelligence capabilities developed, benefiting it in later stages. Around 2011, ISI implemented what was known as Operation Soldier's Harvest after Operation Breaking the Walls. In Operation Soldier's Harvest, ISI targeted security forces with threats and intimidation, after having gathered intelligence information on the families and addresses of officers in the security forces. This was facilitated by Operation Breaking the Walls, through which military commanders of ISI's leadership were liberated, who then provided assistance in planning and implementation and made the movement more professional. During Operation Soldier's Harvest, ISI carried out many assassination operations and bombings.

After al-Baghdadi assumed leadership, he strengthened his ties with the Sunni armed groups in order to gain more legitimacy among the Sunnis. In this way, his ties and coordination were strengthened with Izzat al-Douri's group, Army of the Men of the Naqshbandi Order and the Baathists that were very active in Mosul. This is despite the fact that the two parties do not have the same ideology and, for this reason, Charles Lister calls this relationship a "relationship of convenience." Both parties benefit from this relationship, as the Baathists historically have a relationship with and legitimacy among Sunnis and, on the other hand, ISIS seems ever ready to begin strikes. This relationship is ongoing and it is not known when it will be dissolved. However, it is certain that it will continue as long as both parties are subject to foreign pressure through the currently ongoing bombardments, certainly unless the Americans achieve another breakthrough among the Sunni tribes like that which succeeded in forming the Sons of Iraq.

The Caliphate

An image of Ibrahim al-Baghdadi, who, on 1 July 2014, pronounced himself Caliph of the Muslims in the Islamic State, circulated through social media. This image portrays him as being originally Jewish. This does not even serve his enemies and was a crude manner in a time when it has become difficult to hide information about one's self. The world that Wilbur Schramm, a media expert, described as a village in the 1970s has, due to modern technology, become a small room.

Perhaps what assisted this man's opponents in drawing this picture of him was that he had long remained hidden and tends towards secrecy. He has maintained this secrecy since he was a commander of the Islamic State in Iraq in 2010. It is certain that this disappearance and secrecy were recommended to him by his security apparatus, drawing on their knowledge in security and intelligence and learning from the lack of concern as practiced by Abu Musab al-Zarqawi, which allowed the Americans to target him in a drone strike in 2006.

Al-Baghdadi is Abu Du'a, Doctor Ibrahim Awad Ibrahim, also known by the name of "the Phantom" and "the Invisible Sheikh." He was born in Samarra, north of Baghdad, in 1971 and his full name is Ibrahim bin Awad bin Ibrahim al-Badri al-Qurashi. He is from the Albu Badri tribe, which claims that it is descended from the Quraysh, whose members are known as the "Family of the Prophet" (*Ahl al-Bayt*). He is from a religious family known for producing a number of imams and scholars of the Quran. His mother is from a respected family in the Albu Badri tribe. He received his B.A., M.A and PhD from the Islamic University of Baghdad in Islamic Sharia and Islamic history. As Abdel Bari Atwan states in his book on ISIS, this helped to elevate his success as a religious leader, something that Osama Bin Laden did not have.

Al-Baghdadi is known for talking little and being severe and serious. He was imprisoned by the Americans at Camp Bucca for about two years, beginning in 2004. A companion of his in prison (whom Atwan knows) described him as maintaining a constant smile, calm and self-possessed and having a large amount of charisma, making it difficult for those listening to him to not be affected by his speech, thoughts and convictions. His companion in prison also said that, when he was released from prison, al-Baghdadi said to his jailers at the gate of the prison, "We will find you on the streets somewhere, someday"! This is a clear threat.

It is known that al-Baghdadi understands the importance of "*hijra*" [migration] and believes that the withdrawal from an unwinnable battle is a kind of *hijra*. He enjoys the respect and obedience of his fighters, achieving that through his good reputation among them.

It is said that he has two or three wives. His first wife is named Israa al-Qaisi. Later, in 2010, he married Saja al-Dulaimi. She is the widow of a leader of the mujahideen, called Fallah Ismail Jassem. Her father was an ISIS commander, it is said that her sister was martyred in a suicide or martyrdom operation (according to how you define it) and her brother has been sentenced to death for bombings that he was behind in southern Iraq. It is further said that his marriage into these large tribes (the number of members of the Dulaim tribe is about seven million) aided his caliphate in gaining the loyalty of the tribes. According to information from the Iraqi Ministry of Interior, al-Baghdadi married a third woman named Fawzi.

Based on Atwan's book, like Bin Laden, al-Baghdadi loves sports. Bin Laden played basketball while, according to the London-based newspaper *The Telegraph*, al-Baghdadi loves soccer. The newspaper also said that he was an excellent striker.

Al-Baghdadi began preaching and doing missionary work at the Imam Ahmad Ibn Hanbal Mosque in Baghdad, where he was known as Sheikh Ibrahim. He gave lessons to his fellow prisoners in Camp Bucca. After his release from prison, he and others founded the Jaish Ahl al-Sunna wal Jamaa, a group that fought the Americans, but he did not swear his allegiance to al-Qaeda in Iraq when it was headed by al-Zarqawi or, after him, Abu Hamza al-Muhajir. After the killing of al-Zarqawi, al-Baghdadi joined his group, Jaish Ahl al-Sunna wal Jamaa, with the new mujahideen umbrella organization, called the Mujahideen Shura Council, and pledged allegiance to its leader from the Quraysh, Abu Omar al-Baghdadi. Following the killing of Abu Omar al-Baghdadi in a 2010 American strike, Abu Bakr al-Baghdadi was chosen as emir of the council.

In 2013, al-Baghdadi founded the Islamic State in Iraq and Syria. He occupied Raqqah, which he made the capital of his state. He did so by using powerful attacks, through which he was able to occupy oil wells in Syria and banks in Deir ez-Zor.

Abdel Bari Atwan says, "Al-Baghdadi fully understood and exploited the power of extreme violence. Using the Internet and social media platforms, IS's slick propaganda wing launched a grisly campaign disseminating images of massacres, beheadings, public executions—some by young boys—and amputations. Al-Baghdadi's background as a scholar of the Quran and jurisprudence lent some authority to his organization's harsh justice."

Westerners repudiate al-Baghdadi's actions and his extremism, classifying him as suffering from megalomania. However, opinion about this has not yet been decided among the Arabs. The majority support al-Baghdadi and some repudiate his actions, according to the results of opinion polls.

Al-Baghdadi's Development of the Movement

One of the most important things that al-Baghdadi achieved after becoming the leader of ISIS was to appoint military commanders from the "remnants of Saddam Hussein's regime" and to put them to work in military and intelligence jobs. They added a professionalism that achieved military successes for him in 2014. Thus the system of leadership and authority came to be composed of al-Baghdadi, who represented religious legitimacy, and, under him, military leaders with experience and professionalism.

The second development was to make most of the military leadership Iraqi, with the exception of Abu Omar al-Shishani, previously a sergeant in the Georgian army who who speaks Russian.

The third development was his success in establishing a social welfare system that offers services to citizens. He was able to do this because of the cash flow, which enabled ISIS to subsidize goods and services, leading to a kind of "silent consensus," in the words of Sheikh al-Turabi.

Charles Lister believes that ISIS's ability to care for and support the poor and the destitute "is a factor of strength and a factor of weakness at the same time." He believes this because he predicts that, in the cases of ISIS's failure to offer subsidies and welfare, this will weaken the silent consensus.

To this day, though, ISIS represents a political alternative for the Sunni community.

These developments are considered some things in which al-Baghdadi is superior to al-Zarqawi. Not only that, al-Baghdadi also excels over al-Zarqawi in establishing an effective governmental administration system and his unprecedented success in propaganda and media. Not to mention the tremendous expansion of the territory under his control, which was not possible for al-Zarqawi.

It should be noted here that the administrative system under al-Zarqawi was primitive, causing people to joke about him. Rumors began, at that time, that al-Zarqawi banned the eating of ice cream under the pretext that it was not present during the time of the Prophet (peace be upon him). There were other obscene and improper rumors, like those that said that al-Zarqawi's groups banned women from buying cucumbers because their shape is sexually provocative!

Al-Qaeda Central

After the strike on al-Qaeda in Tora Bora, its members dispersed from its stronghold there, finding refuge among the tribes of Waziristan in the west of Pakistan and among neighboring tribes on the Pakistani border and other areas of Afghanistan. There, al-Qaeda established ties with these tribes and Pakistani jihadist groups. Some of these relationships were further bolstered, even strengthened by the ties of marriage. More importantly than the ties of marriage, al-Qaeda benefitted from the strong and rooted tradition among these Pakistani and Afghani tribes of giving protection to those who seek it, no matter the cost of that protection and even if its price were a violent death.

However, most members of al-Qaeda dispersed throughout other Muslim countries, most importantly—from what developments have shown—to Iraq. Al-Qaeda members surreptitiously snuck into Iraq, finding refuge among the Salafist organizations in the northeast.

Throughout this period and until his assassination in May 2014, Bin Laden remained the leader of al-Qaeda despite the security precautions that froze his movement. As the documents obtained by the Americans in Bin Laden's cache show, the administration of daily affairs was entrusted to Mustafa Abu al-Yazid and then Atiyah Abd al-Rahman. However, al-Qaeda lost many of its commanders and operational experts, such as Adnan el Shukrijumah; the media expert and leader of al-Qaeda in the Indian Sub-continent, Ahmed Farouq; the American propaganda expert, Adam Gadahn; and Khalil al-Sudani, described by US Secretary of Defense Ashton Carter as al-Qaeda's expert in suicide bombings and bombing operations. Outside of its safe havens, al-Qaeda Central lost Nasir al-Wuhayshi, the leader of al-Qaeda in the Arabian Peninsula, killed by the Americans. The Americans, however, are still kept awake at night by survival of Farouq al-Qahtani (known as al-Qatari), whom they describe as being the most capable of al-Qaeda's military commanders.

The branches of al-Qaeda continue to recognize the leadership of al-Za-wahiri after the loss of Bin Laden, as Mohammad al-Julani, the leader of al-Nusra Front in Syria stated to the Al Jazeera network, and to implement his directives to limit their operations to Syria and to not target Americans at this stage. Qasim al-Raymi, leader of al-Qaeda in the Arabian Peninsula after Nasir al-Wuhayshi, has concurred. Al-Qaeda is also missing its security official, Saif al-Adel, who is imprisoned in Iran with his comrade, Sulaiman Abu Ghaith.

We notice, as well, the absence of al-Zawahiri from the media since the fall of 2014. He has not appeared since, except to present Hamza Bin Laden, Osama's son, in a speech that he gave last August that was broadcast on al-Qaeda's website, As-Sahab.

Perhaps al-Qaeda continues to use Afghanistan and the south and north of Waziristan as a refuge and remains in constant movement there because of security precautions. However, its situation there continues to be filled with danger not only because of American drone strikes, but also because the Pakistani army is fighting the presence of jihadist movements, particularly after each attack al-Qaeda undertakes. For example, according to what the Pakistani army announced, in one operation they killed 1,200 al-Qaeda members and seized 200 tons of explosives. There is no doubt that that security situation and the strikes that al-Qaeda is facing have halted its ability to attract sympathizers. Both factors have also halted its ability to establish large training camps. The group has begun to establish small training camps with the cooperation of its colleagues in the Haqqani network and the Pakistani Taliban, despite the fact that the relationship between them has subsided somewhat lately. This is because of al-Qaeda's opposition to the Taliban in Pakistan's targeting of Muslims, according to an al-Qaeda sympathizer that I met in Istanbul for the purpose of this book.

It can be noted, as well, that al-Qaeda's media activity has disappeared recently. It seems that the killing of Adam Gadahn has had an effect. The number of issues of the English-language magazine *Resurgence*, which Gadahn had been editor-in-chief of, have decreased, though the most recent issue, June 2015, maintained the same polished style that it used to be published in. The number of As-Sahab publications, 50 media publications yearly in 2008 and 2009, have also decreased.

After the changes and developments that invaded the Middle East since the outbreak of the Arab Spring revolutions, al-Qaeda began to suffer from the lack of a message clarifying its strategic plan vis-à-vis these developments. This showed that al-Qaeda did not plan for them. Its response to them came late and out of step with the developments, making it seem that the group has lost its concentration. The rise of ISIS also created challenges and competition for al-Qaeda in attracting sympathizers and enlisting them into its ranks.

Because of these consecutive developments, particularly in the Middle East, it seemed that al-Qaeda had not developed a precise plan of action for this region. This led to questions about the priorities that al-Qaeda is adopting now. On the one hand, the Khorasan group, sent by al-Qaeda to Syria, states that it will target America and Hamza Bin Laden said in his latest speech (August) that the plan to target America is still standing. At the same time, al-Julani, the leader of al-Nusra Front, has said that al-Zawahiri has directed him to focus his operations on Syria.

This is one of the reasons that motivated some members of al-Nusra Front to join ISIS, a group that has an openly stated and clear plan, a propaganda and media capability which al-Qaeda cannot compete with and courageous leadership that has even accused al-Zawahiri of deviating from the true path of jihad and following an outdated strategy. This caused al-Zawahiri, in turn, to describe the Caliphate as an emirate of seizure and usurpation, which was founded without a Shura council and which mujahideen are not required to pledge their obedience to.

Despite the weakness suffered by al-Qaeda Central and its loss of Iraq, it gained an active presence in Syria and East Africa. This is represented by the al-Shabab movement in Somalia; the al-Muhajiroun movement, which is somewhat active in Uganda and Tanzania; its presence in Yemen, whose branch announced their responsibility for the Charlie Hebdo attacks in Paris; as well as a branch in the Indian subcontinent, which attempted to seize a battleship from the Pakistani army in September of last year in order to attack the United States Sixth Fleet in the Gulf. Despite this weakness, al-Qaeda Central has not died.

After 14 years, on the day that I write this section of the book, it seems clear that the United States had achieved a victory over al-Qaeda in its stronghold and its safe havens in Afghanistan and in Pakistan. Its members were dispersed and its top leadership and helpers were killed. However, al-Qaeda Central achieved a victory, as well. It spread its ideas throughout a large part of the world, coming to have branches in Nigeria, such as Boko Haram, the northern region of Mali, in North Africa (Morocco, Algeria, Tunisia, Libya and Egypt), Yemen, Iraq (in another manifestation) and Syria. It is active in Pakistan, India, Indonesia, Afghanistan and Bangladesh. Michael Morell, author of *The Great War of Our Time*, says that al-Qaeda's thought produced jihadist groups that work in 20 countries around the world.

Bin Laden became an example to emulate for these groups because of his sacrifices as a millionaire who gave up a life of comfort and money and because of the successes of his group in targeting America on September 11th, the example of the destruction of the USS *Cole* in the Gulf of Aden in 2000, and, before that, its bombing of two American embassies in Dar es Salaam and Nairobi in 1998. Bin Laden became the magnet that attracted them to jihadist thought. When his followers dispersed, they disseminated al-Qaeda's thought and formed subsidiary cells and organizations. Muslim opposition to the American and British intervention in Iraq and Afghanistan added to Bin Laden's followers. There is no doubt that what followed the Arab Spring created safe havens in which branches of al-Qaeda can work, even finding weapons, recruits and money there. Fourteen years after what was called the War on Terror, al-Qaeda may have been weakened in its ability to carry out large-scale attacks, but its branches have been active in carrying out sporadic attacks, which are small but disruptive. However, the latest manifestation of al-Qaeda, as represented by ISIS, and what al-Nusra Front and other jihadist groups are doing around the world led Michael Morell to say, "2014 was the year that saw the most killed by global terrorism in 45 years." The rise of ISIS, which, during the past 10 years was called al-Qaeda in Iraq, the speed of this rise and its expansion in two countries has proven that killing even the top leadership of jihadist groups does not kill these groups. It perhaps even worsened the matter as it emerged in a form that made many, perhaps, wish for the relative moderateness of al-Qaeda when they saw what ISIS is doing.

ISIS was a source of disturbance because they believe the group to be a source of instability in the countries of the Middle East, especially because its propaganda and the lightning pace of its expansion attracted 30,000 fighters from 83 countries, among them close to 5,000 from Western countries. All of them gain fighting experience, which is a terrifying notion whether they stay or whether they return to their countries. Even those that did not migrate to ISIS territory, the group succeeded in attracting them. They have formed branches in the Sinai Peninsula, Algeria and Libya, where they can target Westerners. This happened when a group sympathetic to ISIS killed an American in a hotel in Tripoli, Libya frequented by diplomats and the killing of 21 Copts in Libya, which was attributed to ISIS, using the same manner of cutting off heads followed by ISIS. In March 2015, a branch of ISIS in Libya seized the city of Sirte.

Al-Qaeda Central has been weakened, but its branch called al-Qaeda in the Arabian Peninsula is considered responsible for three attempts to blow up civilian planes in 2009, 2010 and 2012. All the security apparatuses in the West continue to be disturbed by the presence of Ibrahim al-Asiri. Al-Asiri, according to the American Combating Terrorism Center, is the designer of a new type of package bomb that cannot be detected by the electronic screening devices used by security agencies. The center says that he is intelligent and inventive in addition to the fact that he trains members of al-Qaeda on how to make these kind of dangerous bombs. The center even describes him as the "most dangerous terrorist living today," saying that he was the one who invented the "rectal bomb" and who enlisted his brother to target Prince Mohammad bin Nayef using this bomb. Despite the explosion of the bomb, which sent his brother's body parts flying, even reaching the ceiling of the room in which they were in, God saved Bin Nayef. Al-Asiri is also the designer of what is known as the "underwear bomb," which the al-Qaeda member, Umar Farouk Abdulmutallab, almost succeeded in using to down a plane flying from Amsterdam to Detroit in 2009. Al-Asiri is also the designer of the "clothing bomb" made from non-metallic materials, which could be worn by an al-Qaeda member riding on a plane so as to bomb it, as well as other explosives undetectable by scanning devices or trained dogs.

Two brothers, members of al-Qaeda, one of whom was recruited by al-Qaeda in Yemen in 2011, were the ones that attacked the editors of *Charlie Hebo*, the newspaper that was publishing drawings satirizing the Prophet Muhammad (peace be upon him) and Islam in January 2015, killing 12 of the newspaper's editors. The French authorities called the attack, "the deadliest terrorist attack in France since 1961." While the two brothers were besieged by the French security forces, a third, sympathetic to them, took and killed four hostages in a market that sold kosher food. One of the brothers was trained in al-Awlaki's group's camp. This attack was the biggest one since the 2005 London bombings carried out by young Muslims who were recruited by al-Qaeda or sympathized with the group. Al-Qaeda's power has increased since the outbreak of the recent war against the Houthis. It offered them the opportunity to seize weapons and to normalize its relations and form alliances with the tribal groups fighting the Houthis.

The al-Qaeda Central leadership sent one of its leaders and his men to Kunar and Nuristan provinces in Afghanistan. These are some of the most rugged and most extremely harsh in the world, with their towering mountains, steep slopes and severe topography in which rivers flow with valleys so narrow that that make movement extremely difficult. He was sent there to ensure it as a refuge if situations worsened for them in Pakistan and the group was forced to resort to that area. This leader succeeded in gaining the friendship of the two tribes in the area and the protection of the Taliban there, so that branch of al-Qaeda grew larger with the joining of many new members.

This man is of Qatari nationality and is called Farouq al-Qahtani. Al-Qahtani now is a focus of attention by global security agencies. The expert Micheal Morell says of him, "[He] is a US counterterrorism expert's worst nightmare. He is smart and operationally sophisticated. He is also a charismatic leader. He is one of the few al-Qaeda leaders I worry might have what it takes to replace Bin Laden." Al-Qaeda also has a branch in Libya that killed the American ambassador in Benghazi in September 2012 and attacked a mall in Nairobi in September 2013. Its branch in Algeria attacked a natural gas facility in Amenas in January 2013. It was joined by a group that came from Mali and took hostages, killing more than 100 workers at the facility, among them seven Americans. This field is managed by BP and the Norwegian company, Statoil.

In 2012, the commander of al-Qaeda in the Arabian Peninsula advised his Algerian comrade, the commander of al-Qaeda in Islamic Maghreb, not to announce an Islamic state because the right circumstances for this had not yet arrived. He explained to him the necessity of benefiting from their experience in Yemen and that responding to the necessary needs of the people and offering them basic services are the first steps towards governing, but there are difficulties in the way. He also explained that the inability to offer these will lead people to repudiate the model. However, the leadership of al-Qaeda in the Islamic Maghreb did not understand this advice until later.

Al-Qaeda in the Islamic Maghreb benefitted from the chaos that spread through Libya after the fall of Gaddafi and his death. The group obtained many Libyan weapons and found in the security vacuum that resulted from political crisis in Mali at the end of 2012 and the beginning of 2013 an opportunity to fill that vacuum, according to an analysis by the Combating Terrorism Center. Al-Qaeda seized an area of Malian territory equal to the size of Texas, as the center states, implemented Sharia and opened training camps for the mujahideen that flocked from everywhere.

Because al-Qaeda in the Islamic Maghreb did not well understand the international scene nor the reactions of countries with interests, it was punished with defeat. France sent thousands of soldiers to Mali, killing hundreds of mujahideen, while the rest fled to the mountains.

In his book, *The Great War of Our Time*, Michael Morell concludes by saying, "Islamic extremism will stay with us for generations." Similarly, the former US Secretary of Defense Leon Panetta stated, "I think we're looking at kind of a 30-year war," in an article published on him by *USA Today* on 6 October 2014.

Summary of ISIS's Developments

ISIS developed in four stages. They are the following:

The first stage (2004-2006): Al-Zarqawi established a branch of al-Qaeda in Iraq, calling it al-Qaeda fi Bilad al-Rafidayn, which became known as al-Qaeda in Iraq. It launched a guerilla war campaign against the American forces and the Shiites in Iraq. This stage ended with the death of al-Zarqawi on 7 June 2006.

The second stage (2006-2011): This stage saw the establishment of the Islamic State in Iraq (ISI), which worked as an umbrella organization for a number of jihadist groups. It continued its operations against America and its allies in the government and among the Shiites. It was weakened by the Americans establishing the Sons of Iraq.

The third stage (2012-2014): ISI strengthened and established ISIS. After the American withdrawal from Iraq, ISI grew in power. After the outbreak of the civil war in Syria, ISI established a branch there, al-Nusra Front, assigning this mission to Abu Mohammad al-Julani. However, a disagreement occurred between them when al-Baghdadi, alone, announced the foundation of ISIS.

The fourth stage (beginning in June 2014): This stage has witnessed ISIS's dramatic achievements before its seizure of Mosul and establishment of a government center in Raqqah, which is considered its capital. After this, it announced the establishment of the "Islamic State" or the "Islamic Caliphate," led by Abu Bakr al-Baghdadi.

In September 2014, the United States announced its military campaign against ISIS.

Elders of international politics say that the lessons of history inform us of the failure of all invading forces to establish a stable political system. Perhaps recent examples include the failure of the Soviets in Afghanistan. In that country, the invasion resulted in the establishment of al-Qaeda. In Iraq, the branch of al-Qaeda was established after the American invasion. The Israeli invasion of Lebanon resulted in the establishment of Hezbollah, supported by Iran. Of note here is that the branch of al-Qaeda in Iraq was its first branch outside of Afghanistan and began with members of al-Qaeda that came from both Afghanistan and Pakistan via Iran.

CHAPTER THREE

THE IDEOLOGICAL AND POLITICAL

FOUNDATIONS AND OPERATIONAL ROOTING

The Ideological and Political Foundation and Operational Rooting

Few are the Americans, perhaps, that have occupied themselves with thinking about the reasons for the September 11th attacks. Most Americans were possessed by anger and desire for revenge, thus their response came like the raging of a wounded lion. For their part, polls show that most Arabs and Muslims hate the American government. They note that America has intervened in 14 Arab and Muslim countries since 1980: Iran, Libya, Lebanon, Iraq, Somalia, Bosnia, Afghanistan, Sudan, Kosovo, Yemen, Syria and three others! They note America's protection of Israel in the Security Council and that it supplied Israel with weapons to kill Palestinians in Sabra and Shatila, Gaza and the West Bank as well as Israel's destruction of Palestinian homes, establishment of settlements on their land and attacks on all of its surrounding Arab countries. They note America's occupation of Iraq and its blockade before that, that killed 1.5 million Iraqis in addition to hundreds of thousands killed in Afghanistan.

The Arab and Muslim masses felt humiliation and disgrace, which produced a desire for revenge among some young people. People listened to Bin Laden when he said that he decided that it was necessary to take revenge on the Americans when its ships shelled Beirut in 1984. Thus, the majority of the Arab people—according to polls carried out at the time—do not repudiate the September 11ᵗʰ attacks, but consider them a natural response to a tyrannical power that degraded them.

However, some thinkers in the West clarify the justifications for the anger among the Muslims. Graham Fuller has written enumerating the same resentments and reproaches repeated by the Muslims against America and the West, who recall their current practices and colonial history. We can examine what he has written in this regard in a number of articles published on his website and in his books. The importance of what he has written is highlighted by the fact that he worked in the area while employed by the CIA, then he specialized in Middle East affairs and wrote a number of books on the subject. The most prominent of his books is *A World Without Islam*. Patrick Seale, the British journalist and thinker, who specialized in the Middle East, also wrote on the subject, leaning towards Fuller's explanations. He pointed to the "militarization of foreign policy" at the hands of George W. Bush, under whom the Ministry of Defense's budget reached 700 billion dollars in 2012.

Mark Gabriel has written *Islamic Terrorism* and *Journey Inside the Mind of an Islamic Terrorist: Why They Hate Us and How We Can Change Their Minds*. The most dangerous is his use of "changing their minds"! Bridget Gabriel has written *Because They Hate*. However, these last two, while the first two authors are graced with depth, tend towards the style of tabloids that court the masses and try to satisfy them!

On the part of the Muslims, polls show that the majority support attacks on America, despite the fact that they hate violence on principle. For example, a poll conducted by the website The Religion of Peace informs us that 61% of Egyptians, 83% of Palestinians and 62% of Jordanians support the attacks. A poll conducted by the same website after the announcement of the Islamic Caliphate shows that 92% of Saudis believe that ISIS "conforms to the values of Islam and Islamic law." A poll conducted by Al Jazeera in May 2015 shows that 81% of people in the region support ISIS and its operations.

In an article in the November/December 2012 issue of the periodical, *Washington Report on Middle East Affairs*, Patrick Seale writes that 25,000 Yemenis went to fight in Afghanistan. Other sources inform us that 45,000 mujahideen went there from Saudi Arabia, so that the numbers of Arab mujahideen reached 100,000 from various Muslim countries. After America's occupation of Afghanistan, following the September 11ᵗʰ attacks, most of those who had remained in Afghanistan with Bin Laden dispersed to various countries. They dispersed, but kept in mind an experience they considered successful, that led to the defeat of the second largest military force in the world. From this, they gained military experience, capability, rigidity and preparedness to fight the "tyrant," as they call it, anywhere. They were filled with longing to reestablish the Islamic Caliphate after its collapse. In this regard, their literature discussed the role of Great Britain, who deceived the Arabs through its intelligence agent, T. E. Lawrence, famously known as "Lawrence of Arabia." They recalled the correspondences of McMahon, the British High Commissioner in Egypt, with Hussein bin Ali, Sharif of Mecca. In these correspondences, on 30 August 1915, McMahon promised Hussein bin Ali to support the "Islamic Caliphate" when he announced it and that the government of His Majesty the King of Great Britain would welcome the resumption of the Caliphate under the leadership of an "Arab of true race," in negative reference to the Turkish Caliphate in Istanbul! McMahon also promised him to support the independence of all of the Levant—with the exception of Lebanon, considering that it has non-Arab races—as well as Iraq and Egypt, to be, in addition to the Arabian Peninsula, the territory of the Caliphate, on the condition that he fight Turkey with the English. The Sharif of Mecca believed this deception and events occurred according to what Great Britain desired. However, the Arabs and the Muslims have not forgotten this deceit. What happened at that time remains alive in their hearts in countries that live and reside in the past more than they live in the present. Patrick Seale says that the Arabs have not forgotten all this and have not forgotten that "instead of Israel being America's guard-dog, it is the US which has become Israel's guard-dog." He adds that the Islamic revival that became prominent during the Arab Spring should be seen as a phenomenon of rejecting Western control and an affirmation of Muslim identity.

Jihadist groups were seized by the desire to bring back the golden past through reestablishing the Caliphate. This is based on texts in the Quran that reject injustice and oppression and encourage Muslims to oppose the oppressors with whatever power that they have. They also relied on books by scholars that are esteemed by Muslims, such as Sheikh Muhammad ibn Abd al-Wahhab and Ibn Taymiyyah, and quote Sayyid Qutb.

However, more important than all of these texts is young people's natural inclination towards rebellion against the forms of dominance and authority. Even if Islam were not present, these young people would rebel. Proof of this can be seen in that Ho Chi Minh and his comrades in Vietnam were not Muslim, nor were Che Guevara, Fidel Castro, Nelson Mandela, Jomo Kenyatta or Hugo Chavez. In their movement, the jihadist groups rely on a number of scholars that look at the *fiqh* of jihad, just as they look at the philosophy and military operations of the mujahideen, benefitting from their experience in Afghanistan.

Among these theorists is Mustafa Setmariam, who participated in the Combatant Vanguard group as well as the 1980 fighting in Hama, then joined al-Qaeda, where he became known as Abu Musab al-Suri. He wrote on the techniques of war and the foundations of jihad. He became the primary administrator under Mullah Omar, the leader of the Taliban. In 2005, he was arrested by American intelligence officers in Pakistan, who, in 2011, sent him to Syria slightly before the outbreak of the war, according to what Abdel Bari Atwan states in his book, *Islamic State: The Digital Caliphate*, published August 2015.

In 2011, the Syrian Abu Jihad al-Shami also became prominent after writing a guide to planning and carrying out operations called, "A Strategy for the Land of Gathering," the name being an allusion a hadith about Syria. In this book, he recommended that his comrades in Syria establish secret logistics cells and mobile battalions in the regions and avoid centralization in the beginning to avoid being targeted. He then advised them to attack the greatest number of sites in a wide area to disperse the "enemy's forces," according to his expression. He further advises coordinating operations and exchanging support among the mujahideen of Iraq and Syria so that the two parties are able to take advantage of safe havens in any one of the two countries if they are attacked and to facilitate the movement of mujahideen and their supplies across the border. He called for achieving monetary self-sufficiency through the seizure of oil and taking ransom to release prisoners so that they would have a cash flow available to them. He also stated that importance of their comrades forming sleeper cells in neighboring countries, while avoiding Jordan!

The Management of Savagery

However, the most important and dangerous strategic thinker of the jihadist groups is Abu Bakr Naji, who is thought to be Mohammad Khalil al-Hukaymah, known as Abu Jihad al-Masri. His book, *The Management of Savagery* continues to have a direct influence on the military operations of ISIS, as well as on the group's planning of propaganda and media, as I will show below. It is most likely that he is Egyptian. What makes this likely is that most of the examples that he cites in his writing are on the history, circumstances and positions of Egyptian jihadist groups.

Abu Bakr Naji was killed following an American drone strike in Waziristan, Pakistan in 2008. *The Management of Savagery* is even more influential than what the Chinese wise man, Sun Tzu, wrote in *The Art of War* and more dangerous that what Sayyid Qutb wrote in *Milestones*, though it was influenced by Qutb's writing in its ideological structure and its political position on the *Jahiliyyah*. *The Management of Savagery* was published on the Internet in 2004 and has not been printed as a physical book. Assuredly, there is no publisher that would dare to print it.

In the introduction to *The Management of Savagery*, Naji observes the currents of Islamic movements that have written programs. He discusses these and defines these currents as, 1. Jihadist Salafism; 2. Sahwa Salafism, symbolized by Shiekh Salman al-Ouda and Sheikh Safar al-Hawali; 3. The Muslim Brotherhood (the parent movement); 4. The Brotherhood of al-Turabi (as he calls it); 5. Popular jihad, such as Hamas.

He concludes that Sahwa Salafism revolves in a vicious circle, enabling the infidels, the Taghuts [idols or tyrants (cf. Quran 5:60 and passim). This is the word Jihadis use for contemporary Arab rulers who do not implement Sharia law.], and the people of hypocrisy to toy with it." As for the Muslim Brotherhood, he describes their program as innovative [heretical] and secular and a theoretical, "rotten" program based on flashy slogans. As for jihadist Salafism, he states, "the steps of their program are being followed as they were written on paper in accordance with the sharia laws and the sound universal laws." He further states that the struggle of this current with its enemies is the continuation of the struggle between the prophets and the people of unbelief and tyranny.

As for the brotherhood of al-Turabi, he says, "it is a current that took what is suitable for establishing a state...from universal laws. However, that current's neglect of some of the sharia commandments and its corruption of some others makes this state a secular state." His statement is unsurprising, as Dr. al-Turabi's modernizing ideas provoked Salafist groups, especially the extremist ones, some of whom went so far as to call him an infidel.

As for the current of popular jihad (Hamas, the Islamic Jihad Movement in Palestine), he states that it is similar to jihadist Salafism. However, its political thought has been infiltrated by the approach of the Brotherhood and the brotherhood of al-Turabi. Thus, he fears that the fruit of its labors will fall into the hands of the nationalist, secular apostates.

He then explains the stages of building the state. He specifies them as three stages: 1. The stage of the power of vexation and exhaustion, 2. The stage of the management of savagery, 3. The stage of the power of establishment: the stage of establishing the state.

He defines the goals of the stage of the power of vexation and exhaustion: 1. Exhausting the forces of the enemy and the dispersal of its efforts and work so as to make it unable to catch its breath by growing operations, even if they are small, like "the blow of a rod…[on] a (single) Crusader head"; 2. Attracting youth to jihad through qualitative operations that grab their attention, for example the operation in Bali, Indonesia. These are operations which, he says, "do not require consultation with the High Command"; 3. Training the groups of vexation in preparation for the stage of the management of savagery.

As for the stage of the management of savagery, he believes that it will come when chaos prevails in a Muslim country and its people long for someone who will maintain their security. He represents this as the stage that preceded the Taliban in Afghanistan and believes that the management of savagery succeeded in bringing stability and establishing a state: the state of the Taliban. Naji believes that the stage of the power of vexation and exhaustion is what led to the collapse of the Soviet Union and facilitated the stage of the management of savagery by the Taliban.

Naji predicts that the collapse of America will come, like the collapse of the Soviet Union that proved Sayyid Qutb's prediction of the end of Communism true, as well as the sheikh of the mujahideen in Afghanistan, Abdullah Yusuf Azzam's prediction of the end of the Soviet Union and the union's fragmentation. He cites a quote by the American writer, Paul Kennedy, whose prophecies the mujahideen love, saying, "If America expands the use of its military power and strategically extends more than necessary, this will lead to its downfall."

Naji clarifies that the goal of the mujahideen in carrying out qualitative operations, such as the September 11th attacks and the bombings in Nairobi and Dar es Salaam was to lead to the downfall of a large part of the fear and respect for America and to spread confidence in the Muslim people. Most importantly, in my estimation, is his statement that part of this is to "[f]orce America to abandon its war against Islam by proxy and force it to attack directly so that the noble ones among the masses and a few of the noble ones among the armies of apostasy will see that their fear of deposing the regimes because America is their protector is misplaced and that when they depose the regimes, they are capable of opposing America if it interferes."

He states that the second goal of these operations is to replace the human losses sustained by the mujahideen by way of the human reinforcements that will come as a result of their admiration of the qualitative operations and their anger at America's open interference in the Arab world. It seems that this man's experience in Afghanistan produced within him a great confidence in the mujahideen that leads him to disdain the great power and even to disregard it. Thus, he says with confidence, "If the number of Americans killed is one tenth of the number of Russians killed in Afghanistan and Chechnya, they will flee, heedless of all else." He cites the examples of the experiences of the management of savagery in the first period of the era of the Prophet in Medina and John Garang's movement (the Sudan People's Liberation Army) as an example in the contemporary era. He nominated a group of states that he recommends the mujahideen focus on: Jordan, the countries of North Africa, Nigeria, Pakistan, *Bilad al-Haramain* [the country of the two sanctuaries] (by which he means the Kingdom of Saudi Arabia) and Yemen. He justifies his reasons for choosing these countries, but does so in a context that makes it clear that this was a choice made by a group and not him alone. He also sets out the goals of the stage of the management of savagery, of which there are 12.

He further recommends that the "vexation strikes against the Crusader-Zionist enemy" be diversified and widened throughout the world so as to drain the enemy. As examples of this, he cites a tourist resort in Indonesia, a usurious bank in Turkey, a strike on an oil interest in the Gulf of Aden and the killing of two "apostate" authors in one simultaneous operation in two countries, etc. He focuses mainly on economic targets, particularly petroleum.

He believes that whenever the enemy is exhausted, it will incline towards reconciliation, adding, "of course, without a treaty." He warns the mujahideen that recruiting a million mujahideen from the general Muslim population is easier than recruiting them from the young people of the Islamist movement, whom he describes as, "polluted by the doubts of the evil shaykhs. The youth of the nation are closer to the innate nature (of humans) on account of the rebelliousness within them…"

As for military operations, he believes that operations in the form of waves send a message to the enemy that the waves of fear and paying the prices of his deeds will not come to an end. Furthermore, he states that we should consider that wave after wave of operations fills their hearts with a fear and that this fear has no end. He notes that one of the important principles of operations is, "Strike with your striking force and the maximum power you have at the weakest spots of the enemy."

Among the information that Naji reveals is that the attempt to assassinate Safwat El-Sherif, the Minister of Information at the time of Hosni Mubarak, failed because, the night before the operation, the one who was supposed to carry it out the killing stored his weapon in a damp location. When his colleague, who was facing the car, shot the guard and his turn came to shoot the minister, the bullets got stuck because of the moisture and the minister survived.

Naji titles the fourth chapter, "The Adoption of Violence." He states that whoever practices jihad knows that it can only be done through violence, crudeness, terrorism, displacement and demoralizing one's enemy and that he cannot move from one stage to the next, unless the first stage was one of demoralizing and scattering the enemy. He adds that the enemy will not be merciful if it captures them, whether they use force or softness. Thus, it is better to make the enemy think 1,000 times before he fights. He believes that the success of the Abbasids was because of their use of force, adding, "However, praise be to God, we are confronting the Crusaders and their helpers among the apostates and their army... Thus, there is nothing preventing us from spilling their blood; rather, we see that this is one of the most important obligations since they do not repent, undertake prayer, and give alms. All religion belongs to God."

In order to root this violence, he claims that Abu Bakr and Ali ibn Abi Talib (two famous companions and Caliphs of Mohamed) practiced burning people by fire. This is because, "…even though it is odious, because they knew the effect of rough violence in times of need." They cite a quote attributed to Dhiraar bin Al-Azwar, saying, "I saw no one other than the Messenger of God (peace and blessings be upon him) who was more filled with the ruthlessness of war than Abu Bakr. We once informed him of evil news about the apostasy and its magnitude and it was as if what we had told him did not bother him at all. His orders for the army dealt only with the matter of severing the neck without clemency or slowness. And he (may God be pleased him) even burned a man named Iyas b. 'Abd Allah b. 'Abd Yalil, nicknamed al-Faja'a, when he cheated him by taking the money for the jihad against the apostates and then joined them, or more accurately became a brigand." Perhaps this was ISIS's source for burning the pilot al-Kasasbeh, if it is true that they did so. However, stories on the deeds of the Companions of the Prophet such as this have not been vetted with the standards that the narration of the hadith carry. However, ISIS gives them legislative authority, which legalizes the punishment that the Prophet (peace be upon him) banned in the authentic hadiths in *Sahih al-Bukhari* and *Sahih Muslim*. It should be noted here that, in Islam, taking blood is not regarded as lawful, except based on the Quran or on *hadith mutawatir* [hadiths that have been narrated by a number of people]. Even *hadith ahaad* [hadiths that have not been narrated enough to be *mutawatir*] are not accepted by scholars as enough to issue a verdict that declare the shedding of blood permissible, let alone narrations of the deeds of the Companions of the Prophet.

Naji adopts what he calls a "policy of paying the price." He explains this by saying that any criminal deed that the enemy carries out should be met with a reaction from the mujahideen that makes the enemy pay the full price of his crime, so that he thinks a thousand times before undertaking an attack and so that despair fills his soul. He further states that paying the price must happen, even after a long period of time, so as to cause a deterrence for the enemy, making him incline towards reconciliation without any kind of treaty. He adds that this is because, "We do not believe in a truce with the apostate enemy, even if it were possible to do so with lifelong infidels"! The reader might ask himself where in the *fiqh* do we find the differentiation between the apostate infidel and the lifelong infidel. Naji believes that it is better if other groups in other areas carry out operations of "paying the price." For example, if the mujahideen in Iraq were attacked, groups of mujahideen in Morocco, Indonesia or Nigeria should carry out the response in order to confuse the enemy. Or, if the Egyptian government imprisoned mujahideen, then the mujahideen in Saudi Arabia, for example, must direct a strike at the Egyptian Embassy or take its diplomats prisoner, while following the policy of violence. These are his examples in which it can be seen that something other the ministry could end up paying the price for the ministry.

As regards media, Naji focuses on the necessity of the media activity of the mujahideen groups being broad and encompassing and the necessity of using all forms of media, so that their message reaches everyone. He further stresses the importance of filming all of the mujahideen's operations and broadcasting them widely, so as to be a deterrent to the enemy. This is exactly what ISIS has done. He also thinks that the mujahideen's media should carry out a wide media campaign showing the security and justice in the regions that they control. This would act as a way of attracting young people to immigrate to the areas that the mujahideen control to assist them and to live with them, despite the fact that the areas are predominantly lacking in people and wealth.

Naji discusses how to administrate the areas under their control, education and how to establish an effective security system.

The theses that Naji presented represent an "operational guide." This is what ISIS uses now, by implementing it in its military operations, showing violence towards the enemy, filming its operations of cutting off heads, killing the soldiers that oppose them by the hundreds, stoning adulterers, throwing homosexuals off of roofs and widely broadcasting all of these scenes on all of the social media platforms. Westerners admit their inability to keep pace with this, as each time their agencies take them down, a specialist from among the followers of ISIS is quick to broadcast in an even faster and more complete manner. For this reason, Westerners have recognized the skill of ISIS's followers in media, communications and computer technology and we find them constantly classifying these followers as "tech-savvy" and "adept."

They support their opinion on cutting off heads with the saying of Ibn Qayyim, "Striking the neck with the sword is, of the manners of killing, the best and fastest at releasing the soul. God, glory be to him, has prescribed the killing of apostate infidels by striking their neck with the sword without prodding."

The War of Ideas

It is related that Bin Laden said that half the mujahideen's battle should be fought on the media battlefield. The strategist, Abu Bakr Naji, advised the mujahideen to understand the media politics of the opponent and to work with them, as it is "very important" in winning the political and ideological battle, in his words. He decided that the most important thing that would help the political success of the mujahideen was the transmission of their media materials to their targets, whom they defined as everyone. Naji further advised them to widen the scope of the transmission of their media materials and to publish them as quickly as possible across all media, especially those operations that spread fear in their opponents and despair in their hearts, with a focus on the operations that show "severity."

It appears that ISIS is aware of the messages of both of these leaders and sought with seriousness, effort and knowledge to implement it. I have not found a specialist in media or propaganda or an expert in Middle East affairs or jihadist or terrorist (depending on their position) movements that has not recognized ISIS's extraordinary abilities in waging the media battle, especially using new media, as represented by social networking platforms. Instead, all of them are in consensus in recognizing that ISIS has cadres that are skilled in sending its propaganda materials and are proficient in this art, to the extent that some Western bureaus have stated that ISIS has won the "war of ideas" that is ongoing between it and the West. This is due to the fact that the new generation of fighters in the jihadist or terrorist movements (according to your opinion) differs from the al-Qaeda generation and is superior to al-Qaeda in this regard.

Thus, the new media allowed ISIS to expand, traversing the geographical borders of the battlefield through its publications on the internet, including media, activities, battles and even the slaughter of its enemies. Most of these are frightening and terrifying, causing Westerners in particular to classify the group as brutal. However, they recognize that it has conducted a propaganda campaign of publishing its "terrifying"—in their words—successes and re-cruiting young people, even from outside of the Middle East. This is another aspect in which ISIS is superior to al-Qaeda. The latter focused its propaganda more on like-minded people among the Islamists.

James Phillips at the Heritage Foundation says that ISIS is a collective move-ment, led by a new generation of Islamist revolutionaries that have developed a wide-spread propaganda effort via digital platforms in a way that is attractive to young Muslims. Thus, they embrace ISIS's extremist Islamist thought and flock to what this group calls the "Caliphate."

A researcher at the Brookings Institution believes that ISIS's propaganda machine succeeded in enlisting people into its ranks and attracting about 1,000 recruits to Syria and Iraq a month from almost 100 countries. He adds that ISIS transmits global messages that are attractive, bright and romantic of its version of jihad and its Caliphate in a way that attracts young people, as its architects are experts in propaganda!

Though I have not found any others, one person, Professor Max Abrahms, believes that ISIS's use of new media increases the sympathy and the recruitment of their targets, but that it also increases its rate of depletion because it repulses those who look at its media message, just as it motivates governments to respond more strongly in order to "combat terrorism." Perhaps he is referring in this last point to the success of the American Air Force in targeting an ISIS fighter when he sent a "selfie" from an ISIS center in Syria. When he sent the image, the American intelligence services were able to determine the location from which it was sent and to bomb the location in less than 24 hours. Because of the West's failure to this day to keep up with ISIS's media propaganda, some specialists indicate that the problem resides, as well, in America's inability to gain credibility among the young Muslims that ISIS is targeting.

Professor James Phillips believes that the United States should "secretly support" ISIS dissidents that publicly proclaim their critique of the group to confront what they call its extremist efforts. Of course, "support" is a diplomatic term for bribes or for recruiting agents with money! I add that the US Department of State has a Center for Strategic Counterterrorism Communications, whose work is limited to combatting "terrorist messages" that they transmit through social media. Those that are employed there are specialists that speak perfect Arabic, Urdu, Punjabi, Somali and, of course, English, to wage a "war of messages" against ISIS's media message and to strip it of its credibility. This is for the purpose of stopping the influx of foreign fighters to the group, or, in Secretary Kerry's words, "'drying up this pool' of potential volunteers." This is an effort which is, in his estimation, more important than the military effort.

It is worthwhile to note here that an important part of current American general foreign policy includes encouraging Arab religious leaders, Muslim scholars and news channels to condemn ISIS and to describe the group as harming and distorting Islam. However, an assessment published by the State Department in a "sensitive but unclassified" memo painted a bleak picture of the American administration and its allies' efforts in combatting and confronting ISIS's media message. It concludes that the "violent narrative" carried by ISIS's media messages via thousands of messages each day has "effectively 'trumped'" the efforts of the richest and most technologically developed countries, according to quotes in the *New York Times* on 12 June 2015 from that assessment. Even before the publication of this assessment, administration officials admitted that ISIS "...is far more nimble in spreading its message than the United States is in blunting it." This is a dangerous admission from the largest power in the world. The headline of this article in the *New York Times* was, "ISIS Is Winning the Social Media War, U.S. Concludes."

Currently, the United States is considering establishing a communications center that would be headquartered in one of the capitals of the Middle East. Its only mission would be to constantly send messages throughout the day in opposition to ISIS's messages, so as to attack its credibility by focusing on its "brutality" and its "harm to Islam"! This came about after the biggest American newspapers wrote that ISIS won the media and social networking war. It has been proven now that ISIS's media messages worry the entire American landscape, with even an assistant attorney-general saying, "It's an unprecedented threat environment that we're facing" because ISIS's ability to use these media and encrypted messages is superior to the American legal authorities' ability to close in on them. These messages are consistently reaching new sympathizers and encouraging them to carry out attacks against Western targets, even if these are lone wolf attacks. What worsens the Americans' anxiety is what Michael McCaul, Chairman of the House Committee on Homeland Security, has noted: "More than 200 Americans are believed to have traveled—or attempted to travel—to fight in Syria" and sympathizers with the groups in America are in the thousands. What worries them, as well, is that the directives by ISIS and the various branches of al-Qaeda to attack Western targets have found those to implement them on the ground. This is what happened in the Boston Marathon bombing; the attacks by the Muslim soldier who killed his colleagues at a military base inside America; the attacks on the editors of the newspaper *Charlie Hebdo*, which satirized the Prophet (peace be upon him); and the attacks on the kosher grocery in Paris; the attacks in Copenhagen; and the attempted attack on the head of the organization Stop

Islamization of America. Americans, Westerners and many other countries are worried that ISIS's propaganda machine is highly developed and that it uses encrypted messages and sites whose sources cannot be traced, like Kik, as their specialists acknowledged.

ISIS uses the part of the Internet that is known as the "dark web," which consists of encrypted websites. It is not known how many messages pass through it, but thousands of messages arrive daily. Of course, it is known that the internet was, at one point, the method of communication between CIA stations around the world and was, at that time, secret and no one else knew about it. When the agency developed a more modern and complex means, they gave it to the commercial public use market. However, what ISIS is doing these days can be described as giving them a taste of their own medicine! The severity of America's anxiety about ISIS's superiority in the realm of social media can be seen in how much this is written about in their newspapers and broadcast by their various media agencies.

Because ISIS's successes in this realm are so dazzling, so that they have become, in Abdel Bari Atwan's words, "the masters of the digital universe," he has given them the name of "the digital caliphate." This is because they are so adept and tech savvy. In their "jihadosphere," its thousands of supporters around the world use the Internet in a covert manner to post information on their movements through Twitter and other sites like it, in a way that hides their identities and the locations from which their messages were sent. There are innumerable websites that do this on the internet and ISIS itself has created means of concealment and programs that make tracing the group's members on the internet difficult, as Westerners have acknowledged. This is where recruitment, propaganda and the publishing of information take place.

On the Internet, there are websites, like JustPaste.it, that are not under surveillance because of the difficulty of doing so. Atwan states that, after the targeted recruit receives the first messages via Twitter or Facebook from a friend or an ISIS sympathizer, he receives messages on his smartphone via Kik or Whatsapp to strengthen the ties. These applications are also difficult to monitor. Kik is used by 14 million people and is mostly used for licentiousness, prostitution and selling drugs. These are websites on which it is easy for jihadists to conceal themselves, according to Western researchers, through which recruiters converse with potential recruits, as they are encrypted and can be used with the dark web and hidden operating systems.

It should be noted that ISIS, itself, released a cellphone application that transmits ISIS's news. Sympathizers can use accounts and have news about ISIS brought to them automatically and continuously. This application is called "The Dawn of Glad Tidings." ISIS has also produced its own video games, through which players can fight and kill an American soldier in the streets and plant IEDs!

All this has enabled ISIS to craft its image how it wants and to elicit feelings and desires among the Muslim youth to "migrate" to where they "belong," to where all are brothers. They can rebroadcast al-Baghdadi's message that there are no borders or barricades that prevent them from immigrating to Dar al-Islam, as all are one Islamic community. Thus, they should leave the countries of the "infidels" or the "apostates" and hasten to participate in building the Islamic State, quoting verses from the Quran that, no doubt, speak to the souls of Muslims. They show scenes that normalize martyrdom and striving for martyrdom and even celebrating it. Atwan states that this is their most powerful weapon, as the soldier who does not fear death cannot be defeated. ISIS often shows pictures of their dead fighters smiling and this is like magic to young Muslims.

The author of the *Digital Caliphate* informs us that, the man who is in charge of all of this is the Syrian Ahmad Abousamra, the head of ISIS's media department. Abousamra was born in France in 1981 and grew up in Manchester, where his father was a well-known endocrinologist. Ahmad obtained a university degree in IT and worked in England in communications before committing himself to the path of jihad. In his department, he has a full set of employees that publish Al-Hayat, Al-I'tisam and Al-Furqan. All three of these are for the purpose of propaganda. Al-Hayat was established in 2014 and is headquartered in Syria. Al-Furqan is dedicated specifically to matters of the Islamic State in Iraq and began in 2006. Al-I'tisam is a film production unit with headquarters in Syria that produces surprisingly advanced videos. Abousamra employs journalists, professionals, filmmakers, photographers and editors that swear their loyalty to Caliph Ibrahim al-Baghdadi as a requirement for their employment. They use the most modern techniques and qualified employees and, thus, the films that they produced are considered to be at the level of Hollywood production. These films show horror, which include mass executions that ISIS purposefully broadcasts to cause fear in their enemies. They also show the stoning of adulterers and throwing homosexuals off of rooftops. In February 2015, the video of the pilot al-Kasasbeh burning alive while in a cage became famous. This is despite the fact that some doubted in ISIS's ability to produce films of this quality that included the use of sound effects, zoom in on the location of the burning by satellite (or Google) and sliding cameras. The film of the burning of al-Kasasbeh was very widely posted by ISIS and its supporters seconds after its release, using JustPaste.it and its Arab equivalents, Nashir.me and Manbar.me. Via Twitter, the supporters were warned to await a big event and were advised to activate numerous duplicate accounts in case of doubt. Then, tweets were sent to supporters encouraging them to send numerous tweets to those who possess high-speed connections to download and save the films on anonymous clouds or mirror websites. In this way, the supporters overcame the governments' capability of removing the tweets because they bring them back as they were continuously and, each time, by sending thousands of tweets.

ISIS was strengthened by Junaid Hussain and others like him who have IT capabilities joining ISIS. I will discuss Junaid in another location.

ISIS operates a radio station, al-Bayan, based in Mosul and a satellite television channel, al-Tawhid, that broadcasts in Libya. In January 2015, the group announced that it was about to launch a television station that would broadcast over the Internet 24 hours a day on the website KalifaLive.info. ISIS believes that it is in a state of war with the "infidels" and, thus, deceiving them is admissible. Atwan and many others, especially the American think tanks, are filled with talk about ISIS's technical abilities.

Winning over Hearts and Minds

Since ISIS's enemies around the world are more numerous that its supporters and since war has been declared on them, the fog of war has hidden the facts, so that obtaining them has become exhausting, like searching for a needle in a haystack. Despite this, some have been able to remain neutral and to maintain a scientific approach in studying the phenomenon of ISIS. Because security apprehensions and, thus, fear of the West has come to control ISIS, the group has only let one famous global personality visit its territory: the German Jürgen Todenhöfer. He has written and spoken about what he witnessed and heard. I will set aside some room for his testimony in this book. As for the others, they solicit information about the course of events inside ISIS territory by meeting with those who were previously there and then left for Turkey and conduct research and studies based on these testimonies.

Therefore, what I will present here depends on the studies and research carried out by credible experts, writers and journalists.

In this regard, we look to the Washington Institute for Near East Policy, which offered information on ISIS's efforts to win the hearts and minds of the citizens within the territory of the state. In this, it is mention that ISIS is offering necessary services of life through a bureau called the Khidamat al-Muslimeen Bureau. The authors of the book *ISIS: Inside the Army of Terror* offered the testimonies of citizens from the Syrian city of Al-Bab, in which they said, "At first, Lattif said, ISIS treated civilians "gently," even assuming some of the civil administrative duties that had been handled by volunteers and the FSA. They fixed damaged roads, planted flowers in the street, cultivated gardens, and cleaned the local schools. But not long thereafter, Lattif said, ISIS instituted Sharia law, forcing women to wear what he called "the Daesh clothes" — the niqab or full head-and-face covering. "They banned hairdressing. Beard shaving is also forbidden. No woman can leave her house without a male escort now. There's no smoking, no shisha [hookah], no playing cards. They've made everything bad for civilians now. They force the people to go [to] the mosque for prayers, to close their businesses."

Another testimony, from Manbij, informs us that after the opposition brigades invaded the city and expelled ISIS in 2014, some of the citizens expressed their regret at what the brigades did. They said, "People did not see anything but good things from ISIS, even though they did not like its religious ideas…They also know that those who fought it were the worst people in the area." They also testified that ISIS, after reclaiming Manbij, established a complete system of local government. They entrusted their members with responsibilities distributed among them. They made some responsible for medical services, others for operating bakeries, managing and supervising the markets and some responsible for security, government and so on. This caused many to flock to the group, either to fight under its orders or to work in the city's administration. ISIS offered them the safety that they lacked under the domination of the FSA militias.

The authors offer testimonies about the system of justice. Abdel Bari Atwan offers similar testimonies, which demonstrate that ISIS's judicial system is complete and quick as well as effective in implementing verdicts without prejudice and that the verdicts that its courts hand down are logical. The authors of *ISIS: Inside the Army of Terror* provide a testimony from a Syrian citizen, who states, "The reason why people support the Islamic State is its honesty and practices compared to the corruption of most of the FSA groups. Some FSA groups joined it, too."

In this way, through its manner of administration and governance of the areas under its control, ISIS adopted a strategy to win the peoples' loyalty so that they would work under its orders or, at least, not show open hostility to them. This is especially true when they would compare ISIS's governance with the chaos and insecurity that they witnessed under the control of the FSA. Citizens also witnessed that the sway that some people had due to their connections disappeared under ISIS and that the group returned the rights to the people. The group worked to stabilize the security situation, beginning with banning carrying weapons in public, then confiscating heavy weaponry and banning the bribes that had burdened the citizens when the FSA would impose them at roadblocks. One citizen from Deir ez-Zor even stated, "We haven't felt this safe for twenty years."

Others testify that ISIS applies the law, even on its members, no matter their position. It executed a number of its own soldiers, even some of its own leaders, when they discovered that they were taking personal profit and exploiting the use of power. In November 2014, it executed one of its leaders in Deir ez Zor after he was accused of embezzlement and looting. Imad al-Rawi speaks of ISIS executing ten of its own soldiers in the Iraqi city of Al-Qa'im because they sold tobacco that they confiscated from smugglers.

In order to spread tranquility among the people, ISIS banned its soldiers from patrolling the streets in their military uniforms and with their weapons as much as possible. An Iraqi stated that people were terrified of ISIS because its reputation preceded it, so they avoided the soldiers when the first arrived in the city. However, after they had contact with them and met them in the mosques, the people began to feel comfortable with them and loved their dedication and purity. Thus, gradually, they began to work with them, even those that did not join ISIS.

It was noted that, in areas where ISIS did not have a sufficient workforce at its disposal, they invented a new system of membership for the local residents, who they call *"munasireen"* [supporters] in contrast to the *"ansar"* [followers]—who are their committed local members—and the *"muhajireen"* [immigrants]—the foreign fighters. If the *munasireen* declare their loyalty to ISIS, they can be employed in the police or the local authority, under the administration of the Khidamat al-Muslimeen bureau. The *munasireen* get a salary just like the other two groups and, in this way, ISIS began not to enter into competition with local residents over employment in arranging the affairs of their area and further won over the hearts of the people.

As for salaries, in ISIS territory they range from 200 to 2,000 dollars. They are at thus above the average salaries in both Iraq and Syria. ISIS certainly has money: its budget for 2014 was 2 billion dollars and had a surplus at the end of the year of 250 million dollars. For this reason, Western bureaus have dubbed it, "the richest terrorist organization in the world."

The combination of the forceful use of authority and the effectiveness of the system of governance formed an internal insurance for ISIS as the motivation of citizens to revolt against them lessened. Its violence benefitted it by deterring peoples' desires to rebel. In light of the lack of an acceptable implementable alternative , so far, the situations is stabilized for ISIS. Furthermore, with its policies in force, as some researchers say, it will be difficult for any outside force to regain control of ISIS's territory. On the topic of violence, the first facility ISIS establishes after taking over any city town, is a Hudud [punishment] Square. This is where punishments according to Islamic law are carried out, such as crucifixions, beheadings, lashings, and cutting off hands. It then establishes a Sharia police, known as the *hisbah*, which implements Sharia, organizes the markets and regulates prices. The Sharia police are more active in urban areas.

It should be noted here that ISIS has divided the areas into 16 provinces in both Iraq and Syria. There are administrative units that are even smaller, called sections. In each city there is a military commander, a security commander and an emir that oversees them. They are all accountable to the governor of the province. They do all of this for the purpose of implementing an administrative system that attracts and wins over the citizens.

The Social Welfare System

ISIS has a social welfare system in which specialists and professionals are employed. In 2014, the group announced employment opportunities in this field on social media platforms. This system helped the group implement a strict administrative system whose harshest punishments are doled out to those who have embezzled or squandered the public money.

I note here, again, that ISIS's budget of two billion dollars is considered a good amount for a country whose residents are estimated to be around 6 million people. This is especially true when we remember that a country like Comoros had an annual budget in recent years of only 45 million dollars, 30 million of which was spent on salaries. Furthermore, the government of Sudan's budget is about six billion dollars, but Sudan has a population about five times greater than ISIS's territory. The American think tank, the Brookings Institution, reports ISIS's budget according to studies and investigations that were performed based on its sources of income. Even yesterday (1 September 2015), the *Daily Mail* published images of ISIS employees distributing money to those the newspaper said were the poor in the area of Raqqah, the capital of the Caliphate. ISIS also distributes food rations to the poor, widows and the needy. Since October 2014, it has distributed daily meals to needy families, as well as weekly rations of grains and vegetables. Furthermore, the poor, those with special needs, widows, orphans and families that have lost their breadwinners receive monthly stipends.

ISIS also has a consumer protection office, whose establishment was announced in the September 2014 issue of *IS Report*, which is published on the Internet and headed by Abu Saleh al-Ansari. In order to ensure that goods are not leaked or smuggled, merchants are only allowed to sell their products to those that carry cards with the ISIS emblem. The group has also established a postal system; however, it only works within ISIS's territory.

All of these responsibilities are carried out by the Khidamat al-Muslimeen Bureau. This bureau also oversees health services and social services, which include an "orphans' bureau," restaurants to feed the poor and vaccination programs. ISIS has also distributed boxes for recommendations and complaints.

CHAPTER FOUR

LIFE UNDER ISIS

Life under ISIS

On 18 September 2014, Alastair Crooke wrote an article for the *Huffington Post* in which he stated that Obama's claim that ISIS is not a state is wrong. He argued that it is a state that controls territory, has a well-trained army, possesses modern weaponry and a well-spoken leader. He further writes that ISIS is different from al-Qaeda, as al-Qaeda was an idea, whereas ISIS has a vision and a goal: establishing the state of God on earth, based on the first Islamic experience, through which the Prophet Muhammad established his state. Crooke adds that ISIS controls a territory the size of Great Britain and large financial resources, as well as having capable military commanders. Furthermore, he states that this development—ISIS—must be taken seriously, as it has dug in its heels and has come to have a pull more than the current Western simplifications, based on cursing it and describing it as a gang of butchers and crazy killers, allows it.

Crooke is not the only one that argues that ISIS is a state. Jürgen Todenhöfer, the German judge, parliamentary representative and writer, has made similar statements. Furthermore, the Pope has called for negotiations with ISIS to achieve peace in the region, despite the fact that he condemned the group's treatment of Christians. Fareed Zakaria, editor-in-chief of *Newsweek International*, has also called for negotiations with ISIS and Graham Fuller has said that Zakaria's ideas are worthy of attention and study. Obama has argued that ISIS is not a state because no state has recognized it as such; however, this is not a required condition in the definition of a state.

Zakaria justified his call with the precedents of America recognizing the Soviet Union about two decades after its establishment in 1917 and Nixon's recognition of communist China in the 1970s, despite the fact that it was established in 1949. He added that both Nelson Mandela and Yasser Arafat were previously categorized by America as terrorists, though, soon after, America began to treat them as statesmen. America did the same thing with Cuba and a number of leftist groups in South America. Jürgen Todenhöfer, instead, argues for the necessity of recognizing the facts on the ground. He believes that ISIS is performing all the tasks of the state: it raises its own flag; controls its territory with an army, a security force and a police force; offers education, health and other services; and has a head of state. Thus, as he sees it, we must recognize the facts on the ground.

These five all are global personalities who are notable in their fields. Although they are not in consensus on the topic of the recognition of ISIS, the simple fact that three of them call for negotiations with the group demonstrates that it is a force that must be seriously considered. In any case, glimpses of normal life could give us more knowledge about ISIS. We begin with the film made by Ghadi Sary, which was shown on the BBC on 9 June 2015. In this film, "Hanaa" discusses how she asked her husband to take her to a restaurant in Mosul, as she had not left her house for days since ISIS had seized the city. Her husband warned her that she would have to wear the niqab over her face. When they arrived at the restaurant that they had been going to since their engagement and, thus, had an emotional connection to, her husband told her that she could remove her veil because there were no ISIS members in the restaurant and it was a family-oriented restaurant. As soon as she did so, the owner of the restaurant came to her, begging her husband to have her put on the niqab, as ISIS members could come by surprise to visit and search the restaurant. If they did so, the owner of the restaurant would be flogged as punishment for allowing a woman to show her face. Hanaa stated, as well, that she heard of husbands being flogged because their wives did not wear the veil and of a father who was banned from driving because his daughter did not wear the niqab.

However, men being flogged because of their wives not wearing the niqab is a topic of controversy. It seems that there is another side to this discussion. ISIS has shown films on YouTube in which there are women with their faces uncovered. In one of these films, there is a woman with a doctorate lecturing ISIS women in an elegant lecture hall on Islam's justifications for polygamy and women whose faces are uncovered. However, it is true that all the women in the lecture hall are wearing "black abayas." The film also shows walls of houses on which the Arabic letter "*nun*" [n] is written and, under that, the phrase, "property of ISIS." The narrator states that these had belonged to the "Nusayris" [Christians], that the "*nun*" was a symbol of this and that, as they fled the city, ISIS took their property into its custody.

In its 26 June 2015 edition, *The Independent* offers a testimony by one of the residents of Ramadi, who says that he does not love ISIS, but life under their rule is better than under the Iraqi Army or the Shiites. He adds that, before ISIS took control of Ramadi, someone he knew was arrested by the police and, although he was innocent, he was not freed until his family paid a 5,000-dollar bribe to the police. *The Independent* offers other testimonies that work in the favor of ISIS, by comparing between ISIS and the Shiite government in explaining why the citizens prefer ISIS. The newspaper states, "This is one of the great strengths of ISIS." The author quotes the statement of one of the residents of Ramadi, who says that "…under government rule Ramadi had no electricity, no fuel, no internet and no clean water for drinking and cooking. The local hospital and medical center were not working despite vain pleas to the government from local people. "Under the rule of ISIS," says Salem…"many big generators have been brought to Ramadi from Fallujah and Raqqa. In addition, they are repairing the power station at Khesab. As for the hospital, Isis brought in doctors, surgeons and nurses from Syria, so it is working again." The newspaper notes that the person who they met hates ISIS because the group closed his business and punished him savagely.

On 10 June 2015, in an article entitled, "Life in Mosul one year on: 'ISIS with all its brutality is more honest than the Shia government,'" *The Guardian* wrote that, after ISIS's seizure of Mosul, they treated the people with respect, took down the roadblocks that the government's army had set up and opened the roads. *The Guardian* states, "People could not believe their eyes that there was no Shia army in the city, no more detainees and bribes." The newspaper states that ISIS does not allow male doctors to treat women, except in the case of there being no women doctors. In such a situation, they allow male doctors to treat women, as was the case with the only neurologist in the Mosul hospital; however, he refused to do so unless they gave him a written fatwa, as he feared punishment.

The newspaper writes that ISIS established bureaus for health, complaints and preaching, and mosques as well as departments for education, *zakat* [alms-giving, one of the pillars of Islam], *hisbah* [religious police] and services. The article further states that the *zakat* department gives each family 25 dollars a month, which is raised to 50 dollars a month during the harvest. This is in addition to giving families good-sized rations of wheat, rice, sugar, cooking oil, fuels and pickles!

The newspaper also writes that ISIS does not employ any doctor who has not sworn loyalty to the Caliphate but that it does not send any doctor outside of his own city if he does not want to. Furthermore, ISIS opened a market only for women in Mosul so that they are able to shop comfortably.

The Guardian testifies that ISIS does not ban women from driving. Furthermore, they write that the municipality is exerting its utmost efforts to fix, clean and light the roads, provide water and power and to renovate buildings destroyed by coalition planes. They cite Bashir Aziz, who says that he supports ISIS and that he is proud to be a part of ISIS because it gave him freedom. He says that the residents of Mosul live and feel pride, with the exception of the coalition airstrikes that spread fear and panic among the civilians.

Bashir also states that he does not agree with ISIS's treatment of Christians, Yazidis and other minorities in Mosul and that he is still in communication with his Christian neighbors. He also hopes that they will return. Furthermore, he says that all the people in Mosul oppose ISIS's destruction of historical sites and that even some ISIS extremists did not agree with the destruction of these sites. He continues that he discussed this with some members of ISIS that share his opinion and that he does not know who issued the orders for their destruction because "the sharia court in Mosul was in astonishment too."

The newspaper writes that people in Mosul are suffering from a financial crisis because of a lack of jobs and that they are anxious and depressed because they fear that they will be attacked by another military group that will take revenge on anyone that worked with ISIS. Bashir states that most people are opposed to the return of the former politicians, who they describe as corrupt, or the Shiite militias that will destroy the city and not liberate it as is claimed. He adds, "Isis with all its brutality is more honest and merciful than the Shia government in Baghdad and its militias."

The Guardian also offers the testimony of Shaima Yousif. She says that her husband was killed by the coalition planes and that, during the days of his funeral, ISIS men brought a car full of food and gave her 300 dollars in cash and 100 dollars as a monthly pension. Shaima admits that she stole a gold ring and that, because of this, ISIS's court cut her left hand off from the wrist.

The newspaper cites the statement of a citizen sympathetic with ISIS in which he narrates that an ISIS fighter hit the owner of a bakery. The next day, two ISIS men came and interrogated the witnesses, who all condemned the fighter. They forced the fighter to publicly apologize to the owner of the bakery and fired him from his position. This sympathizer states that ISIS won the hearts of the people in Mosul from the first day that the city was liberated. ISIS men were modest, unbiased and cooperative. He states that they brought back the dignity and pride of the Sunni man in Mosul after he had been subjected to much contempt and revenge under successive Shiite governments since the American occupation of Iraq. This man, who is loyal to ISIS, said that corruption had been widespread, leading to the erosion of all the facilities of Mosul, a city that had become more like a big military camp that was suffocating the people. According to him, the city had not experienced any construction over the past ten years, despite the billions of dollars being poured into the city council's treasury, but that now Mosul is living a golden age. He claims that, despite the fact that the world media is expending rapid efforts to distort ISIS's image and to portray them as terrorists, the opposite is true. People are very welcoming of the sacrifices that the group has made to protect Sunni citizens from the inhumane practices that the Shiite army has perpetrated in Mosul and other Sunni governorates. He goes on to say that the ISIS fighters, both local and foreign, deserve all the love and respect of the people of Mosul. He wonders why the Shiite militias in Iraq are allowed to bring Lebanese, Iranian and Afghani fighters and the Sunnis are not allowed to seek assistance from foreign Sunnis to protect them. He states that the foreign fighters have integrated excellently into Mosul society and that many of the tribes whose members joined ISIS last year have accepted offers of marriage made by foreign fighters, proving that they are brave and trustworthy. He says that the falsehoods attributed to ISIS about the foreign fighters forcing families to marry their daughters to them are completely untrue. There is no one among those that have sworn loyalty to Caliph al-Baghdadi that want the Shiite militias to get close to Mosul. He says, "I would be the first to fight these militias who come to sow destruction and killing among Sunnis. We have seen their atrocities in Tikrit and Jurf al-Sakher against unarmed civilians." He adds that Mosul is now stable and safe and that "...my father can leave his shop open and go for prayers, and no one dares to steal a straw from the shop. Civil services are better now, like power and water, and roads are more clean. I spend most of my free time praying in mosques and attending courses in Islamic sharia and hadith."

The newspaper also mentions the story of another person, saying that ISIS cut off his hand because he stole five cigarettes. This is despite the fact that the value of cigarettes does not reach the legal minimum necessary for enforcing the punishment for stealing. All Muslims know this, not to mention the judge. Thus, it is difficult for Muslims to believe this story. Perhaps this kind of illogical falsehood helps ISIS's media to argue that what is said about the group is all lies, despite the fact that ISIS's media, itself, sometimes shows things that most Muslims consider monstrous.

As for those that worked in the Iraqi army, security forces or police, and they do not fall into ISIS's hands, but rather come to the group repentant, the group pardons them and issues them what is called a "repentance card" that they carry to safeguard them from anyone who is watching them or doubts their loyalty. I have seen images of people carrying these certificates.

As for the website *Vice News*, they published a report on 24 June 2014, two weeks after ISIS took control over Mosul. They titled it, "Mosul Residents Enjoy Calmer Lives Under ISIS Control, For Now." In this article, they cite many testimonies. They state, as well, that many of those that fled the city returned after they had been reassured, though they had been expecting massacres and brutal violence. The article states that ISIS has remained moderate in its measures and, for this reason, has found support among the residents, who informed the author of this report that they are happy under the command of their new leaders. The report states that people are easily passing through both sides of the borders between that area controlled by the Peshmerga (Peshmerga means those that do not fear death in Kurdish) and the areas controlled by ISIS forces. These locations are 500 yards from one another, but people can pass through them easily. It further states that the roadblocks erected by the Iraqi Army have been removed by ISIS from all of Mosul and that ISIS is employing a strategy to win the hearts and minds of the citizens.

According to the report, ISIS brought back water and electricity services and treated people with kindness so that the people began to love them. One of the residents of Mosul described ISIS's seizure of the city as, "an uprising against the tyranny of Maliki." The report states that ISIS has not imposed its laws with brutal violence (as was expected) and that the facilities and services are better under ISIS than they were under the government.

Most of the businesses have opened and normal life has begun to return to the city. The report also states that the residents' biggest fear is that the government's army will return. However, the removal of the roadblocks is evidence that ISIS is holding the reigns of power. As an example of ISIS's moderation in implementing its approach, a musician, Amin Ali, stated that he played in a concert and ISIS did not interrogate him. On the availability of necessities, one citizen said that all necessities are available; however, prices for goods, particularly fuel, have gone up. Of course, discussion about ISIS's "moderateness" is only accepted by a few.

The Atlantic wrote about the subject, using the headline, "Mosul under ISIS: Clean Streets and Horror." By horror, the article means the implementation of punishments under Sharia law, like stoning, cutting off hands, decapitation and crucifixion, which Westerners are generally repulsed by and describe as brutal and barbaric.

This article was published on 10 June 2015, exactly a year after ISIS seized control of Mosul, the second largest city in Iraq after the capital, Baghdad. The author states that the details about life in Mosul that reached him are "shocking" and contradictory. The group carries out punishments in the public square in order to scare people and The Atlantic even claims that ISIS forces people to watch these Islamic punishments being carried out. The article refers to a report published by the BBC, which states that ISIS is turning churches in Mosul into its own facilities and that it is destroying mosques (perhaps the article meant tombs and mausoleums, which are forbidden in Islam). It also refers to the fact that ISIS forces women to wear the niqab, which I indicated earlier is not true. It is true that the group prefers that kind of dress, but it does not impose it.

On 4 June 2015, Nicolas Pelham wrote that Sheikh Taha Hamid al-Zaydi, the speaker for Baghdad's Sunnis, stated that life in Mosul is normal since ISIS took control and people in Mosul fear for the future, not their present reality under ISIS.

Clarifying another aspect of the image, the Wall Street Journal published an article on one of the residents of Mosul, who said that, in 30 years, he has not seen the streets and markets of Mosul this clean and praised ISIS's efforts in this regard. The Atlantic writes that ISIS mixes between strict laws and fear, on the one hand, and creating infrastructure, on the other. This has become ISIS's model of governance in any place it controls. The article concludes that this is a model that is very difficult to dislodge.

In another aspect of daily life and an indication the changes that ISIS has effected, it should be noted that, since 27 October 2014, the group has used the lunar calendar. Thus, the *hijri* date is the one that is primarily relied upon, as a way of escaping the Gregorian calendar, which was imposed by Western colonialism when it took control over the Islamic countries in the 18th and 19th centuries.

It should be noted here that the Islamic countries were not familiar with the Gregorian calendar until that time. In Sudan, for example, the lunar calendar was used until the end of Mahdist regime. The day ended with the setting of the sun and the next day would begin. Accordingly, 7 p.m. was considered 1 a.m. of the next day. This tradition is the same one used by orthodox Jews to this day. The Sabbath, on which they refrain from working, begins with the setting of the sun on Friday.

However, the problem that Muslims face today in using the *hijri* calendar, despite the fact that it is one of the practices of Muslim identity, is that Muslims in various countries do not agree on when the lunar month begins. Thus, each state or group of states would have different dates for the beginning of the months and different dates for the beginning of the year.

Another aspect of the application of Sharia law, as ISIS sees it, according to investigations carried out by Abdel Bari Atwan and published in his book, *ISIS: The Digital Caliphate*, is offering housing to unmarried male arrivals and separating the residences of women and men. Women live in what ISIS calls the "headquarters." As for married couples, ISIS offers them one of the houses left empty when its residents left the city or the village. If there are none available, ISIS assists them in renting a house by giving them money towards the rent.

Atwan cites the testimony of a resident of Manbij, a city close to Aleppo, who says that crime has been entirely non-existent in his city since ISIS took control. This is because of ISIS's zero-tolerance policy towards those who commit crimes and its steadfast reliance on one approach to implementing its punishments. He says that ISIS levies the *zakat* and then distributes the income to the poor and displaced in Manbij, who have come to be about half the residents of the city. He says that its educational system focuses on teaching the sciences and that the group has adopted a strong curriculum in this regard, just as it intensively teaches Islamic studies. Furthermore, teachers have begun to regularly receive their salaries, after these had been cut off for months. He states that the citizens are worried that their city will face attacks by another armed movement, which could force them to flee, but that they are happy with the current situation. Despite the positive picture painted by the citizens of the situation in Manbij, he adds that people do not think that ISIS control will last more than two years. This is because he expects that people will rise up due to ISIS's implementation of the laws that it follows. The second reason he believes this is because he thinks that there is a "symbiotic" relationship between ISIS and the Syrian regime! The Syrian regime does not attack ISIS's areas because ISIS is fighting the regime's enemies among the other brigades. The lack of regime strikes on ISIS areas was a reality until parts of 2014, but the picture now has changed, and the regime has begun to bomb ISIS.

The Management of the State

According to the criteria of international law and the 1933 Montevideo Convention, there are specifically two kinds of states: "declaratory" and "constitutive" states, as Professor William Worster at The Hague University writes. He clarifies that the declaratory state must have a defined territory, residents living within this territory and a government capable of exercising its authority over its residents, territory and resources. The Montevideo Convention decided that it is not necessary for the declaratory state to be recognized by any other state. As for the constitutive state, as opposed to the declaratory, it must be recognized by other states. However, we should indicate that the condition of recognition is difficult to achieve because there is no official international body that has the authority to recognize states in the name of the community of the states of the world. Abdel Bari Atwan notes in his book, *ISIS: The Digital Caliphate*, that even the United Nations cannot do this.

Here, I note that the only international personality that ISIS has allowed to visit its territory and promised safety to through a letter from Caliph al-Baghdadi's office is the German writer Jürgen Todenhöfer. Jürgen visited ISIS's territory and resided there for 10 days in the period between 6-16 December 2014. He visited Raqqah, its capital, Mosul, its largest city and Deir ez-Zor. After leaving, he stated, "Whether we like it or not, we must understand now that ISIS is a nation"! In saying this, he relies on what he saw during his visit and confirms it with knowledge about the elements of the state that Professor William Worster noted. Why would he not, when he is a writer, before that, a member of the German parliament and, before *that*, a judge? I will allow a space for his comments, observations, and testimony within what we are outlining about ISIS.

ISIS controls half of Syria and a third of Iraq, an area no less than the United Kingdom. Its population in this area is estimated to be 6 million, which is more than Finland, for example.

ISIS also has an Islamic bank in Mosul that has minted its own currency, according to an ISIS announcement in 2014. Jürgen has stated that the group has its own license plates, traffic police and other cars with the slogan of ISIS on them and a uniform.

Fuad Hussein, chief of staff of the Kurdish President Massoud Barzani, told Patrick Cockburn that he estimated ISIS's number of fighters to be 200,000. *The Independent* published Hussein's statement in November 2014.

At the end of August 2014, the Iraqi security expert Hisham al-Hashimi estimated the group's numbers to be close to 100,000 fighters. Abdel Bari Atwan notes that his sources have informed him that ISIS's number of fighters has reached 100,000.

The website War on the Rocks suggests that the number of *inghimasis* is 15,000. These are the elite paramilitary forces ready to plunge into the ranks of the enemy and to carry out dangerous operations as well as suicide/martyrdom operations (according to your opinion on ISIS).

On 16 November 2014, *The Independent* reported that a Kurdish official stated that the strength of ISIS's army has reached 200,000 soldiers. He notes that, while al-Qaeda was an idea and a limited military force, ISIS has developed from this idea into a political entity that controls territory and has a flag, a security service, a military and a police. It also offers services to the citizens of its territory. A report published by *CNN* on 14 January 2015 states that ISIS has a government structure in which provincial and city governors as well as legislative and judicial bodies work. The report states that the bureaucratic hierarchy is very similar to what is present in some Western states, whose values the group rejects (like its rejection of democracy).

What is known about the emirate is that al-Baghdadi, president or caliph, has two deputies, Abu Ali al-Anbari and Abu Muslim al-Turkmani. Both of them were generals in Saddam's army and in the security services of that army, facts that I will return to give more detail on later. The first of the two is responsible for Syria and the second for Iraq. In Iraq, ISIS has appointed 12 city or regional governors, as well as a similar number in Syria. ISIS has a Shura Council whose task is to make sure that ISIS is being led according to the principles of Islamic Sharia. It has the power to depose the caliph if it perceives that he is in violation of Sharia.

ISIS also has a Financial Council, a Legal Council, which is dedicated to legal and judicial matters, a Military Council, tasked with matters of defense, in addition to an Intelligence and Security Council and a Media Council, responsible for media on traditional and social networking platforms.

The Americans say that al-Baghdadi uses the American military slogan, "clear and hold," in his military operations. According to Western sources that wrote about ISIS's occupation of Mosul, in June 2014, the group attacked with 1,500 fighters, causing 30,000 Iraqi soldiers to throw down their weapons, some of them even taking off their military uniforms, and to flee from the city. ISIS was aided in this by psychological warfare campaigns published on social media, which contained images of decapitation, throwing off of rooftops, stoning and cutting off hands, sending fear into the hearts of the soldiers. It should also be mentioned that ISIS killed the 1,500 soldiers that they captured while they fled from Camp Speicher. The group killed them over three days and filmed the operations of mass execution, broadcasting this over the Internet. According to Abdel Bari Atwan's book, the group killed 13 imams in Mosul that refused to swear their allegiance to the caliph. Among them was the imam of the Great Mosque, in which al-Baghdadi announced his Caliphate. This is the same mosque in which Saladin al-Ayyubi announced the beginning of his campaign to fight the Crusaders.

It is true that the experiment of jihadists in administration has failed in the past, perhaps because they did not have the knowledge or the experience in administering governorates, let alone an entire country. However, it seems that ISIS became aware of this weakness and redressed it. Thus, ISIS strategists planned for the Caliphate to have a more stable and flexible system of administration than it may appear to the outside observer.

It seems that Caliph Abu Bakr al-Baghdadi is called the leader, but it is unclear how much authority he has. To clarify this point, I read that envoys sent by Ayman al-Zawahiri, the leader of al-Qaeda, met Haji Bakr and his intelligence officer companions. They did not meet with al-Baghdadi, though it would be supposed that they would meet him, as they were envoys to him. It is reported that the envoy said in sorrow, "these phony snakes who are betraying the real jihad."

In the Islamic State, there is a system, a bureaucratic state structure and authorities. However, there is also a parallel leadership structure. There are elite units alongside the regular forces and there are additional military leaders alongside Chief of Staff Abu Omar al-Shishani. Then, there are deputies that make the decisions to move the emirs of governorates and to promote or fire them. Decisions as a rule are not made by the Shura Council, which is, in name, that highest decision-making authority in ISIS; rather, they are made by *"ahl al-hal wal aqd"* ["those with the power to loose and bind": a traditional Islamic term referring influential people in the Muslim community who have the power to appoint the caliph]. To this day, this is a secret circle few know about.

The ISIS Economy

ISIS's financial capabilities are clearly improving as a result of its expansion and control over a growing number of cities. The resources available in cities under its control constitute its income and help boost its revenue. According to the Financial Times issue of July 1, 2015, ISIS's seizure of Ramadi and Palmyra, and its subsequent levying of taxes on citizens and businesses, led to a significant increase in its income.

It is noteworthy that the measures implemented by the United States-led coalition of countries to prevent oil purchases from ISIS, with the goal of drying up one of its most important financial resources, do not appear yet to have yielded results.

According to the American think tank RAND Corporation, ISIS's income from taxes and tariffs in 2014 alone reached 600 million dollars, which they believe to have been obtained through extortion. In addition to the 600 million, ISIS has also managed to get its hands on 500 million dollars from banks that it seized.

It is impossible for Turkey to secure its border with ISIS due to the fact that it is 856 kilometers long. This has resulted in ISIS smuggling to and from the country, which plays a role in its ability to secure both its necessities and cash, obtained through the sale of smuggled goods.

Westerners describe ISIS as "the wealthiest terrorist group in the world," and its economy as self-sufficient. ISIS owns a number of oil fields and small refineries in Syria, and sells its oil on the grey market at discounted prices that reach about 30 dollars per barrel (in October 2014, the average prices were between 80 and 85 dollars per barrel). ISIS's daily oil production is estimated at 80,000 barrels, resulting in a daily income of three million dollars. According to other reports, its daily income from oil sales is 1.6 million dollars. Given all the estimates, ISIS's yearly income from oil sales is between 750 million and 1.2 billion dollars. In addition to this amount is profit from the sale of ready-to-use petroleum derivatives, through smuggling to neighboring countries, for which the exact total revenue is unavailable.

ISIS benefits from its alliance with Saddam's men, who over the decades of sanctions against Saddam's regime managed to gain significant experience smuggling oil.

It is well known that ISIS pays the salaries of employees in its territories, despite reports of both the Iraqi and Syrian governments still paying the salaries of those same employees. According to presently available information, ISIS pays salaries that range from 200 to 2,000 dollars monthly, exceeding the average salaries in Iraq, Syria and Sudan and other Arab countries.

What distinguishes ISIS when compared to other jihadist groups (or terrorist, as they are called by their adversaries) such as al-Qaeda, is its lack of dependence on donations and charity from sympathetic benefactors. With the resources it seizes in territories of influence, ISIS has become able to fund itself. However, this fact does not completely negate their ability to obtain a level of financial support from sympathizers, although in small amounts due to the strict measures taken by countries against suspicious financial transfers.

Returning to the issue of oil, Western sources state that ISIS has seized Syria's largest oilfields, including the al-Omar oilfield, which can produce 75,000 barrels per day. In Iraq, ISIS has six small fields in the Saladin and eastern Diyala governorates. It has also seized oil refineries in the two countries (control over the Baiji refinery is going back and forth between ISIS and the Iraqi government); however, near Mosul, it controls the small Qayyara refinery, according to claims by a number of sources, the Wall Street Journal's publication on August 28, 2014, and other highly credible sources. When American aircraft bombed a number of ISIS refineries, it subsequently designed and began operating small refineries that continue to refine one barrel at a time.

In the pages of its magazine *Dabiq*, ISIS published pictures of the designs of its future coinage, which consists of a gold dinar, a silver dirham, and a copper fils. According to ISIS, one gold dinar equals 139 dollars, and five dinars equal 694 dollars. Each silver dirham equals one dollar, ten dirhams equal nine dollars, and the copper fils equals 5.6 cents. On one side of the currency is written the phrase: "Caliphate based on the prophetic method," and on the other side is a map of the world. This map is significant for a "Caliphate" whose Caliph who said he would conquer Rome and recapture Al-Andalus. When his forces destroyed the border gate between Syria and Iraq, he refused to recognize borders between Muslim countries under the premise that they were built by the infidel "English Sykes and French Picot" in their 1916 agreement.

It is difficult for ISIS to mint gold currency to internally administer the economy of a population of six million people. This process is even more complicated externally, since the world neither recognizes ISIS as a state, nor deals with it economically. Even if we assume that ISIS survives and gains international recognition, there is still the problem of no "par value" for gold and silver currencies in the world today. While it is true that gold and silver can be internationally bought and sold by weight, they are not currently used as currency.

ISIS's economy is now based on monetary circulation, as it is a cash economy both internally and externally, through the sale of oil to smugglers who then sell it abroad. The two factors of ISIS's classification as a terrorist organization and the international sanctions it faces have made financial transactions between the banks it owns and international banks impossible. Inside ISIS, business is conducted with the Iraqi dinar, the Syrian pound, and the American dollar.

The narratives and reports about ISIS's actual financial situation are inconsistent. Some paint a highly negative picture, others an average one, and a few state that with their budget in 2014, ISIS achieved a decent living for its population. For the purposes of this book, I spoke with a Syrian mujahed that sympathizes with al-Qaeda and opposes ISIS. He stated that the average person lives a normal life, in which all goods are available and he can freely enter and exit Syria. He added that electricity, water, and food products are available in stores, though some prices have gone up because goods reaching ISIS are smuggled in. The Syrian mujahed also said that the people's standard of living is better now than when Free Syrian Army factions controlled the checkpoints and imposed exorbitant tariffs on trucks carrying goods.

Also for the purposes of this book, I spoke with a relief organization employee that has a number of branches in Syria, and their answer reflected the al-Qaeda sympathizer's claims.

On January 5, 2015, the *Financial Times (FT)* stated that, "If ISIS's "caliphate" were a state, it would be a country of the poor... In Syria, the price of bread has nearly doubled to almost a dollar." It also said that the Iraqi government removed Mosul from the national electricity grid, but people bought powerful generators and lit up the city. According to testimonies from Western sources, it was ISIS that purchased the generators, a more likely possibility given that their budget last year was two billion dollars and by year's end, they had achieved a surplus. As we previously mentioned, *FT* stated that both the Iraqi and Syrian governments are still paying the salaries of employees working in ISIS-controlled territories. They added that the Syrian government and ISIS appear to have reached an agreement that gives the government access to fuel for its electric power plants in exchange for electricity. In accordance with the deal, ISIS agreed to have the government send electricians to fix malfunctions and provide spare parts. According to *FT*, a Syrian living in

ISIS-controlled territory told their journalist: "I'm against ISIS with all my heart...But I can't help but admire their cleverness." An Iraqi researcher told the *Financial Times* that ISIS is suffering financially, but service facilities are still up and running because Baghdad continues to pay the salaries of its previously-employed civil service employees that now work in ISIS territories. Though *FT* claims ISIS takes half of these salaries, other sources say they only collect 2.5% as a tax, a more logical claim. *FT* stated that basic service facilities work poorly, yet its report also complained that they did not have a clear picture of the situation. This is due to the fact that ISIS does not allow journalists into its territories, making reports based on observations and follow-ups impossible. *FT* thus depends on verbal testimonies collected mainly from activists, which weakens their credibility. *FT* claimed that the supply of electricity, fuel, medicine, and water was low, but people were managing to survive. They also stated that people think some of ISIS's policies are an improvement from those of previous regimes, and businessmen from Kurdistan, Iraq who send trucks of goods across ISIS-controlled lands, revealed that they see the ISIS system as "friendly to business." Since ISIS does not impose fees for opening new businesses, doing so has become relatively easy, but business owners must pay 2.5% of their profits in tax at the end of each year. According to families FT spoke with, coalition aircraft bombing small ISIS-established refineries is having a minimal effect because ISIS obtains most of its income from selling crude oil to neighboring countries through middlemen. It attributed to some residents of the Syrian city Deir ez-Zor the idea that ISIS aims to present itself as a just ruling entity by specifying the prices of all goods, from bread loaves to Caesarian sections.

Despite the inconsistency in reports, price increases are a logical and natural outcome of war conditions and ISIS's inability to perform business transactions with the world. Making matters worse are the sanctions that are undoubtedly causing ISIS great suffering. I have taken a look at the tweets of Western female mujahedeen living in Raqqah that complain of power supply cuts. This is clear evidence that the rosy picture ISIS is trying to paint about the course of affairs in its territories is exaggerated and an attempt to improve their image.

Bitcoins

It is well known that the Security Council has imposed international sanctions on ISIS, banning fund transfers and business transactions with them. However, the Islamic State has circumvented this by using other means to ensure economic activity and global trade that bypass the sanctions regime. ISIS now depends on new systems that have made bank transactions – impossible given the sanctions – and the embargo, obsolete. The new systems have so far proven significantly effective.

To bypass the embargo, ISIS has turned to using "crypto currency," which is a digital, electronic, intangible and impalpable currency called "bitcoins." Bitcoins are a hidden encrypted currency whose trail authorities cannot track, and whose transactions they cannot follow or monitor because they do not go through a bank or center with a specific location. All transactions are done through the Internet, and despite the fact that they are not a contractual, or backed by assets or official currency legislation, they allow you to buy real commodities and services. Though no central authority governs bitcoins, nor are they a palpable commodity, they can be sent to anyone with Internet access. The first step is to make a virtual wallet in which you store bitcoins and transaction dates. This wallet acts as a headquarters for secure digital keys that are used to reach public bitcoins addresses and a transactions index. Business transactions require you to give your wallet's secret identification number to your business partner, i.e. the person with whom the business transaction will be completed. The wallets then become a means to store digital records for bitcoins amounts, through which users can obtain their bitcoins expenditure. In reality, there are different types of virtual wallets, the most secure of which are desktop bitcoins wallets.

As an example, bitcoins are used to buy weapons, and because they are electronic cash, the authorities – even the American – cannot monitor or track their operations. Due to the impenetrable encryption system and the need to have "keys," mafia gangs and organized crime groups also use bitcoins for trafficking drugs, child prostitution, and so forth.

Since it is difficult for ISIS to exchange this electronic cash for tangible money in its territories, it likely does so through its supporters in Middle Eastern countries with bitcoin aggregators (most likely Turkey and Dubai), that host special bitcoin ATMs. Bitcoin ATMs work exactly like regular bank ATMs, in that they allow you to transfer all bitcoins into actual tangible cash without a human teller. If no bitcoin ATM is available, anyone can sell bitcoins through the Internet, or wait until they are able to reach a place with an ATM.

Thus, ISIS has become able to bypass some of the sanctions and the embargo through bitcoins, or the related dogecoins. Through these currencies, it has definitely received donations and conducted trade.

Military Force and Expansion

To describe itself, ISIS has taken up the slogan "remaining and expanding," relying on volunteer fighters who join and fight under its banner of their own accord. These volunteers do not expect material reward and are willing to protect ISIS's banner at any place or time out of their own conviction. They have adopted a dogma that makes them desire rather than fear death.

When Alaa, Ayman, and Abd al-Aziz arrived in Syrian ISIS territory, they ripped up and burned their passports as a pledge to the Muslim mujahedeen line: "The sea is behind me, the enemy is in front of me, and heaven is preparing for me." By burning their passports, they were announcing their lack of recognition of their native countries' governments, and their readiness to fight them. Most new arrivals to ISIS burned their passports in similar ways.

When the group arrived, the "Islamic State" had announced its "Caliphate." As a prelude to the announcement, groups of mujahedeen led by al-Baghdadi launched a massive campaign that paved the way for future successes. The campaign culminated in the occupation of Mosul, the second largest Iraqi city and home to one and a half million people. A campaign of suicide bombings had been launched, reaching 30 suicide bombings in one month at its peak at the end of 2013. The campaign involved attacking the Abu Ghraib prison after shelling it with one hundred mortar shells and detonating car bombs in front of its gate and walls. The mujahedeen-supporting prisoners lit areas on fire to distract the guards from the attackers, who seized the opportunity to intensify their attack. They were able to free 500 prisoners, including their leaders and senior mujahedeen with experience and war know-how. They repeated the same attack on the al-Taji prison, where they freed more of their mujahedeen (Breaking the Walls campaign). The campaign also included the intensification of attacks on Iraqi security forces and army centers, with the goal of scattering the forces and preoccupying them with the protection of numerous distant neighborhoods (Soldiers' Harvest campaign).

This campaign proved its effectiveness. At the end of 2013, the American Institute for the Study of War described the jihadist movement in Iraq and Syria as "an extremely vigorous, resilient, and capable organization that can operate from Basra to coastal Syria."

According to journalist Patrick Cockburn's analysis, ISIS's expansion depended on two factors: the 2011 Sunni uprising in Syria, and al-Maliki's pro-Shiite government policies. The latter drove away the Sunnis, especially after killing dozens of peaceful protesters in al-Hawija in April 2013. The al-Maliki government was also behind a history of subjugation and repression that began with the fall of Baghdad in 2003. Since then, al-Maliki's sectarian policies have enabled the Islamic State in Iraq and Syria to ally with about seven Sunni militant groups: thus, al-Maliki's sectarian government threw the Sunnis into the arms of ISIS.

In the first half of 2014, the Islamic State occupied Fallujah, only 40 miles away from Baghdad. In March, ISIS drove American military Humvee cars through the streets of the city to display its strength, and as an indirect slap in the face to America. With ISIS's control over the Fallujah dam, it also gained control over the southward flow of water in the Euphrates. Occupying Fallujah was a warning that the balance of military power was shifting in favor of ISIS. The Iraqi army suffered crushing defeats during fighting in Al Anbar province that year, which led to 5,000 soldiers killed by ISIS, and the desertion of 12,000 more in Al Anbar.

In parallel with the military campaign, ISIS launched a "digital" psychological campaign by using social media to disseminate videos of its suicide bombings, attacks on security, police, and army centers, mass killings, and beheadings. These films were streamed online for two reasons: to encourage youth to join them as a victorious jihadist movement that implemented "God's rule over his enemies," and to instill fear and alarm in the hearts of its opponents.

In June 2014, the total Iraqi military force in Mosul equaled 30,000 soldiers. When ISIS attacked after a four-day long siege, Mosul fell on June 10, 2014. The soldiers shed their military attire and fled the city, leaving behind more than 2,300 American military Humvee cars, hundreds of tanks, artillery pieces, small arms, and tons of other supplies. It is noteworthy that the attacking ISIS force was equal to only 1,300 soldiers, who managed to seize 500 million dollars in cash from the Mosul branch of the Central Bank of Iraq. The surprise crushing victory stunned "friends and enemies of ISIS," said Abu Mohammad al-Adnani, the official ISIS spokesperson. ISIS repeated the same technique on three small neighboring cities, securing the neighboring oilfield and massive dam, before continuing to seize ten cities in the Saladin governorate, including their oilfields and an important dam. Also in June, ISIS seized the largest Iraqi oil refinery in Baiji when 400 Iraqi soldiers evacuated it willingly and saved their lives by not putting up a fight. On June 19, ISIS seized the chemical weapons facility built by Saddam Hussein in

Muthanna (Western sources claim that ISIS used poisonous chlorine gas against Iraqi forces in the city of Balad).

It is important to note that ISIS began selling oil on the black market one month after its seizure of Mosul, and that its stunning victories, most importantly Mosul, led hundreds of mujahedeen to break away from other factions and come from abroad in order to join ISIS.

When ISIS fighters entered Mosul, witnesses say the public welcomed them with joyful cheers. This situation likely resembles the Afghani welcoming of Taliban forces that brought safety and stability after the post-Soviet departure fighting amongst rival mujahedeen groups.

According to Western sources, the majority of weapons sent from Arab states to Syrian opposition have fallen into the hands of ISIS forces after ISIS defeated them. The same fate befell the limited shipments of light weaponry that America, the United Kingdom, and France sent to the Syrian fighters. The three countries stopped this marginal support when it became evident that any weapons sent would be captured by ISIS or the al-Nusra Front, classified as a branch of al-Qaeda (reports have been published in the past few months of this year that claim al-Nusra and ISIS reached an agreement to stop fighting, and to work towards conciliation and cooperation).

In his book on ISIS, the veteran journalist Patrick Cockburn wrote that the military force in Mosul was 60,000 soldiers; however, a third of the force was actually outside of Mosul. This is because the soldiers used to give part of their salaries to the officers in exchange for permission to return to their cities. He also wrote that a number of those he met painted a bleak picture of the behavior of the Iraqi military force in Mosul, stating that it used to blackmail people at road checkpoints, as well as impose exorbitant tariffs on business owners, to the extent that some of them closed their businesses and fled the city.

The nominal role and effectiveness of the Iraqi military force is evident in the fact that al-Qaeda was active in Mosul and surrounding areas, despite heavy military presence. According to a number of reports and witnesses from the city, members of al-Qaeda were imposing tariffs on business owners and on ordinary trade, with their representatives passing by businesses in the light of day to collect the tariffs.

A businessmen told Cockburn that one of the Islamic State's emirs demanded, in the name of the Islamic State in Iraq, 500,000 dollars in exchange for "protection" – or else. When he informed the Iraqi authorities in Baghdad of this, they did nothing. They instead directed him to add this on to his usual al-Qaeda payment, as per the contract he had signed with the Iraqi government, on the basis that ISIS was just al-Qaeda under a different name.

The source of the Islamic State's strength is undoubtedly their ability to work in two countries and thus to implement extended military maneuvers. The ISIS force attacking Mosul included other Sunni factions such as Ansar al-Islam, the Army of Mujahedeen, and Saddam Hussein's incumbent Izzat al-Douri's Army of the Men of the Naqshbandi Order.

The defeat of the Iraqi army was achieved on June 9 when three of its leaders, the Deputy Army Chief of Staff Abboud Qanbar, Commander of Ground Forces Ali Ghaidan, and the Commander of Nineveh Operations Mehdi Azzawi, used a helicopter to flee to Kurdistan. This led to a collapse in the force's morale and eventually its complete disintegration.

According to a soldier, the commander of his force asked the men to stop shooting, take off their military attire, hand over their weapons to the ISIS force and leave the city on June 10. Before they could obey the command, a mob of civilians stormed their barracks, throwing stones at them and yelling: "Get out of our city you sons of al-Maliki, you sons of whores, you soldiers for Iran!" ISIS men emerged from among the masses, reassuring the soldiers that if they placed down their weapons, they would not be killed. The civilians then gave them robes so that they could escape.

In a letter quoted by Cockburn, a woman from Mosul informed her friend of the city's fall to ISIS. In her letter, she said that the situation a day after the city's fall was calm, that the ISIS men were treating people with respect, and that they had secured all government facilities from being looted. In Baiji, the force surrendered to ISIS without putting up a fight. In Mosul and Tikrit, the leaders of the force and senior officers quit and fled via helicopter. In Tikrit, the surrendering soldiers were divided into Shiite and Sunni. The Sunnis were told that they were free to go, and the Shiites were executed, with the killings recorded and aired over the Internet.

A Reuters report on October 14, 2014 stated that the fall of Mosul, which followed ISIS's consecutive seizure of surrounding cities, was the latest result of a domino effect. The authorities were paralyzed, and bewilderment prevailed in the capital of Baghdad. People even began storing food and water, and remained in their houses for days, expecting the arrival of ISIS forces to Baghdad after the shocking destruction of thousands of soldiers in Mosul, Baiji, Tikrit, and surrounding areas. The residents of Baghdad were filled with alarm, and even cancelled wedding parties. Newspapers published that no less than seven ministers and their families, as well as 42 parliamentary members had fled the country and arrived in Jordan.

When ISIS forces headed in the direction of Saqlawiyah in September of 2014, aiming for the military base and chanting "Allah made me victorious over my enemies through awe for the distance of one month's journey" they killed most of the thousand soldiers, and only 200 were able to flee. With Saqlawiyah only 40 miles away from Baghdad, experts said that the end of Shiite control over Iraq had begun with the fall of Mosul. On the international scale, a serious fear of ISIS escalated after the fall of Mosul.

A major factor of ISIS's military strength is its leadership and ability to control. It has executed three decades of operations, beginning with Afghanistan, the Chechens, and Iraq after the occupation. Its leadership has stood out, especially during the American invasion of Iraq. Al-Baghdadi has himself been described as intelligent, resolute, and charismatic. He is known to have excelled at leading ISIS, and reading the battlefield and military tactics. For this reason, he has chosen to withdraw from any military operation when it became evident that his forces will lose. This is apparent in his decision to utilize guerilla war tactics since the beginning of the American airstrikes in August 2014. On the 9th of July 2014 the Guardian reported that Al-Baghdadi has two deputies, both of whom were major generals in Saddam's army, as well as an intelligence apparatus headed by Abu Yahya al-Iraqi that Westerners have described as both developed and disciplined.

Many Western sources , among them *The Guardian* on the 9 July 2014 and Carnrgie Endowment on May 14th 2015 ; have stated the leadership of ISIS in the following manner: Al-Baghdadi's first deputy was a Baathist during the Saddam era, and one of al-Baghdadi's prison friends in Camp Bucca, where the Americans imprisoned them. Fadel Ahmed Abdullah al-Hiyali, known as Abu Muslim al-Turkmani, would listen to al-Baghdadi's preaching in the prison. Prior to being killed by an American drone strike in August 2015, he was an intelligence officer in the Special Forces. Originally from the city of Tal Afar in the north of Iraq and ethnically a Turkmen, he was a major general close to Saddam and his incumbent head of the army Izzat al-Douri. Al-Baghdadi gave al-Turkmani responsibility over Iraq (general governor of Iraq), presiding over local rule and the councils. He also served as a political emissary for ISIS when it wanted to communicate with tribal elders and senators.

According to *The Guardian,* the second deputy is Abu Ali al-Anbari, from a village near Mosul, who goes by Ali Qurdash al-Turkmani as well as Abu Jasim al-Iraqi. He was a major general in the Iraqi army after the invasion, and then joined the resistance under the banner of Abu Musab al-Zarqawi. At that time, al-Zarqawi was allied with the jihadist movement "Ansar al-Islam," before the latter joined al-Qaeda, and then along with its leader al-Zarqawi came under the umbrella of the "Islamic State" in Iraq. Al-Anbari then became a member of the "Mujahedeen Shura Council" and headed the intelligence and security councils coming out of the Mujahedeen Shura Council, where he worked consistently with Abu Yahya al-Iraqi. He is now the "general governor" of Syria. The man has gained a reputation for success in intelligence operations behind enemy lines that has allowed ISIS fighters to achieve stunning victories that have led to massacres and stunned ISIS's enemies. A report by International Business Times, published November 10th 2014, stated that, should al- Baghdadi be killed ISIS has prepared for the succession. Those among his many deputies most likely to be on the shortlist would be Abu Ali al-Anbari,   Abu Muslim al-Tukmani and Abu Suleiman.

The leadership of the security and intelligence council is composed of four senior officers that were in Saddam's security apparatus, famous for its severity and strength, all of whom have extensive professional experience. ISIS's security apparatus has branches in every country, and is quick to eliminate dissidents and spies. It plays a major role in keeping the "Caliphate" together, and is responsible for roadblocks and border control. The military council is responsible for protecting the State's territories and expansion operations. It is run by Abu Ayman al-Iraqi, who was previously a lieutenant colonel and intelligence officer in Saddam's air force and had very close relations with Izzat al-Douri. He was also a prisoner at Camp Bucca, and was known for his intensity, ruthlessness and violence. The ISIS chief of staff is the Chechen Tarkhan Tayumurazovich who goes by Abu Omar al-Shishani. Before joining the al-Qaeda branch known as the Caucasus Emirate, he was an officer in the Georgian army. Al-Shishani arrived in Syria in March 2012 with a group of Chechen fighters that were known for being well trained and "sons of war." Al-Shishani swore his allegiance to al-Baghdadi in mid-2013.

According to American experts, the reason behind ISIS's military success is their ability to combine "traditional military operations, guerilla warfare, and mafia operations."

The weapons ISIS captured from the other factions in Syria formed a major source of armament. Before the United States and United Kingdom realized the arms they were sending were falling into ISIS hands, these factions were armed with light weaponry by the two Western states as well as Arab countries. Another source of armament is the weapons ISIS seized from Iraqi forces during their major invasion in 2014. In a statement to Reuters in early June of 2015, the Iraqi prime minister said that, in Mosul alone, ISIS had seized 2,300 American armored military Humvee vehicles, which are strong multi-purpose military vehicles. In its campaigns against Baiji, Ramadi and other towns, it seized hundreds more. The value of the Humvee vehicles that ISIS seized in Mosul alone is estimated to be over one billion dollars, based on the Iraqi government deal to buy 1,000 Humvees from the Americans the previous year at 579 million dollars. It had also agreed to buy M1 Abrams tanks at a value of 1.204 billion dollars. The Americans have expressed concern over American military technology falling into the hands of its enemies, who could sell their technological secrets to countries competing with the United States. The Americans were stunned by the sight of ISIS forces riding aboard their Humvee military technology, after having previously depended solely on civilian Toyotas in their operations.

Saddam's Precautions

Learning his lesson from what happened during the 1991 Iran-Iraq War when the Shiites in the South of Iraq and Kurds in the North rebelled, Saddam was expecting the Shiites and Kurds to repeat their rebellion when the Americans attacked in 2003. In preparation, he established a secret system to store massive amounts of weapons, ammunition, and explosives in hiding spots throughout Iraq. He created what is known as Fedayeen Sadaam, as well as a network of safe houses as hiding places for his quasi-security forces and Baathist supporters, if the situation suddenly turned against them.

American colonel Derek Harvey, the U.S Defense Intelligence Agency officer that worked under the command of the U.S commander in Iraq Ricardo Sanchez, estimated that 95,000 people were fired after Paul Bremer, the post-invasion Administrator of Iraq, decided to disband the Iraqi army and security forces (the digital Caliphate). These included republican guard forces, intelligence, and Fedayeen Sadaam. Over the course of a day, 95,000 officers and soldiers found themselves unemployed. In addition, "de-Baathification" led to the unemployment of no less than 2 million people. This number swelled to millions when those who depended on or sympathized with them erupted with bitter rage against the U.S-British invasion forces. These two decisions lacked wisdom and vision, and were taken based on hatred and a desire for revenge without full consideration of consequences and results. These millions were now mobilized against the Americans, and ready to flock to any "rallying cry" with the goal of defeating them.

Due to economic sanctions placed on Iraq after the first Gulf War, the Baathists worked to find alternative sources of funding, one of which was circumvention through oil smuggling. They excelled and gained important skills and experience, building networks for this purpose from which ISIS benefits today. Izzat al-Douri, Saddam Hussein's deputy, was responsible for these networks and has today opened them up to ISIS. Al-Douri belonged to the Naqshbandi order, whose preachers claim descent from the companion Abu Bakr as-Siddiq, an affiliation that has helped him create an effective resistance against the Americans composed of Sufi order supporters called the Army of the Men of the Naqshbandi Order. This group allied with the Islamic State in Iraq and Syria to gain control over Mosul. Al-Douri's network was also able to smuggle cars in network workshops, to equip them with explosives and use them as lethal weapons that killed many Americans.

After the Iran-Iraq war, Saddam worked to fortify his Baathist regime against the religious critics in Iraq. He partially Islamized it through a faith campaign by including "God is Great" on the flag and implementing measures such as amputating the hands of robbers and cutting the ears of those evading and deserting military service. To distinguish these two constituencies from those wounded or disabled in war, he used a hot iron to mark their cheeks with an "X." As the Americans know, he sent army officers to religious classes until they became closer to Salafists than Baathists. After the invasion, some of them even disappeared and joined the Americans while secretly working with the resistance.

Another example of the security campaign's effect was the ascension of Saddam's intelligence agent Abdallah al-Janabi to the position of President of the Mujahedeen Shura Council in Fallujah. After the invasion, it is said that al-Douri and a number of Baathists fled to Syria, where they found an appropriate environment for planning and launching their operations. Their work served both their purpose and, indirectly, the Syrian regime, which was not pleased by the American occupation of Iraq, since if it succeeded, it would open up the West and the US's appetite for occupying Syria and elsewhere. This Syrian stance gained significant respect among the Arab masses.

All of these factors helped create an appropriate environment for launching resistance operations that were essentially Sunni, due to this group's feelings of marginalization and exposure to repression. They had lost the regime that once considered them essential elements, as well as the Baathists that were running it. With authority having slipped from between their fingers, the Sunni and Baathist sides began working together.

Suicide/Martyrdom Operations

The first to have initiated suicide operations were the Buddhist Tamil Tiger rebels, who fought Hindus in Sri Lanka. They were responsible for killing the Indian Prime Minister Rajiv Gandhi, and 18 others, on May 21, 1991 with the same suicide bombing technique.

Muslim scholars differ in regards to the permissibility of these operations. Some of them consider them as forbidden suicide; however, the majority of them believe that it is permissible if necessary, if a Muslim fighter has no other way out, and it is done within the conditions of waging war in Islam. Sheikh al-Qaradawi is a proponent of delineating the numerous conditions required for suicide bombing. On the other end of the spectrum is the jihadists, who rely only on their scholars' rulings. They ignore the rulings of those they call idle scholars, considering that "they have chosen to be with those who remained behind." Classifying this war as defense against attackers, they thus remove it from falling under *fard kifaya*. The jihadists exclude themselves from the rulings of non-jihadist scholars, and work based off of their principle that "An idle scholar does not impose legal rulings on a mujahed!" Yet it is a principle that, no matter how much zeal it draws, has no basis in Islamic jurisprudence. This is due to the fact that waging defensive or offensive war is not a legal obligation.

Suicide/martyrdom bombings are considered the Islamic State's most acute weapon. They have led to the rapid annihilation of its enemies, and exhausted and deprived the American forces of sleep. ISIS's jihadist factions are known to have excelled in everything from target selection, precision in manufacturing and mixing explosives, and their effect on the target area. The Islamic State's intelligence and security systems have helped hide both its secrets and the overwhelming majority of individuals in charge of designs and operations. The Islamic State divides responsibilities, and then isolates each operation and their point people from others as a way of internal fortification. The security and intelligence apparatuses sternly implement the principle of "knowledge only as needed," making each individual equivalent to a small cog in a machine, performing its role and being replaced at any moment if it breaks or is unable to perform its duty. In this way, none of the Islamic State's members can gain complete information about developments and operations, and are not privy to its details and facts beyond what is required for them in order to perform their roles.

The authorities are disturbed by suicide/martyrdom operations, and anticipate their destructive effect on facilities and structures, as well as the human losses they cause. They anticipate the terror, alarm, and feelings of insecurity, as well as the extremely weakened morale of the forces, the leadership, and the citizens. The battle between security/police forces against ISIS bombings is more of a war than a crime-fighting operation. ISIS bombers blow themselves up in consecutive waves, and in Baghdad, they successively bombed Shiite assemblies, specifically markets in Shiite neighborhoods, Shiite commemoration ceremonies, and their imams' shrines. They do not distinguish between men, women, young children, or newborns, which is strange given that targeting women and children in war is clearly forbidden in war against infidels, tyrants, and others. ISIS follows its own jurisprudence, which does not bat an eyelash at extreme violence and savagery. Bombings also target security checkpoints and police stations, and an Iraqi police officer described its precision in such bombings as "...works of art... They were so sophisticated that they destroyed everything; there was nothing left of the car and nothing to investigate how the explosive charge was assembled." During the first years of the American occupation of Iraq, the number of suicide/martyrdom operations reached 17 explosions in one day in Baghdad alone.

Christoph Reuter informs us that, ISIS fighters and leadership carefully avoid falling captive, to the Americans previously, and the Syrian and Iraqi forces today. In some cases, they resort to carrying with them and swallowing poisonous pills or blowing themselves up, if wearing an explosive belt. In other cases, they fight until the death in order to avoid captivity.

Though this is what usually happens, Abu Abdullah had unfortunate luck. Abu Abdullah was an ISIS leader in Baghdad, commissioned with the task of preparing suicide/martyrdom operations in the capital. His role was to specify the bombing target, design and prepare the explosive belt or car bomb using ISIS's famous complex, technical methods, and accompanying the car bomb to a spot nearest to the explosion. Abu Abdullah was surprised by a large number of security forces surrounding him; thus, he had no time to neither swallow poison nor blow himself up. Abu Abdullah was subsequently held in a high-security prison.

The Iraqi forces began hiding the locations of prisons after ISIS broke into the Abu Ghraib and al-Taji prisons and freed hundreds of their supporters and leadership. They transfer the prisoners that are important both for them and for ISIS between prisons, yet the location of these prisoners and their names are unknown.

Abu Abdullah was arrested in late July of 2014 in the explosives factory disguised as a car repair shop he ran. He had supervised bombings over the course of a year and a half in Baghdad, and carried out about 19 that led to the death of hundreds of civilians and military personnel.

The journalist Christoph Reuter conducted an interview with Abu Abdullah from inside his cell. He relayed that the authorities stipulated he not expose the location or name of the prison, despite the fact that he did not find a sign at its entrance with a name. They also stipulated that he conduct his interview at night, because the chances of such bombings were lower at night. According to the journalist, the period of al-Maliki's governance was one of corruption in which dangerous ISIS members would escape from prisons, occasionally in groups. The jurists, politicians, and police offers were corrupt and would often accept ISIS bribes.

Reuter said that 30-year old Abu Abdullah al-Naheel entered the cell blindfolded, with his hands and feet cuffed. Though he answered questions in a monotone, his answers provided the opportunity to travel through the mind of an ISIS man. He could become acquainted with the way ISIS thinks, its vision, and its beliefs. It gave a glimpse, even if brief, of a small part of ISIS's system of power. Abu Abdullah was a Shiite that left his Shiite school of thought and became a Sunni quite some time before being captured.

Abu Abdullah told Reuter that his standard for choosing bombing locations was striking the largest number of people, especially officers, police forces, soldiers, and Shiites. The places he targeted were checkpoints, and Shiite-only markets and mosques. He claimed that he does not feel sorry for the deaths his bombings resulted in on the basis that the dead were Shiites, and as he says, "Shiites are infidels, I was convinced of that." When the journalist told him that they are Muslims like him, he responded by saying that the bombings are thus a means and opportunity for them to repent and become Sunnis. He said that he would use explosives from artillery shells and plastic C4 explosives for car bombs, and for explosive belts he would use highly explosive explosives from aircraft shells. Abu Abdullah said he used to make explosive belts and vests of different sizes in order to fit a wide range of bombers. Over the course of three months, he alone had prepared 19 suicide missions.

Abu Abdullah was not responsible for selecting those that would implement the missions, which was the job of military strategists above him in rank, nor was he commissioned to care for bombers' families, which was the task of other ISIS members. Most of the volunteers came to him from Fallujah, and he recalls: "I was only responsible for…preparing the men in my workshop and then bringing them to the right location. I received the person's measurements in advance from the leadership in order to be able to make a well-fitting belt. But I always had belts in different sizes prepared." Abu Abdullah said most volunteers came from Saudi Arabia, Tunisia, and Algeria, ten came from Iraq, one from Australia, and one German of Turkish roots, all of who ended up completing missions. Regarding the latter two specifically, ISIS released an announcement that said: "Two knights of Islam and heroes of the caliphate were launched," as if they were artillery. Abu Abdullah said the Christian convert to Islam felt great joy and happiness because he sacrificed himself for Islam so soon after converting. He also felt close to this man because "…I also only found the true faith later in life.

Suprisingly, Abu Abdullah came from an old Shiite family in Baghdad, which happens to be related to a leader of the Asa'ib Ahl al-Haq, an extremist Shiite group.

Abu Abdullah says that not one of the men that came to him to blow themselves up doubted the reason of the mission that they carried out. They had been ready for it for a long time. "When they came to me, they were calm, sometimes even joyful. When they put on the belt they would say, for example, "Fits well!" He cites the example of Abu Mohsen Qasimi, a young Syrian man who made jokes even two minutes before his deployment, "then, when he drove off by himself, he bid a friendly farewell." With one young Saudi man, "I was wondering how we could inconspicuously change spots, because I was sitting behind the wheel at first. We pretended to have car trouble, both got out and then pushed the vehicle for a bit. Nobody noticed anything. We both laughed"!

The only time Abu Abdullah flinched during the interview, when he appeared as if caught red-handed, was when Reuter asked him if he would repeat what he had done. He turned pale, and said that he couldn't answer that question.

When preparing the bombers, Abu Abdullah said they made sure they resembled regular young men. They didn't have long beards, wore t-shirts, and had combed and jelled hair. The ages of the bombers were between 21 and 30 years old. Since Abu Abdullah was born and raised in Baghdad, Reuter asked him if he avoided bombing the places in which he had good memories. Abu Abdullah responded, "No, absolutely not! That played no role whatsoever. I didn't do it because I am bloodthirsty."

According to Abu Abdullah, he was implementing the bombings because it was jihad. For a while, he believed the Shiites would either convert to Islam or leave Baghdad. "I am not a butcher, I was implementing a plan," he said. He thought that once people were exposed to a suicide bombing, they would begin to think and this would scare them. When Reuter confronted him with the fact that his acts had not led to desired results, he said it didn't matter. Abu Abdullah's goal was to continue until they converted or emigrated, it didn't matter when. That didn't matter.

When asked if he would ever blow himself up, Abu Abdullah answered that he had never thought about it because it wasn't his job. He was chosen to plan the operation, not implement it. He said, "I was a coordinator, not an executor." Before that, Abu Abdullah said that he was a planner and a thinker, not a follower. Regarding his future, he said it was uncertain.

Al-Qaeda in Iraq became famous for its use of suicide/martyr bombers and *inghimasis* until such operations became its business trademark. Bin Laden told his group in Iraq to use this type of attack against the invasion forces, and directed them to use *inghimasi* bombers in the city streets to scare the Americans. Bin Laden's men implemented their leader's orders in the first two years of the American presence in Iraq when 270 *inghimasis* implemented 18 suicide/martyrdom bombings.

In 2013, ISIS implemented 98 *inghimasi* bombings in Iraq, and 50 in Syria. These operations disabled al-Maliki's efforts at regaining stability and security. According to Time magazine's report, during the period between September and December of 2013, these attacks led to the death of 3000 people, and bombings continued during 2014.

Jürgen Todenhöfer

The 74-year old German Jürgen Todenhöfer is an advocate for human rights, opposes the repression of the Palestinians, and is against the war on Iraq. He lives in Munich, and is a writer with a number of published works in German. The press frequently asks him to contribute, and he has worked in the media, served as a member of the German parliament, and prior to that was a judge. In his search for the truth, he met with Saddam Hussein and the military factions that fought against the Americans in Iraq during the occupation. He also met with President Bashar al-Assad, and leaders of the anti-Assad Free Syrian Army. Jürgen says that his experience as a judge has taught him to listen to and meet with all sides in order to avoid a life filled with false judgments and mistakes. A brave man, Jürgen has clearly defined opinions, and speaks openly about what he sees as the truth. Jürgen's openness about his opinion on the insolent American policies in Iraq and Afghanistan, and the American stance on Palestine, brought about the discontent of the Americans to the extent that *Foreign Policy*, in its December 2014 issue, described him as "a man that detests the United States and loves al-Assad!"

In the Libyan city of Benghazi, Jürgen met the American journalist James Foley. They stayed in the same hotel and got to know each other a month before Foley traveled to ISIS territory where he was captured and beheaded. ISIS recorded this horrendous act and broadcasted it on social media, causing waves of grief and horror, and fueling the world's fear. These videos realized ISIS's goal of spreading fear in keeping with how the author of *The Management of Savagery*, as described above, advocated spreading fear in the land then broadcasting the dreadful acts far and wide "until our enemy thinks 1,000 times before attacking us." The fleeing of 30,000 Iraqi soldiers in Mosul when faced with hundreds of ISIS fighters confirms the validity of this approach in terrorizing their enemies. Some analysts believe that the hesitance of the 60 countries allied against ISIS to send even a single soldier to fight on the ground is a result of the fear ISIS has instilled through their actions and well-utilized fear-propaganda machine that repeats: "Allah made me victorious over my enemies through awe for the distance of one month's journey" However, this will not last for long, for some countries can no longer be patient with ISIS.

The awful way in which the American journalist James Foley was killed both infuriated and saddened Jürgen, but it also sparked his curiosity. He insisted on getting to know this strange organization whose actions had at the least drawn quite a bit of attention. Through social media, Jürgen got in touch with 80 Germans that supported ISIS and immigrated to its territory. Fifteen of them responded to Jürgen's letters, and they had talks and debates about the legitimacy of their actions from the perspective of religion. These conversations continued until Jürgen reached an ISIS official responsible for speaking with journalists, who explained to him the Islamic State's policies and stances. Jürgen expressed to the man his desire to visit the Islamic State, to see up close how affairs are run. This was met with opposition from his 31-year old son Frederic, who had been helping him communicate with the German ISIS jihadists. He opposed his father's travel to their territory because of the terrifying videos he had seen, but Jürgen insisted. After communications that lasted almost seven months between Jürgen and German ISIS jihadists, and finally their media representative, composed of Skype conversations that lasted hours and in which ISIS fighters reassured Jürgen that nothing bad would happen to him if he visited, he received an official invitation from the Caliph al-Baghdadi's office. That is when Frederic told his father that he would not allow him to take this frightening journey alone, but that he would accompany him to provide help and support. The father and son thus boarded a plane to Istanbul, then to the Syrian border, and ISIS smuggled them across the border to their lands.

Jürgen Todenhöfer is the only international public media figure that has visited ISIS territory, remaining there for ten days from December 6 until December 16, 2014. He is the only writer or journalist in the world that has written about the Islamic State from the inside, after living with its leaders and soldiers, roaming its cities and streets, and frequenting its public and popular facilities. Jürgen and his son lived with ISIS combatants in the same building, and on the same floor. They ate together, and had heated and dangerous discussions and debates. He visited Mosul, the ISIS capital Raqqah, and the city of Deir ez-Zor. Countless media agencies have drawn on Jürgen's testimony, since he is the only eyewitness of conditions inside the Islamic State, and because his visit sparked a buzz among official circles in his country and beyond.

There is no doubt that Jürgen remembers ISIS's letter to Foley's family, published by the Global Post on August 22, 2014, which contains the following:

> "A message to the American government and their sheep like citizens: We have left you alone since your dis-

graceful defeat in Iraq. We did not interfere in your country or attack your citizens while they were safe in their homes despite our capability to do so!

As for the scum of your society who are held prisoner by us, THEY DARED TO ENTER THE LION'S DEN AND WHERE EATEN!

You were given many chances to negotiate the release of your people via cash transactions as other governments have accepted. We have also offered prisoner exchanges to free the Muslims currently in your detention like our sister Dr Afia Sidiqqi, however you proved very quickly to us that this is NOT what you are interested in.

You have no motivation to deal with the Muslims except with the language of force, a language you were given in "Arabic translation" when you attempted to occupy the land of Iraq!

Now you return to bomb the Muslims of Iraq once again, this time resorting to Arial attacks and 'proxy armies', all the while cowardly shying away from a face-to-face confrontation! Today our swords are unsheathed towards you, GOVERNMENT AND CITIZENS ALIKE! AND WE WILL NOT STOP UNTILL WE QUENCH OUR THIRST FOR YOUR BLOOD. You do not spare our weak, elderly, women or children so we will NOT spare yours! You and your citizens will pay the price of your bombings! The first of which being the blood of the American citizen, James Foley! He will be executed as a DIRECT result of your transgressions towards us!"

On August 22, 2014, all newspapers and channels published this letter, including CBC and the website Bustle.

ISIS e-mailed the letter to Foley's family in the United States, who decided to hand it over to the media. This led to a "Twitter storm," to use Atwan's terminology, along with unprecedented media coverage of the situation. The free advertising "sent by God" filled ISIS with delight. The letter, sent on August 12, 2014, attempted to draw a connection between the events raging in the Middle East and Western involvement in the region. ISIS wanted to make clear that its actions were the revengeful result of Western involvement, which led to panic and alarm in the West – a fear ISIS loves to see afflicting its enemies. On the other hand, publishing the letter aroused sympathy and respect for ISIS among a number of Muslims. Overlooking Foley's human suffering, they saw in the letter the humiliation and defiance of the America that had oppressed them in their countries through both direct involvement as well as supporting regimes that restricted their freedom. The horrific letter gained ISIS the respect of Muslims that saw it as an organization rising up for the dignity of those humiliated and disrespected by the West. Feelings of rebellion and revenge had risen to the surface, blurring in their eyes Foley's human suffering. Meanwhile, Jürgen had not forgotten Foley and their meeting in Benghazi.

Foley was executed in an on-screen beheading on August 19. To quote the eloquent Atwan, Foley wore the orange Guantanamo uniform to "sanctify a message sent in orange." Foley's execution was an injustice prohibited in Islam, and an act of barbarism void of any humanity. In September of 2014, the American-Israeli Steven Sotloff was killed. His case was far more wretched than Foley's, since he embodied ISIS's two greatest and most unjust foes. News reached Jürgen, and the media storm claimed the decapitator spoke English with a native British accent, later becoming known in sensationalist newspapers as "Jihadi John." Although his identity was not yet known, the U.S and British press recently revealed that his real name is Mohammed Emwazi. The media reported that he is a resident of London and was known to British security forces prior to his joining ISIS. Inside ISIS, John and the other British jihadists became known as "the Beatles," nicknamed after the popular mainstream musical group.

ISIS's list of executions include two other Westerners, David Haines and Alan Henning. Both of them British, authorities revealed that they were aid workers, but ISIS classified them as spies using aid as a cover. The two men were beheaded in September and October. There is no doubt that Jürgen knew, and ISIS would have killed them even if they were not spies. It believes that the Western states, led by the United States and Great Britain, do not show mercy on civilians in Iraq, Afghanistan, or Palestine through their ally Israel; thus, it will not be the respectful one and show mercy on their own civilians. Jürgen's answer to what assured him that ISIS would uphold their security agreement was that it was in the Islamic State's interest to act in a way that paints them as a legitimate state. By not upholding their agreement, they would thus be hurting themselves. Jürgen had a love for Syria and Iraq, having visited them dozens of times during the past fifteen years. . He stated, "As a former judge I have learned to speak with all sides, so I met all the players but I didn't know exactly what IS was and I thought, 'if you want to defeat your enemies, you have to know them.'" He lived among the jihadists and interacted with them. One of the most important questions Jürgen asked was, "In the Quran, 113 out of 114 chapters start with in the name of God, the most Gracious, the most Merciful, so where is your mercy? You kill and enslave people, so where is the mercy?" Jürgen continues, "We discussed this repeatedly, because I truly wanted to make sure they were convinced of their actions. Had they thought deeply about what they were doing? I discussed this with them nightly, which caused them to be averse to speaking with me, since I was conversing with them as an infidel. I was not about to go to such a country and be content with merely listening, but I still had to be careful. I told them repeatedly that I had read the Quran three times, and the God I found in the Quran was much grander than the God they had showed me. The God they knew says that the hands of anyone that steals something worth more than forty dollars must be cut off, but the God I knew from the Quran was much grander than that. This infuriated and enraged them, but they couldn't accuse me of disrespecting God, because I was claiming him to be grander. Every time we had this conversation, our trip nearly came to an end. My son truly believed on multiple occasions that our trip was over. I visited a welcome camp for new recruits, where, more than fifty young men arrive each day from all over the world. They come from the United States of America, Canada, the Caucuses, and other places, most of them beaming with a worrying excitement."

Jürgen said: "The Islamic State is very strong militarily because it has combined terrifying excitement and religious fanaticism with exceptional training provided by Saddam Hussein's officers – a dangerous combination. I tried to figure out where all this excitement was coming from, and what I found is that many of these men felt discriminated against in their own countries. They feel that we, as Western states, have attacked the Middle East over the past two centuries through our colonialism and then through oil-driven wars, killing over one million people. They feel the importance of creating a glorious history for themselves, a history of good fighting evil. And with that, they believe that they will conquer the world."

Over the past fourteen years, Jürgen has learned that fighting ISIS with air strikes is wrong. After September 11, there were less than one thousand terrorists worldwide. Today, there are more than 100,000 terrorists. Thus, there is a clear mistake in the strategy of bombing all of these countries. For every child the West kills, a terrorist will be born. "It has been said that ISIS cannot be contained with diplomacy, but I would like to reiterate what Obama said weeks ago (the statement was made in January 2015) – that the Islamic State is a product of our war on Iraq. The Islamic State is supported by Iraqi Sunnis, who compose 35% of the population that were discriminated against after the American invasion of Iraq. Put simply, the solution is to involve all Sunnis of Iraq in the political process. If not, the army of fear belonging to the Islamic State will continue to expand not only in Syria and Iraq, but also in Yemen, Egypt, and elsewhere. We must find a way to spread that Abu Bakr al-Baghdadi is not a true Muslim, and that what he says about Islam is laughable," stated Jürgen.

On his Facebook page, Jürgen wrote that ISIS knew prior to his visit that he strongly criticized them both on Facebook and in the German media: "Thus, I did not underplay the danger of my trip. The conversations I had with the ISIS fighters and the experience I obtained were dramatic, as was the security situation there. Only yesterday, I was crossing the Turkish border, heading to the ISIS territories (12/16/2014). I had sped up my steps to enter through the Turkish border, my belongings on my back on the road that smugglers take, next to the Turkish watchtower. As I crossed, I felt like the weight of the world had been lifted off of my shoulders. Now, I feel an overwhelming happiness because I have safely returned to my country of Germany. My family was so happy that we broke out into tears upon my arrival," recounted Jürgen.

He continued, "I didn't set out upon this difficult journey because Pope Francis had recently called world leaders to open dialogue with the Islamic State. Rather, I took this trip because throughout fifty years of my life, I have refused to close the door on dialogue with any side. For example, I had spoken with President al-Assad, al-Qaeda, and the Free Syrian Army. In Afghanistan, I held a number of meetings with President Hamid Karzai, as well as Taliban leadership. I spoke with the Shiite government in Iraq, and the Sunni resistance during the war on Iraq. I did all of this amid significant criticism from certain bureaucratic offices."

According to Jürgen, "United States involvement in Afghanistan, Iraq, Libya and other countries has resulted in a catastrophe. The United States has not been open to dialogue with its opponents, and knows very little about them. Thus, I think that the prevailing lack of information should become the trademark for Western policy in the Middle East."

Those that want to defeat their enemies must first know them well, and the Islamic State is stronger and more dangerous than any Western politician realizes, claims Jürgen.

On December 21, 2014, five days after Jürgen Todenhöfer's return from ISIS territory, *The Independent* wrote that the only Western journalist ISIS has allowed entry into its territories claims the truth on the ground is different than what anyone in the West believes. He returned with the warning that the group is "stronger and far more dangerous" than what Westerners believe, and that it now covers a territory larger than the United Kingdom. It is supported by an "ecstatic enthusiasm" from its supporters, the likes of which he had not seen in any other war zone. Each day, hundreds of eager militants arrive from all parts of the world, something he did not understand.

Jürgen was able to move between the militants and note their living conditions and equipment. He took a picture of the German MG3 machine gun that ISIS fighters use, who told him that it would one day point at Germany. Jürgen also relayed that ISIS fighters sleep in barracks made out of buildings that airstrikes have transformed into carcasses. The number of fighters in Mosul alone is 5,000 and they are spread throughout a wide area. If the United States wanted to kill them all, they would need to turn all of Mosul into a heap through its strikes.

Jürgen said that this means that the Islamic State cannot be defeated through Western involvement or airstrikes, despite the United States' claims in December 2015 that its bombing had been effective. He said, "With each bomb that falls and kills a civilian, the number of terrorists will increase." Jürgen relayed that the Islamic State has social welfare and education systems, and he was surprised to learn that the latter is planning to provide education to girls (Westerners usually have the impression that Muslims and extremists oppress women). *The Independent* said that most worrisome of what Jürgen had said was that ISIS militants believe all religions that agree with democracy must be wiped out. They repeatedly state that ISIS will conquer the world (militarily), and that anyone who doesn't agree with their interpretation of the Quran must be killed. The only religions they plan on allowing to remain are the religions of the People of the Book: Judaism and Christianity, adding, "This will be the largest planned religious cleansing in human history."

The Islamic State celebrated and was filled with delight over the media broadcast of Jürgen's remarks. It subsequently tweeted, "The German journalist Jürgen: The Islamic Caliphate is trying to create a life modeled off of the Caliphs that lived after the Prophet Mohammed, peace be upon him, and they can move mountains." Jürgen finished his statement by saying that he thinks the Islamic State will try to communicate with the West soon regarding negotiations for a certain level of coexistence. Nine months have passed since Jürgen's statement, and ISIS has not shown any initiative in this direction. Lastly, he thinks that the only people who can stop ISIS are moderate Iraqi Sunnis, which is a highly difficult matter.

Jürgen told Al Jazeera English that during his communications with the ISIS media representative prior to his visit, he was honest about not supporting them. He said that they knew his critique of them, as well as that he had previously met al-Assad; however, they replied to him by saying, "Yes, that is not our problem, we don't care about your opinion, we want you to tell what you have seen here, not the opinion that you had beforehand." According to Jürgen, ISIS is to a certain extent a security state. On a number of occasions, they requested that he not videotape while driving along the road to avoid raising suspicion. His son had taken 800 pictures, and they erased nine of them for reasons he considered reasonable, since they could have exposed the families of fighters to danger if published. Regarding the difficulties he faced during there he said, "Everything was uncomfortable. Sometimes there was no food or water, like on the last day when we had nothing to eat. It was very simple because they chose houses where nobody thinks they are or may be. They have to hide because there are American bombs out there. One of the most difficult situations was in Mosul when a drone identified some who were with us, and the bomb came down. It was also very unpleasant when we returned to Raqqa after some days in Mosul. We were three days late and two days before that, when we were supposed to be there, our apartment where we lived was destroyed by Syrian bombers. No more windows, no more doors. There was glass everywhere. We knew that if we were back in time, we would have been dead. Crossing the border at the end was also unpleasant. A few days before we were to cross, there was some shooting and at the end, close to the border, you have to run about 1,000m to cross the border with all your bags and equipment in order to get to safety. Running 1,000m is very far when you're running for your life and there are gun towers with armed men inside."

About their time with the fighters, Jürgen recounts, "the discussions were very hard. I have read the Quran many times in German translation, and I always asked them about the value of mercy in Islam. I didn't see any mercy in their behavior. Something that I don't understand at all is the enthusiasm in their plan of religious cleansing, planning to kill the non-believers... They also will kill Muslim democrats because they believe that non-ISIL-Muslims put the laws of human beings above the commandments of God. These were very difficult discussions, especially when they were talking about the number of people who they are willing to kill. They were talking about hundreds of millions. They were enthusiastic about it, and I just cannot understand that."

Jürgen said that his trip left him with three strong impressions, the first being that "ISIL is much stronger than we think. They have conquered an area which is bigger than Great Britain. Every day, hundreds of new enthusiastic fighters are arriving. There is an incredible enthusiasm that I have never seen in any other war zones that I have been to." His second impression was the brutality of ISIS's plan for religious cleansing, and third was his conviction that "the strategy of the western countries regarding the Muslim world is completely wrong. With our bombardment, we have never been successful. We have not been successful in Afghanistan; we have not been successful in Iraq. The bombardments are a terror-breeding program. We had much fewer terrorists before 2001 and these bombardments, which killed hundreds of thousands of people have created terrorists and increased terrorism."

Jürgen Todenhöfer believes that the best way to deal with ISIS is to treat Muslims in "a fair way, to see them as equal; inside Western countries and societies, Muslims have to be considered as compatriots. Secondly, we should stop our bombardments, we have nothing to gain from bombarding in the Arab world; it is not ours. Thirdly, I think only Sunni Iraqis can defeat the ISIL. They have done this once before. In 2007, they fought them down, but then ISIS was much weaker. But this is the only possibility and way forward. But the Sunnis in Iraq are discriminated against and excluded from society and that is a big mistake made by the old and the new Iraqi government. As long as these Sunnis are not integrated, they will not fight against ISIL, but if the Iraqi government and if the American government would arrange the integration of the Sunni Iraqis in the Iraqi society...then they would be ready to fight ISIS. So I say western countries will not defeat ISIL. Only Arabs, only Sunni Iraqis, can defeat them. But this is a long way away."

As expected, Jürgen's statements aroused a storm of reactions, a ton of written responses and analyses, and discussion online and in major television networks. For example, Michael Ashcraft and Mark Ellis wrote that Jürgen had visited ISIS, exposing himself to incredible danger, after ISIS gave him unprecedented permission to enter. They quoted him as having called it a "movement with the power of a nuclear bomb." Moreover, an ISIS fighter told him that, "We will conquer Europe one day. It is not a question of IF we will conquer Europe, just a matter of when that will happen. But it is certain. For us, there is no such thing as borders. There are only front lines. Our expansion will be perpetual. And the Europeans need to know that when we come, it will not be in a nice way. It will be with our weapons. And those who do not convert to Islam or pay the Islamic tax will be killed." Jürgen said in reaction that, "I don't see anyone who has a real chance to stop them." He told the BBC that, "I don't see anyone who has a real chance to stop them," "Only Arabs can stop ISIS. I came back very pessimistic. I thought I would meet a brutal terrorist group, but I met a brutal country. They are so confident, so sure of themselves. At the beginning of this year, few people knew of ISIS. But now they have conquered an area the size of the UK. This is a one per cent movement with the power of a nuclear bomb or a tsunami."

According to the two writers, allowing Jürgen to visit was ISIS's way of proving to the world that the Islamic State is working. They said that Jürgen found ISIS to have effective systems of social welfare and education, and that he also saw child soldiers of about thirteen years old carrying AK-47s. He saw prisoners and slaves, and the writers related one of the fighters telling Jürgen that, "Slavery absolutely signals progress. Only ignorant people believe that there is no slavery among the Christians and the Jews. Of course there are woman who are forced into prostitution under the worst circumstances. I would say that slavery is a great help to us, and we will continue to have slavery and beheadings; it is part of our religion. Many slaves have converted to Islam and have then been freed."

Jürgen met with an ISIS prisoner from the Iraqi Kurdistan region. He told him, in the presence of his prison guards, that they had not tortured him. Yet Jürgen did not believe him, and said that he saw terror in his eyes. Who knows what he would have said given the context of the people surrounding him. He was a broken man, and Jürgen was saddened to see a person in such a state of weakness and fear of his captors.

The captive told Jürgen that he didn't know what would happen to him, and that even his family didn't know if he was alive. His hope was to either to die or for a hostage exchange to occur. A fighter told Jürgen that they will kill all of the Shiites, whether their numbers are 200 million or 500 million. "We will kill them all," said the fighter.

Jürgen stated that despite the rule of terror resulting from The Islamic State in Iraq and Syria's stern implementation of Sharia law, the people in the region give you the feeling that they are accepting of this rule, to the extent of adopting it eagerly. Jürgen followed with "There is an awful sense of normalcy in Mosul."

He added that ISIS's stunning success in controlling these territories is derived not from their military tactics, but from their zeal and religious fanaticism. They had told him that, "We fight for Allah, they fight for money and other things that they do not really believe in." They added that they attacked 20,000 Iraqi soldiers with a force of 200 fighters, capturing valuable weapons and ammunition, and military vehicles left by the soldiers.

The two writers said that the Islamic State had two billion dollars as a result of donations they receive from Arabs in the Gulf, oil sales, tariffs, and seizure, as well ransom revenue they obtain as a result of kidnappings.

On January 12, 2015, *Huffington Post* quoted Jürgen as saying that the zeal and ardor of the ISIS fighters is unparalleled, and that they speak of victory with full confidence. They are the largest threat to world peace since the Cold War. Jürgen wrote on his website, that "we are now paying the price of George Bush's unparalleled stupidity in invading Iraq. Until today, the West remains ignorant regarding how to face this challenge."

Jürgen recounts that on the day of their arrival in Mosul, the ISIS men requested that he and his son remain in the apartment. He wanted to walk around the streets, so contestation rose up between them, with Jürgen accusing them of trying to hold him prisoner. The confrontation intensified, despite Jürgen knowing that they are in a state of war, and in the end ISIS calls the shots. That evening, when faced with Jürgen's urgency, they gave in and allowed Jürgen and his son to walk around the streets of Mosul with accompaniment. Fifteen minutes later, they were no longer interested in monitoring them, so they allowed them to speak freely with the people without ISIS men eavesdropping. Jürgen did not at all get the impression that the people they spoke with were saying what ISIS wanted to hear. They organized a number of meetings for us, including one with a prisoner they captured from the Peshmerga. They also met new fighters, one from the US state of New Jersey, a German, and one from the Caribbean islands. Shortly before joining ISIS, the Caribbean militant had only recently passed his law exam.

Jürgen was bothered by the beheadings and killing of Muslims that the Islamic State was performing, so he told them that he had not found a single verse in the Quran, which he read numerous times, that permitted killing all Shiites or Hindus. He told the ISIS militants: "How can you say, 'Yeah, but Muhammad has said this?'" The gap between them widened day after day, until they stopped eating with Jürgen and his son. However, the nature of the relationship changed, and things became normalized once again.

According to Jürgen, the danger of provoking ISIS men was combined with the danger of American and Syrian airstrikes. One time, he was walking around Mosul with a group of combatants, and an American drone began to fly lower and lower to the ground. The group they were with then ran to a football field in which a match was taking place, in hopes that the plane would not strike them, and this is what saved them.

Jürgen aired his meeting with a German Muslim mujahed, the famous 30-year old German author Christian Emde from the city of Solingen. The German confessed that ISIS had inspirations beyond its borders, and that it is now advancing in Libya, Egypt, Yemen, and Saudi Arabia (he referred to Saudi Arabia as "what is known as Saudi Arabia"). He said that they "For us, there is no such thing as borders. There are only front lines. Our expansion will be perpetual." Regarding ISIS's desire to control Europe one day, Christian said: "We will conquer Europe one day. It is not a question of IF we will conquer Europe, just a matter of when that will happen. But it is certain." Christian confirmed to Jürgen that Jews and Christians could enjoy freedom of worship, as long as they pay the jizya tax (which is a method of exemption of military service for non-Muslims, and the confirmation of their protection). However, he said that the Shiites whose numbers have reached 150 million "apostates," will all be killed, unless they convert to Islam. He said that even if it would be considered unprecedented genocide, every apostate will die. He defended beheadings by claiming it was a part of religion, and described slavery as progress. He said that ISIS would move its militants to Europe, and especially Germany, because it arms the Peshmerga. He said, "Once we return to Germany, I don't know what will happen... Only God knows what will happen," with a clear threatening tone. He followed with "However it is certain that we will return, and when we come, it will not be in a nice way. It will be with our weapons. And those who do not convert to Islam or pay the Islamic tax will be killed."

A German channel aired this meeting with Christian, and at the end of it Jürgen Todenhöfer described this mujahed as "Highly intelligent with a strong dogmatic vision, knowledgeable and very barbaric and stable. He is fully convinced that he is doing the right thing."

Jürgen Todenhöfer told BBC, "ISIS appears to be a functioning state. The terrorists are putting forward a security system, and a fully functioning system to care for the poor. These systems are accepted by many of the societies that fall under ISIS's control."

He said, "Life is more normal than I expected. The residents tolerate them, and accept them for being Sunnis, after being discriminated against by the Shiite government for so long." Regarding ISIS's severity and barbarism, he says that the barbarism of the Cambodian Pol Pot (leader of the Khmer Rouge) is nothing compared to ISIS, and al-Qaeda is simply insignificant. He said that among the ISIS fighters he had met was a man who had given up a position in his field of expertise – law – in order to come and fight with ISIS.

Bunyamin Aygun

The well-known journalist Amberin Zaman lives in Istanbul and covers Turkey for prominent international newspapers including the *Los Angeles Times*, the *Washington Post, The Telegraph* and *Voice of America*. She has previously appeared on Turkish television, and is currently a correspondent for *The Economist*.

Amberin met Bunyamin Aygun in the Turkish city of Hatay in January of 2015. She then told his story, which she refers to as a "gold mine" for any journalist that loves investigative reporting. In her piece on Aygun, Amberin wrote:

"We met on a recent evening in a cafe facing Gezi Park, where Aygun had shot powerful images of the mass demonstrations that rocked Istanbul the summer before. 'I'll only be drinking coffee, lots of it,' he announces."

Aygun was one of the first Turkish journalists to cover the Syrian conflict from its start in 2011. "Being Turkish was a real advantage," he claims. "The people loved us, the Free Syrian Army (FSA) loved us." He was able to record the suffering that afflicted the Syrian people, the suffering that unfolded in front of his eyes. Like other journalists at the time, Aygun painted a romantic image of the Syrian rebels during the early days of the war. Perhaps with the intention of romanticizing the rebels against the Syrian government, Aygun told Amberin that, "Ordinary people sold everything they owned to keep the revolution going." He was not bothered by news of journalist kidnappings, and continued covering the events in Syria.

On November 25, after hearing of Islamic State massacres happening in a series of Turkmen villages, Aygun snuck across the border to put together his report. Along with an FSA commander, he was subsequently captured during an attempt to conduct an interview with a senior Islamic State militant near Salkin, a town facing the Turkish city of Hatay.

To ensure he couldn't see anything, Aygun was blindfolded and hooded. His hands and legs were bound most of the time, and his captors repeatedly transferred him between different damp cells. Fighters wearing black clothes interrogated him daily, asking, "Are you Muslim, Sunni, Alevi? Recite a prayer. Give us all your passwords. Who are those women on your Facebook page? Do you drink? Who are you working for? Give us some names. What is your real name?"

Aygun told Amberin that these interrogations lasted too long for him to keep track of the days. In reality, the interrogations lasted forty days, but to Aygun they felt like forty years.

Amberin asked him if ISIS had beaten or tortured him like the Americans had done to their captives, at which Aygun tensed up and refused to reply. He did say, however, that the Islamic State has a strong network in Turkey. He was likely afraid of being punished by ISIS again, "so I decided not to ask," writes the journalist.

Aygun told Amberin, "We were forced to take ablutions and pray five times a day. I didn't really know how, but Heysem Topalca [his fellow hostage and FSA commander] taught me what to do. It was the only time they would unbind my eyes and hands."

The militants would threaten Aygun by saying, "If you are a Muslim you have nothing to fear, but if you are lying we will kill you." On the 17th day of their captivity, Aygun was separated from Topalca. He was moved to a house filled with Turks, which led him to think that his end had come, and that they would surely kill him.

The days that followed were depressing, yet they were also fascinating. "It sheds light on the mindset of the IS fighters," writes Amberin.

Aygun insists that he has no personal agenda. When Amberin asked about the atrocities ISIS commits, he responded: "What of American atrocities in Guantanamo, in Iraq?" He added, "We need to understand the circumstances that led these people to choose this path." Aygun was trying to humanize ISIS.

In the safe house where Aygun spent the rest of his captivity, most of the ISIS fighters were Turks and Germans. He recalls, "Their faces were covered. You could only see their eyes. It was clear from their voices that they were young. Some were university educated. All they did was fight and pray. They said they went into battle praying to be martyred. This is what they lived for, to die as martyrs and to establish an Islamic state in which all citizens would live as the Prophet Muhammad did, to live by the rules of the Book."

"They asked me if I wanted to become a suicide bomber or go to battle with them. They gave me a Turkish language Quran to read and a book about the jihad. There was no singing, no whistling, no women, no cigarettes. They rained curses on Erdogan, and Davutoglu, saying they were 'infidels.' They claimed that if Turkey sealed the border gates that were under IS control they would hit one Turkish village after the other and trigger a civil war inside Turkey," recalled Aygun.

The ISIS piece on Turkey, published on their website *Land of the Caliphate* and republished by *Al-Monitor*, is an example of some of ISIS's severe and extreme stances. In the article, ISIS calls President Recep Tayyip Erdo an the devil, and the Turkish Prime Minister Ahmet Davutoglu the devil's son. The website, written in Turkish, mocks the name Davutoglu. Since Turks do not pronounce the letter "g", Davutoglu is thus pronounced "Davutolu" which translates in Turkish to the word "son." The name Ahmet Davutoglu thus comes to mean Ahmet, son of Davut. Secondly, because Turks pronounce the letter "d" as "t" in most words, the name Davutoglu is pronounced as Tavutolu, which translates roughly to "son of the taghut" (because Tavut is similar in pronunciation to taghut). "Taghut" has a number of different meanings, but one of them in Arabic is Satan. On its website *Land of the Caliphate*, ISIS calls the Turkish leaders apostates, despite their support for the causes of poor Muslims in countries including Somalia, as well as Muslim minorities such as the oppressed Rohingya in Burma. Davutoglu is the only Muslim leader to have visited the Rohingya people, supporting them and discussing their plight with the Burmese government. Similarly, Erdo an is the only Muslim president to have visited Somalia and facilitated projects to aid and support the infrastructure of Somalis.

According to an issue of *Land of the Caliphate*, ISIS vows to conquer Constantinople. It does not recognize the Ottoman Mehmed the Conqueror's taking of the city, referencing the Prophetic hadith that predicted the city's seizure. The hadith states: "Verily you shall conquer Constantinople. What a wonderful leader will her leader be, and what a wonderful army will that army be!" It is said that after the conquest, the Turks named Constantinople Islambol, which then became Istanbul. They hung a plaque inscribed with this prophetic hadith on the wall of the Hagia Sophia entrance, where it still hangs today.

Even al-Julani, the leader of al-Nusra Front – a branch of al-Qaeda in Syria – was deemed an apostate after breaking with the "Caliph of the Muslims." The ease with which ISIS declares apostasy is, at the very least, worrisome to many Muslims. Calling a Muslim an apostate, a label ISIS bestows with ease on their adversaries, is worse than being an infidel. It is a label more worthy of fighting and killing than the infidel; thus, ISIS's priority is fighting those it calls apostates, even if they had, like al-Julani, been previous jihadist comrades.

The captive journalist told Amberin that he "was told that a qadi [an Islamic jurist] was reviewing my case. One of them said that my slaughter would avenge their brothers who were rotting in Turkish prisons. I was mentally and physically drained." Amberin states that, "these scenes were repeated until, as Aygun put it, his 'guardian angel' appeared."

Aygun recalls, "It was a cold, dark night. A pair of men entered my cell. One of them sat next to me and began to talk. He said he knew what I was going through. He had fought with al-Qaeda in Afghanistan for 10 years where he had been held and tortured in an American detention facility for six months. I could tell he was older than the others. He told me to call him 'Dayi' (the Turkish word for maternal uncle). He said Turkey had strayed from Islam. He would loosen my handcuffs and bring me tea. We chatted normally; he was very kind. He said he was very saddened by my plight, because he knew I was a good person and that he had told the others to treat me well. Sure enough they did. One of the fighters brought me honey and bananas. He asked me if I wanted him to erase my Facebook conversations with women. He brought me extra socks so I could keep warm. He even stroked my cheek."

However, as Amberin puts it, "his 'good' days were short-lived." Aygun told her that, "It was around my third day there. Dayi told me that the qadi had ruled in favor of my execution because I was working for a newspaper that was working against the interests of Muslims. He was very upset. I was paralyzed with fear. I needed to find a way to be shot dead rather than be beheaded. I would feign to escape."

"On the day Aygun was meant to be executed none of his captors showed up, not even to take him for his ablutions for prayers. The silence was finally broken by a cat," wrote Amberin. "I wanted nothing more than to be able to touch that cat, to have it at my side," recalled Aygun.

Three days after the agonizing loneliness, the fighters returned. They had been fighting a rival militia. "One of the fighters asked me whether I wanted to see Dayi. I said I did. They [took] me to a room where they made their explosives. Dayi was lying on the floor in a pool of blood. I saw his face for the first time. He had a bullet mark on his forehead. He was dead. They asked me if I wanted to smell his blood. The blood of martyrs smells good, they said. I knelt by his side. I smelled his blood and stroked his beard. I was devastated. My only friend was gone. They moved to a new place. Now I would be killed for sure," said Aygun.

Aygun did not know at the time that the Turkish intelligence was working quietly behind the scenes to secure his release. The happy ending came when the Ahrar al-Sham faction saved him from ISIS and handed him over to the Turkish authorities. Yet this only happened after a trial was staged for him in which the judge ruled Aygun innocent. "When I heard Davutoglu's voice on the telephone [to] me, that is when I knew I was finally free," recalled Aygun.

Aygun has now returned to his job in the newspaper *Milliyet*. He no longer drinks alcohol, and prays regularly.

Treatment of Minorities: The Yazidis

Many prominent Western newspapers have written about ISIS's treatment of minorities and vulnerable groups including women, children, and racial minorities. They have painted a dreadful picture of the Islamic State as exceedingly brutal, barbaric, and lacking humanity. They claim that ISIS actions are the reason behind this, but it is noteworthy that not a single one of these newspapers has attributed what they have written to an eyewitness correspondent.

While it is true that prominent journalists such as Patrick Cockburn have written about these abominations, not a single one of them is an eyewitness. None of them have traveled to ISIS territory to relay to us a reality they themselves witnessed and experienced. Instead, they depend on oral accounts of those who escaped from the Islamic State out of fear. These escapees often develop narratives, fabricating stories for the sake of their political leanings or interests, such as easing the process of seeking asylum in Western countries.

My position is not to defend ISIS, but what I read reminded me of what I experienced as a diplomatic in Washington, Nairobi, and Geneva, and as an ambassador in London. I remember the intense campaign launched by Christian Solidarity International (CSI) in Sudan with full clarity. It accused Sudan of reviving the slave trade, selling Southerners as slaves, and using them as servants in the homes of Northern Muslims. The target was Sudan's Arab and Islamic character, and we were portrayed as vulgar slave traders, devoid of even the minimal standards of humanity. We were savage monsters that "rape Christian African women" in the south of Sudan. The result of the CSI campaign was Western civil society organizations and associations condemning the Arab Muslims as slave traders in Sudan, and describing them as animals.

Prominent politicians, ministers, governments, and parliamentarians all began supporting the campaign, the most famous of whom was Baroness Cox. All major Western newspapers, magazines, and well-known television stations covered it, until this image of Sudan became ingrained in the minds of all Westerners. It became merely another one of life's givens.

However, Divine will interfered and was manifested through the Italian priest that worked in the south of Sudan. He came forward to testify that the film put together by the campaign was forged and fabricated. In his testimony, he said that he saw, with his own eyes, members of the Sudan People's Liberation Movement, the anti-Sudan armed movement, dressed in the garb of the northern Muslims and acting in the film. They acted in front of the camera as Arab Muslim slave traders from the north of Sudan, buying southern children. The reality was that these People's Movement members where the ones who had brought the children and lined them up in front of the camera to shoot the sale scenes. On May 14, 2002, Father Mario Riva revealed to Dan Rathers, the prominent host of CBS's show "60 Minutes," that all of this was a hoax.

This silenced the campaign, but the defamation and damage done to Sudan was beyond repair. Not everyone who witnessed and lived through the dreadful campaign against Sudan at the time saw the Italian priest's refutation of the lie. His refutation didn't receive the same media coverage as the campaign about our enslavement of the southerners; however, even if it couldn't erase the campaign's effect on our image, his testimony thankfully stopped it. Despite the fact that the *Denver Post* published Jim Jacobson's testimony that cast doubt on the slave trade in Sudan, along with complaints from the German Der Spiegel and prominent British writer Alex de Waal, their voices were not loud enough to overpower the initial lie.

During my time as a diplomat in Washington, I remember being responsible for covering Congress. During that time, I witnessed a meeting in which the Coptic Sudanese priest Makram Max testified. The priest spoke – with a cross hanging over his chest – about the slave market in the city of al-Ubayyid, where southerners are sold as slaves in auctions in the light of day. The hall was packed with journalists, cameras, and seated Congress members. Father Max spoke, dressed in full church attire, with a tone of forged sadness. It resembled his forged anger at the lack of humanity, backwardness, and degradedness of the Arab Muslims in Sudan, who outwardly sold slaves in the 20th century. He claimed to have personally bought fifty slaves from the al-Ubayyid auction, and then freed them – what a great show of humanity! He named some of the slaves he claimed to have freed, and as Father Max spoke, no one batted an eye. The entire audience believed him, showering us with looks of contempt and hatred, since we represented such a base country. We tried to hand out the announcement we had prepared beforehand in anticipation of what the priest would say, since it wasn't his first time giving this speech. However, a number of Congress employees prevented us from doing so; how could they allow slave traders to hand out an announcement in Congress? In their opinions, this man of religion could not, under any circumstances, be wrong. Throughout my entire life, I have never seen someone as "frugal in telling the truth" as this man.

I still remember that the Archbishop of Canterbury issued a statement during my time as an ambassador in London. In it he claimed that Sudan destroyed five churches in Kadugli. When I presented to him pictures of the churches taken from all four sides that same morning, invited him to accompany me to Kaduqli to see them standing untouched, and told him that my government had given me permission to rent a plane that would bring us there whenever he pleased, he looked at his watch, as if to indicate that the meeting was over. The Right Reverend distorted our image, and when I brought him the truth, he refused to listen.

Also running through my mind at the time were the two incidents of the Al-Shifa pharmaceutical factory bombing under the pretense that it was manufacturing chemical weapons, and when it was said that Sudan was storing Saddam Hussein's rockets.

These thoughts came to my mind as I read the October 3, 2014 *New York Times* piece on ISIS's poor treatment of Christians and the seizure of their churches. I remembered the testimony of an Iraqi Christian in which he said his family continues to live in ISIS territory – carefree, safe, and reassured – worshipping their God without any trouble. This made me doubt the factuality of what I was reading in the newspaper. In fact, it made me doubt the content of the article itself, which was a United Nations report. Some may say that what this Iraqi Christian claimed was done to protect his family; however, the person making the claim must provide evidence, and undoubtedly Christians in Mosul are not living through the best of times.

On March 19, 2015, *The Guardian* wrote that a United Nations Human Rights Office report claimed that ISIS used poisonous chlorine gas in its fight against Iraqi forces in the west of the Al Anbar province. The report stated that Islamic State forces committed genocide against the Yazidis, crimes against humanity, and war crimes against civilians. However, it also admitted to have depended on the testimonies of 100 victims and witnesses. The United Nations requested the case be transferred to the International Criminal Court, claiming that attacks were committed on Yazidis, Christians, and other minorities. The report claimed that ISIS captured women and children as spoils of war," and in many cases subjected them to rape or made them "female slaves." The newspaper wrote that the Mosul Sharia court ruled for 13 children to be executed because they were caught watching a soccer game. On this last point, I have nothing to say, aside from the fact that al-Baghdadi loves soccer, plays it, and is known for being a skillful goalkeeper!

On October 3, 2014, the *New York Times* wrote that a United Nations report explained, in detail, how ISIS soldiers abducted, raped, and gang raped Yazidi underage girls. According to the report, ISIS had kidnapped and enslaved 150 virgins and minors, making them what Westerners call "sex slaves." It wrote about an underage girl that was kidnapped on August 3 from her village, gang raped, and then sold in the market as a slave. The women and girls that are brought to the market are labeled with price tags so that the buyers can see and bargain for them. Most of the buyers are young men, and such incentives are meant to encourage them to join ISIS. The report stated that two women had tried to resist what was happening, and so revenge was taken on them; however, the report does not clarify how the revenge was taken.

The article added that on August 21, 2014, ISIS soldiers beat the women in the Mosul market because they were not veiled. Some of the women resisted by throwing rocks, but after four days of this alleged incident, three of the women's bodies were found in Western Mosul with marks on their bodies that revealed torture prior to their execution.

Many people have cast doubt on these narratives, and even Patrick Cockburn has said that details surrounding what happens in Mosul are unclear due to a lack of dependable sources on the ground (page 75 of his book). Earlier, we published testimonies claiming that ISIS treats civilians with respect. In Mosul and a number of other neighborhoods, it sought to prevent civilians from fleeing, instead aiming to win them over to its side. Cockburn himself said, as did many others, that many civilians welcomed ISIS in Iraq, preferring it to the Iraqi government and the actions of the Shiite militias. They prefer ISIS in Syria because it marked an end to the excesses of the Free Syrian Army, other factions, and even the Syrian government.

The *New York Times* wrote that ISIS raped children, killed 60 Yazidis and Turkmen in front of their children, and then placed them into shelters. It also wrote that ISIS recruits child soldiers as young as 12 years old that fight and perform patrol duties in Mosul. I have seen videos of ISIS training children clothed in military attire, but have yet to come across videos that capture their participation in battle, despite the fact that ISIS meticulously records all of its activities and battles for propaganda purposes, as well as my legitimate efforts in searching for such videos.

The *New York Times* also wrote a long report entitled "ISIS Enshrines a Theology of Rape," in which it said that the ISIS magazine *Dabiq* wrote in its May 2014 issue that it "is reviving the sunnah of capturing infidel women." In the October issue, it blamed its followers who doubt the revival of this sunnah.

The same article reported that an ISIS fighter, before raping a 12-year old Yazidi girl, explained to her that his action was not a sin, but in fact an act of worship. He claimed that the Quran encourages him to do this because she is not a Muslim. Before raping her, he got on his two knees to pray. When she complained of pain, he explained yet again that Islam permits him to rape infidels, and that by doing so he was getting closer to God. It noted that the interview with the child was conducted in the presence of her family at a refugee camp in Kurdistan. According to the newspaper, raping girls and women has become ingrained in ISIS members' behavior, and the organization says it is reviving a well-researched sunnah. The article discussed the facilities built by ISIS for Yazidi victims of rape. They are equipped with inspection rooms that allow the buyer to choose from amongst the women. The day that the auction is scheduled, the girls are lined up and displayed one by one to the buyers. On their chests hang a price tag, and buyers ask them to stand and turn around so they can see the girl from all angles.

In the same article, the newspaper reported that 5,270 Yazidi women were abducted the previous year, and no less than 3,144 of them are still in custody, under the supervision of the "female slave bureaucracy." ISIS created this system to supervise their affairs, and it is in charge of preparing purchase contracts notarized by the Sharia court. This practice is a strategy meant to attract soldiers to join ISIS in the context of conservative societies that ban extramarital sex, decrying it if committed without a marriage certificate.

It is noteworthy that the Yazidis are an Iraqi sect that the Muslims claim worships Satan. This stems from their holy deity "Melek Taus," who they claim is Angel Azrael, and is the most important of their seven holy angels. In Iraq, the Yazidis make up only 1.5% of the total population of 34 million. They reside in the Mount Sinjar region in the north of Iraq that ISIS invaded about two months after seizing Mosul.

The report states that ISIS separated the men from the women, shooting the men and driving away the girls, children, and women in trucks. According to Professor Matthew Barber, specialist in Yazidi affairs and professor at Chicago University, the ISIS attack on the Yazidi region was "as much a sexual conquest as it was for territorial gain," since some of the women were sold, and others distributed to head fighters in Syria and Iraq.

Countless newspapers, magazines, and television networks, as well as the organizations Human Rights Watch and Amnesty International, have addressed the topic of the Yazidis. All of them have presented the issue in the same dreadful manner as the *New York Times*, which wrote that until today, capturing female prisoners of war has been limited to Yazidi women; however, a ruling recently issued by the Fatwa Department of the Islamic State make capturing Jewish and Christian women permissible if they resist the Islamic State. In their opinion, the focus on Yazidi women was due to claims of blasphemy and idolatry, in which case Hindus, Buddhists, and other religions outside of the Abrahamic religions consisting – the People of the Book – would be classified in the same way. In this way, the Islam of ISIS is the strangest of all Islams.

In this article, the newspaper contradicted their previous claim that ISIS treats Christians poorly. It included a testimony by a Yazidi who said that, "In Kojo, residents decided to stay, believing they would be treated as the Christians of Mosul had months earlier."

The October 2014 issue of *Dabiq* addressed the topic of "The Revival of Slavery Before the Hour." In the article, ISIS stated that the Yazidis would not get the opportunity to pay the "jizya tax" like the Jews and Christians. Rather, their women and children would be divided amongst the ISIS fighters that participated in the Sinjar operations. This would come after one fifth of the slaves were transferred to the Islamic State's authority as war spoils.

On its website, the newspaper aired a video of men it claimed to be ISIS fighters, reveling in their joy at the arrival of the Yazidi market. One of them gleefully says: "Today is the day of 'those whom your right hand possesses,'" and the men then speak together, with each one describing the traits of the girl he wants: some of them prefer a young girl with green eyes, and joke around about "old women."

The Islamic State relies on texts in the Quran and Sunnah on slavery the same way that churchmen used to make excuses for the West African slave trade. They enslaved millions of Africans, carrying them in boats across the Atlantic to America and Europe. The churchmen found excuses for their disgraceful act in the Bible. ISIS has clearly overlooked the repercussions of this act on the Muslim image, on Islamic proselytizing, and on preachers' ability to promote Islam. They overlooked the fact that one of the rules of jurisprudential understanding is changing rulings to accompany changes in time and place, and acting in accordance with the surrounding environment in issuing judgments. This is what al-Shafi'i did when he changed many of the rulings he had issued in Iraq when he later moved to Egypt. It has even been said that al-Shafi'i had two doctrines: one in Egypt, and another in Iraq. ISIS has forgotten that the Caliph Umar nullified distribution of charity to those "whose hearts are to be reconciled," despite the explicit stipulations in the Quran because, in his words, "Allah has strengthened Islam and made us no longer need them." The Caliph Umar also nullified the punishment for theft during the Year of the Drought, despite the explicit text in the Quran. In Islam, warding off evil takes precedence over bringing benefits; thus, reviving slavery brings evil to Islam greater than any benefit. They have missed the fact that Islam does not prescribe slavery, but instead prescribes drying up its origins and sources. It has made emancipation for the sake of pleasing God one of the greatest atonements, so why do they interpret in this way?

In the slave market, each girl was told to stand, and those who covered their heads were unveiled and told to remain uncovered so that their hair could be seen. They were told to turn around, so as to be seen from behind. They were also asked questions that are private and embarrassing for any woman, such as the date of her last menstrual cycle, or if she was pregnant.

In 2014, ISIS published a pamphlet on the jurisprudence of slavery from its perspective, answering a number of questions about the practice. In all honesty, ISIS should be embarrassed of both the questions and answers their printing press, al-Hama, published in Muharram 1436 (October/November 2014). It appears that the pamphlet came as a response to the fuss caused by the enslavement of the Yazidi women, even among ISIS fighters and sympathizers. The title of the pamphlet was "Question and Answer on Slavery and Captivity," and was commissioned by the Research and Fatwa Department of the Islamic State.

In answering the questions, the pamphlet states that having sexual intercourse with a female slave is permitted by the Quranic verse: {Successful are the believers who guard their chastity, except from their wives or the captives and slaves that their right hands possess, for then they are free from blame.} If she is a virgin, sexual intercourse with a female slave is allowed immediately after obtaining her; but if not, it is permissible after confirming that she is not pregnant. It is permitted to sell, buy, or give female and male slaves as gifts, since they are considered property that may be dealt with in any way as long as it does not cause harm or injury to the Muslim community. The pamphlet says that "it is not permissible to separate a mother from her prepubescent children," and forbids two men from having intercourse with the same female slave even if they purchased her jointly, unless one of them gains exclusive ownership. It forbids selling a pregnant slave, and says that if the owner dies, "female captives are distributed as part of his estate, just as all other parts of his estate are distributed. However, they may only provide services, not intercourse, if several people inherit them in partnership." The pamphlet forbids a husband from having intercourse with his wife's female slaves because he does not own them. It forbids kissing another man's slave due to the idea that a kiss is pleasure, and pleasure is only permissible with exclusive ownership. In regards to whether sexual intercourse with a prepubescent female slave is permissible, it is, given that she is fit for intercourse. If she is not fit for intercourse, then she may be enjoyed in other ways. The pamphlet does not clarify what standards qualify a minor fit for sexual intercourse, but it does clarify the permissibility of "*al-'azl*" and of owning either two sisters or a slave and her aunt on either her mother or father's side; however, having intercourse with both of them in forbidden. The pamphlet permits beating the slave for discipline, but forbids "breaking beating," beating for the purpose of achieving gratification, and torture beating. It mentions that one of the gravest sins is a slave running away from its master; thus, upon their return, they may be punished and reprimanded. A master cannot have intercourse with the slave if she is married to another man, but she does still have to serve him. The pamphlet clarified that in terms of legal punishment, the slave should receive half of the torture (legal punishment) in cases that allow reduction by half, such as flogging. At the end of the pamphlet, it notes that the reward for those that free slaves is emancipation from hellfire!

If I hadn't looked at the ISIS pamphlets, it would've undoubtedly been difficult for me to believe the revival of slavery, captivity and servitude. This matter has transcended causing harm to the Islamic State's image, and has harmed the reputation of Muslims and Islam.

This policy of enslavement has decreased the number of supporters and advocates of the Islamic State. It has increased the number of those who feel outrage and hate towards ISIS. In the following defamatory poem, the Tunisian poet Ahmed Omar Zaabar mocks them:

> Ignorance has come upon us,
> From among the scum.
> Hatred has come upon us,
> Wearing religion as a mask.

Oppression has been imposed on us,
Viewing women as property,
And seeing obvious victory
In fornication and intercourse.
O you filled with mud,
Intellect is a ray of light.
O you who have snuck in among us,
You've brought nothing but lies.
You've come and destroyed the city,
Flipping the place upside down.
You've brought us abominations
And criminal barbarism.
Some of those who lost the way
Lived in a cave for years,
They permitted killing among us,
Like predators in the pasture.
In the lands of the Muslims,
A sickness that reached the spine.
Ignorance has come upon us,
Saying goodbye to knowledge,
Parting with mindful speech,
It bought religion and sold it.
A need for patience is upon us,
As long as there is a cause for patience
They are not followers of our prophet,
But purely a headache.

Though it saddens me to say, some Muslim scholars today promote sex slavery, other types of slavery, and servitude. According to Sheikh Saleh Al-Fawzan, member of the Council of Senior Scholars, as long as Islam exists, female enslavement will continue since it is an integral part of jihad. He describes scholars that disagree with him as ignorant and not true scholars. He claims that they are mere clerks, and anyone who disagrees with him is an infidel. Similarly, Sheikh Saad al-Biraik has been accused of encouraging the Palestinians to enslave Jewish women since God has permitted them to do so. In 1993, the Shiite Sheikh Fadlallah al-Hairi similarly permitted slavery during times of war, or for those born into slavery.

The Boko Haram leader Abubakar Shekau has also said that he will enslave those he captures. In 2014, he rationalized kidnapping girls from the Chibok school in Nigeria by claiming that capturing the 200 girls was in compliance with God's command as stated in the Quran.

It appears as though these supposed ISIS jurisprudents are completely cut off from the modern world, and from the developments of the human race, both Muslim and non-Muslim. ISIS's so-called scholars fail to understand that Islam does not permit their fearful acts of slavery, nor does it accept in principle waging jihad against non-Muslims simply because they are non-Muslims. Jihad, in essence, is waged against whomever commits aggressions or injustices, regardless of their religion; Muslim or non-Muslim. It seems that they only have a tenuouss connection to the Islamic jurisprudence of higher intentions and purposes. I wonder how many arguments they have provided to those who accuse Islam of oppressing women, undermining human capability, as well as those that accuse Islam of savagery and targeting non-Muslims.

In today's world, keeping secrets is growing increasingly difficult in light of the communications technologies that have turned anyone with a cell phone into a correspondent. Despite this, if it were not for ISIS's open rationalization of slavery through religious justification, Muslims may have believed that their enslavement of the Yazidi women was a Western fabrication.

Given the fabrication in 2003 of the lie that Saddam Hussein possessed weapons of mass destruction – the basis for Iraq's destruction – Muslims may have believed any accusation against the West. However, ISIS has doomed itself twice: first with its action, and again with its confession.

The Treatment of Christians

Reports about ISIS's treatment of Christians vary, partly due to the fact that some Christians in Mosul and other ISIS-controlled cities deny having been harmed. However, it is true that ISIS took crosses down from the domes, towers, and exteriors of certain churches. Its jurisprudents declared that although Christians have complete freedom of worship, it is on condition of the obliteration of crosses displayed on churches. This is no longer accepted in today's world, and has caused more harm to Islam than benefit.

It is also true that, after ISIS took control of Mosul, many Christians fled out of fear. This number increased after their priests and monks rejected an invitation to a meeting called for by ISIS in which they were planning on explaining their policy. They claim to have been afraid after hearing about the experience of two clergymen in Syria with jihadists. The two priests had joined the jihadists for negotiations, but afterwards were nowhere to be found. News spread to Christian circles in Mosul that anyone who met with ISIS would face the same fate; thus, they chose not to attend the meeting called for by the Caliph.

ISIS considered the refusal of a meeting called for by the "Caliph of the Muslims" an act of disobedience and rebellion against the Islamic State. It thus issued a decree that gave Christians the choice between paying the jizya, converting to Islam, fleeing, or being killed, the most reasonable of which was the jizya. Paying the jizya is equivalent to the alms collected from the Muslims, but exempts Christians from military service and ensures their complete security. To highlight the contradictory narratives, *The Guardian* published on July 24, 2014 that ISIS reassured Christians during its initial days in Mosul; however, other reports stated that Christians began fleeing Iraq beginning with the siege Saddam imposed on the city.

In its July 18, 2014 edition, the *New York Times* wrote that it had spoken via telephone with a Christian living in Mosul who denied that all Christian residents had fled Mosul. He said that some of them still live in the city, even after ISIS delineated the four options, and it appears that they have chosen to pay the jizya. The newspaper mentioned that there were 30,000 Christians in Mosul at the start of the century, but many of them, like the Mandaeans, fled Iraq at the onset of wars against Saddam. In 2015, only a couple thousand of them remained, and some fled after the arrival of ISIS. This narrative is stronger than the others that claim all Christian residents of Mosul fled after ISIS released a decision in their regard.

The newspaper confirmed that ISIS had destroyed the shrine of the prophet Jonah in Mosul after people started using it for prayer, since it believes that the prophet forbid using graves as an area of worship. According to testimonies the newspaper collected from Christians living in Mosul, ISIS destroyed the statue of the Virgin Mary in the Mosul church, and replaced the cross with the Islamic State flag; however, they did not touch the church itself.

The Destruction of Antiquities

In May of 2015, when ISIS seized the Syrian city Palmyra – known as the "bride of the desert" and located on the historical Silk Road connecting China and the Roman Empire – it destroyed monuments dating back 2,000 years that UNESCO classifies as part of world heritage.

Prior to that, ISIS demolished valuable tombs and shrines, some of which were parts of mosques, including the Prophet Jonah mosque in Mosul. In the Mosul museum, ISIS destroyed antiquities that were thousands of years old. Some of them date back to the Assyrian and Chaldean era and in a video aired by ISIS about their destruction, the speaker said that the Assyrians and Chaldeans were idolaters; thus, the first thing the Prophet (PBUB) did after conquering Mecca was destroy their idols. If the Almighty God commanded the removal of these statues and idols, then they are of no value, despite being worth billions of dollars. Some of the destroyed antiquities date back to the 7th century B.C, the time of the Assyrian civilization.

The monument destruction operation sparked overwhelming international outrage. UNESCO deemed it an act of "cultural cleansing" of cultural treasures in a country considered to be the birthplace of human civilization, and which contributed to erasing its historical memory and identity.

It is strange that the monuments ISIS destroyed were present prior to Islam. The noble companions of the Prophet were aware of their existence, yet let them be both in Syria and Iraq. With that said, are the ISIS jurisprudents more knowledgeable of their faith than Abu Bakr, Umar, and Ali? Nowhere in the religious biographies does it say that the companions destroyed statues of the Virgin Mary, or burned religious Christian images like ISIS did in the Mosul churches. What ISIS did was met with severe international condemnation, and led to the implicit condemnation of Islam.

Since the beginning of history, Iraq has been known for its plurality of religions. In addition to the three well-known Abrahamic faiths, Iraq is also home to a sect of lesser-known religious groups, including the Yazidis that worship Melek Taus. It is rumored that they worship Satan, and are thus angered when Muslims damn him. Among the religions in Iraq are the Mandaeans, who are the Sabaeans mentioned in the Quran and follow John the Baptist. The Sabaeans resided in the Nineveh plains that were mentioned by the Bible thousands of years ago. They spoke Mandaean – a Semitic language that developed from Aramaic and is the language of Jesus – however, aside from the residents of Ma'loula in Syria who still speak Aramaic today, modern Mandaeans speak Iraqi Arabic, and Mandaean is confined to the temples, having become a ceremonial language similar to how Coptic became confined to the monasteries of Egypt.

At the beginning of the century, the number of Mandaeans in Iraq was between 60,000 and 70,000 people; however, they fled Iraq during the sanctions and wars. As of ISIS's entry into the Nineveh plains, the number of Mandaeans was less than 10,000.

When the Muslims conquered Iraq, the leader of the Mandaeans contacted them, showed them their holy book and indicated that their prophet is John the Baptist. The first Muslims dealt with them as People of the Book, particularly because of their mention in the Quran.

Yaqut al-Hamawi mentioned them, saying that the Mandaeans consider themselves descendants of Adam's son, Seth. They acknowledge the existence of Adam, Noah, and a number of other prophets, but they deny Abraham, Moses, and Jesus. They have a dualistic view of life that encompasses good and evil, and light and dark. They consider the body and all material things to have come from the dark, while the soul (indicated sometimes by the mind) is a product of the world of light. Their world of light is ruled by a celestial being named the Lord of Greatness or the King of Light, and they have an appreciation for the sun as a source of light.

CHAPTER FIVE

ISIS AND THE WEST

The Roots of Hatred

It may be incorrect to say that the Western attack on Islam started as a reaction to the events of either September 11th, the 2005 London bombings, or al-Qaeda's bombing of Madrid in 2004. The attack on Islam undoubtedly began during the religion's early days, when the church described it as a religion of apostasy and blasphemy, characterized by ambiguity. It claimed that the Prophet Muhammed was a lying agent of Satan that loved sensory pleasures. The attack continued until it turned violent, spilling the blood of thousands of Muslims as well as civilian Palestinian Christians that did not participate in the Crusades. The hatred reached a new peak after the conquest of Constantinople and the Ottoman wars waged on Europe, the most famous of which was the 1526 Battle of Mohács in Hungary. During the battle, Hungary was joined by forces from throughout Europe that reached a number of 200,000 soldiers, blessed by the Pope. Seven of the Vatican's senior cardinals were in attendance. The battle broke out after the king of Hungary killed the messenger of the Ottoman sultan, Suleiman the Magnificent (also known as Suleiman the Lawmaker). The Europeans participated in the battle and called their party the "Holy Alliance," giving it a Christian flavor. About 10,000 European soldiers were killed in the battle, and Hungary was subsequently fragmentized.

Orientalism, particularly orientalist writings in the 18th and early 19th centuries, played a role in inciting Western hatred and contempt of Islam and

Muslims. Some orientalists wrote that Muslims "are nothing but children that believe in Judgment and Fate. They expose the tyranny of their mental and psychological composition, and the tyranny of their scholars and political leaders with their barbaric philosophies. They fight against the West and progress." The orientalists presented the East as a cradle of exoticism, backwardness, and the antithesis to the West, as well as a source of annoyance and fear. In their writings, they laid the foundation for the belief that, in contrast with the West's excellence, Muslims are the definition of backwardness. However, Islam, despite its backwardness, possessed a dangerous, destructive, covert force because it challenged and waged war on Christianity, they wrote.

The orientalists went to great lengths to denigrate and degrade Islam. The impact of their writings continued through what they passed down to successive writers. Even the intellectual Professor Edward Said said: " I have not been able to discover any period in European or American history since the Middle Ages in which Islam was generally discussed or thought about *outside* a framework created by passion, prejudice and political interests." Edward Said also said that there is a strong relationship between everyone that writes about Islam, or specializes in Muslim countries, and ruling powers in the West. Orientalists have exploited their knowledge of Muslims to serve the Western leadership that controls Muslim countries. Proof is found in the fact that Napoleon consulted the orientalists before invading Egypt in 1798, and they were behind the French decision to colonize Algeria in 1830. Said reveals that orientalists are the ones who encouraged the European governments to colonize the East, and convinced them that the East can be viewed and studied. Most importantly, it will bow to administration. The orientalists convinced them that these were wealthy countries, and Europe would be able to turn them into extensions of itself. Said believes that the orientalists' knowledge thus became a form of aggression against Islam.

The campaign evolved after OPEC raised oil prices in 1974. OPEC was portrayed as a "cartel" owned by Muslims that posed a threat to the West. The campaign escalated until President Carter's adviser called on him to prepare the American nation for a war through which America would gain control over oil wells in the Gulf. Writings, images and cartoons were circulated, mocking these backwards Muslim Arabs who wanted to strangle the West because they were a "barbaric band and destructive element."

When the Saudi Arabians abstained from approving the Camp David Accord in 1978, articles filled with fabrications and deceit were published against them and against Islam. According to what David Lee wrote in the *Washington Post* on July 30, 1980, it then became evident that the Central Intelligence Agency was behind the anti-Saudi Arabia campaign. It was unjust and characterized by what has become known in the West as double standards. Newspapers wrote about the status of women in Saudi Arabia despite the fact that some Jewish rabbis have unbelievable opinions about women, hygiene, and punishments. The newspaper didn't write about this, nor did the media focus on it. However, how can Saudi Arabia act independently and not acquiesce? "This was Saudi Arabia's crime," writes Said in his book *Covering Islam.*

During this period, books such as *The Warring Islam* and The *Dagger of Islam* were published, along with Eric Hoffer's piece about "Muhammad's laziness" in the *American Spectator* under the secondary title "Muhammad, Messenger of Plod." The *New York Times* then wrote, on January 6, 1980, its famous article about Islam entitled "The Islam Explosion," along with another one entitled "The Revival of Jihad" that accompanied a picture of a minaret and a muezzin.

When Khomeini began his revolution and the Iranian students occupied the American Embassy, holding American diplomats hostage for 444 days starting with November 4, 1979, it was considered another doomsday for the spread of hatred and slander of Islam and Muslims. Some articles were sadly laughable, since they referred to Iranians and Khomeini himself as Arab. Khomeini's book *Islamic Government* was published with the new title *Ayatollah Khomeini's Mein Kampf* to draw a link between Islam and Nazism. Some of them referred to the Iranians as the "crazy fundamentalists," which is exactly what is written about ISIS today – that it is not a limited group, but a representation of all barbaric Muslims.

During the hostage crisis, the Americans forgot that this was a reaction – even if it was, in my opinion as a diplomat, unacceptable to take diplomats hostage – to a history of American encroachment on Iran. One such example of encroachment was the 1953 American-British conspiracy, implemented by the American Central Intelligence Agency with the Anglo-Persian Oil Company, to overthrow Mohammad Mosaddegh. If America had forgotten this, then the Iranians surely had not. The Americans shrugged off the fact that they had hosted the Shah that Iranians accused of stealing their wealth and placing it in Chase Manhattan Bank, as well as the fact that his SAVAK service oppressed, tortured and killed thousands of his people. After the revolution, even the American banks joined forces with the government by nullifying all post-1977 Iranian loan contracts, under the premise that the country had not paid interest on time. This came despite the fact that Eric Rouleau, the prominent *Le Monde* journalist, claimed to have seen proof of Iran paying its interest before the deadline. Major newspapers including the *New York Times* wrote that the Iranian revolution was over. On October 14, 1979, they wrote that the revolution had failed, and Iran was a soldering lava-bed of resentment, fear, and dislike of the revolution. Said believes that the article was not a reflection of reality. Yet despite our opinion of ISIS, similar articles are written today about conditions in Mosul, Raqqah, and other ISIS territories.

One of the strangest slogans that Americans chanted during the hostage crisis was "Go back to your countries you Arabs!" After September 11, the chant "Go back to your countries you sand niggers!" spread. Racists in America classify Arabs and Africans as niggers, with the difference being that Arabs are sand niggers. In 1979, during the hostage crisis, the *New York Times* also wrote about the "Outburst of Islam" and the "Crisis of Islam," claiming that the Muslims cannot progress in thought, and making fun of the Arabic language – the language of the Quran so revered by the Muslims. At that time, an American professor said on an American television network, that simply "accepting Islam is anti-American." It is also noted that Western media networks do not mention the origins or religion of any defendant, unless he is Muslim or from an Islamic country.

In this regard, Edward Said stated that the West views that "merely confirming the Islamic identity by a Muslim, and almost for every Muslim, is a kind of universal challenge … It seems that war from the West is a logical consequence against this Muslim." Edward Said does not consider himself religious or Muslim, but he is known for his bravery and scholarly integrity.

Islam's problem may be that it is the only society that has not completely submitted. From the Western perspective, the Hindu and Chinese societies have submitted, and are not a source of danger. When the Tatars were in control and invaded the Islamic State, a paradox occurred that is not consistent with the natural trajectory as defined by Ibn Khaldun in his saying: "The conquered will always emulate the conqueror in every detail, down to his dress and mode of behavior." An exception was made to Ibn Khaldun's rule when the Tatars surrendered and the defeated Islamic civilization absorbed them. The reason behind this is that Islam imparts on its believers an internal inviolability that makes them stronger in battling cultures that clash with its basic principles. It is difficult for the West to realize to what extent Muslims respect their religion, and they speak of their surprise at "Islam's grip" over its believers in rejecting Western dominance. The Islamic slogans chanted during the Iranian revolution were thus quite confusing for Westerners.

Westerners are irritated by Muslim politicians that promote Islam, labeling and fighting them, despite the fact that many of these politicians espouse democracy and are brought into power by the polls. Meanwhile, they were not embarrassed when in 1980 two Republican presidential candidates announced they had been born again under Christianity. Nor did they mind when Bush *fils* announced the same thing, or when he said that God had spoken to him and commanded him to invade Iraq – the three of them had broadcasted their loyalty to Christianity. The West's stance on religious Muslim politicians reveals that all of Islam is rejected: the Muslim Brotherhood's Islam, Salafist Islam in Saudi Arabia, and ISIS's Islam – there is no distinction between moderates and extremists. To the West, Islam is a state of authoritarian theocracy that espouses methods from the Middle Ages; thus, they reduce Islam to punishments, calling it "barbarism," and the rule of men of religion. On April 1980, *The Economist* wrote that, "Islamic law to most Westerners means Islamic punishment."

In his book *Covering Islam*, Edward Said stated that the Western media accuses Muslims of opposing liberalism, and thus wages campaigns against it. However, they do not mention Pope John Paul II's announcement that he is against liberalism. Israel calls itself a Jewish state that is religious at its core, yet no one attacks it. The extremist Jewish organization "Ghosh Amniyum" builds forced settlements on Palestinian lands, yet that, along with all of Israel's transgressions, does not receive the same condemnation and media coverage that any Muslim act receives.

During the Cold War, the West divided the world into two parts: the communist part and the anti-communist part. After the Cold War, the world was reduced into terrorist and anti-terrorist. Unfortunately, most of its terrorists were Muslims. Western journalism began focusing on this principle with each terrorist attacks, spreading naive beliefs about Muslims. Journalists do not speak Arabic, nor do they understand the region's culture, yet you find them bold enough to analyze circumstances and jump to conclusions. Aside almost from David Hearst and *Le Monde*'s Eric Rouleau, no Western journalists specializing in the Middle East speak Arabic.

The overwhelming influence of Western mass media has brought the extent of the repugnant stereotypes to light. Both the public and political leaders have adopted these stereotypes and used them as a basis for decision-making.

The spread of stereotypical thinking has had a major impact on the perceptions both of experts and security and intelligence agencies, dimming their understanding of the true state of affairs in the region. It is the reason behind the failure of Western intelligence organizations to predict major events that have drastically affected the region and determined its path. They have underestimated certain developments in the Arab world, and failed to predict the Iranian revolution, the fall of the Shah, the Iraq-Iran war, and the Lebanese civil war. The Western media and intelligence had in fact spoken of Lebanon's stability just a short while before civil war broke out. Western intelligence also failed to predict what is known as the Arab Spring, in which it lost its allies – the presidents of Egypt, Tunisia, Ali Abdullah Saleh, and even Gaddafi. Likewise, they failed to predict, and were shocked, by the rise of ISIS.

On September 28, 2001, our friend Yvonne Ridley, the famous British journalist that writes for prominent British newspapers, was captured and subsequently released by Taliban forces in Afghanistan. When she returned to the United Kingdom, she found hundreds of journalists and television cameras waiting for her in Heathrow Airport. She was shocked by their displeasure when she told them that the Taliban did not torture, bother, or act harshly with her. The Western media were displeased with her statement, and media interviews became more like intelligence interrogations that pressured her to lie and say exactly what they wanted to hear. Her story shook the stereotype the media had created of the Taliban, and contradicted what was "acceptable" when it comes to Muslims. How could Yvonne claim that the Taliban did not torture or rape her when they are Muslim, and Muslims treat women poorly, oppress them, and force them to wear the hijab! With her testimony, Yvonne destroyed the rules that had become the norm for hundreds of years. Even worse, Yvonne claimed that *she* was the one that was verbally violent and provocative with her captors, which they accepted with patience and smiles. The Western media met Yvonne's statements with disbelief and shock, which led them to accuse her of "Stockholm Syndrome."

Yvonne Ridley was just as shocked as the Western media when her colleagues nudged and pressured her to lie. According to Yvonne, she told some of them that she could not believe that they insisted on generalizing and ascribing this static image of Muslims to every single Muslim. She said that during her time with the Taliban, she never saw proof of this image, despite their many faults.

The actions of the Western media opened Yvonne's eyes to the fact that this was not a pursuit of precision, truth, and professionalism, but that what happened was comprised of a loathsome hatred of every Muslim under any circumstances. The situation filled Yvonne with resentment, but also awakened her instinctual curiosity. She began searching for what was behind it, which led her to read a translation of the Quran given to her by the Taliban. She had refused to read it while in captivity, but was amazed by its harmony, lack of contradictions, the perfection of its verses, and the certainty regarding the issue of oneness and values it encouraged; thus, she converted, and a firestorm erupted against Yvonne!

A side note irrelevant to this topic but related to Yvonne's days in captivity is the story of the man clad in white. The Taliban had sent him to inform her of her release, and she recalls being afraid of him because his face shone with light. Yvonne told me that she was truly terrified – how can the face of a human light up? She added that now, after her conversion, she understands how a human's face can shine. She said that she has sent someone to Afghanistan to search for that man, for after having finally understood, she desires to meet him.

The fabrications and Yvonne's experience with media pressure to lie reminded me of Elizabeth Swift's story. Elizabeth was one of the 52 American hostages in Tehran. At a press conference organized for the hostages after their return to America on January 2, 1981, Elizabeth Swift said that the magazine *Newsweek* wrote that she had been tortured as a hostage by the Iranians. However, she denied that ever happening, saying that she was neither tortured nor treated poorly by the "crazy Muslim fundamentalists."

It is odd that the Afghan jihadists about whom Yvonne Ridley was told to fabricate lies were the same ones Western media had deemed the "righteous Muslims" when they battled the West's enemy, the Soviet Union. In this same media, not every struggle against occupation and injustice brings you to righteousness, for you may have been a terrorist, like the terrorist Palestinians that fight against the Israeli occupation of their land! The righteous Muslims are the men like Anwar al-Sadat and the Shah of Iran, and the Pakistani Zia-ul-Haq. In this regard, Edward Said says that, "Westerners love the submissive Muslims that repeat the obscene history of collaborating with invaders."

In his book *Orientalism*, Edward Said states that the West's interest in foreign cultures has always been either for trade or colonial reasons, or as a result of military expansion, invasion, and building empires. Orientalist writings supported the realization of the political interests of governments and companies, so a correlation and collusion were achieved between knowledge and power, and force and interest.

In his book *Covering Islam*, Said believes that the Western media is truly covering, in the literal sense of the word. It is covering up and hiding the truth while spreading deceitful stereotypes about Islam and Muslims. He talks about the "acceptable coverage" of Islam in academic circles, which does not deviate from what pleases the official institutions, in order to connect the researchers and academics with official circles. This is because many academics and researchers work in government-run organizations, or as consultants for multinational corporations. If not, then they aim to work for the state and such companies, who in turn strive to secure their interests in the course of affairs in Muslim countries; thus, they ask their academics for research that is "acceptable" and compliant with the official plan, thus being consistent with their interests.

It is difficult for Westerners to realize that one of the reasons Muslims find refuge in clinging to their religion is feelings of danger and threat. Islam has become a refuge and effective way to confront danger and threats. It is also an effective way to congregate and to mobilize.

In light of the region's diversity, Islam acts as the only distinct channel that can satisfactorily unify varying races. It is able to absorb these varying identities and provide legitimacy to any political regime in charge of a diverse country.

It is noteworthy that as the attack on Islam from non-Muslim forces intensifies, Muslims rush to join together. They rush to rescue their brothers that are in danger, because Islam is the most effective religion in creating a brotherly bond between its believers throughout the world.

Despite the Western media's prejudice and deception against Islam, there are still voices in the West that can be considered objective and neutral, that have integrity and stand with the oppressed against the injustice of their countries; however, the impact of these voices is limited.

I end this section by saying that ISIS has grave and dangerous flaws that may even affect Islam itself; however, the campaign against them is not a representation of the truth.

The Barbarity of Islam

Scholars divide world civilizations over the past 2,000 years of humanity into the following:

- Antitheist civilization
  Represented by the communist bloc
- Buddhist civilization
  Represented by East Asia and parts of South Asia
- Christian civilization
  Represented by Europe, the Americas and parts of Africa
- Indic civilization
  Represented by India, Nepal and Mauritius
- Islamic civilization
  Represented by the Middle East, parts of Asia and parts of Africa
- Primitive-Indigenous civilization
  Represented by parts of Africa, the Americas and Australia before colonialism
- Sinic civilization
  Represented by China and some neighboring states

In 2009, Professor Naveed Sheikh of the University of Louisville and other researchers conducted a research project under the patronage of the Royal Aal al-Bayt Institute for Islamic Thought in Jordan. The study tracked violent conflicts over the past 2,000 years, then identified 276 of the most violent conflicts in history. To be considered one of the most violent conflicts, it had to have caused over 1,000 deaths. It then organized the results along civilizational lines, and recorded the frequency of these conflicts in accordance with each civilization. The study tried to confirm the number of deaths caused by each conflict by using a number of difference sources, studies and reasonable estimates, supported by scholarly accounts. It took into consideration a 10% margin of error, and reviewed each conflict, recording its date, number of deaths, and which of the seven civilizations was responsible. It then classified the conflict as war between two nations, genocide, civil war, or structural violence, which includes wars waged on racial bases and apartheid. After analyzing the statistics, the study came to the following conclusions:

- Using the entire data set for the period 0-2008, politically and religiously motivated violence has cost humanity between 449.39 million and 708.61 million lives.
- Christian civilization's share of this is between 119.32 million and 236.56 million victims (median 177.94 million victims).
- Antitheist civilization comes in second, and has a median of 125.29 million deaths.
- In third place is Sinic civilization, which has a median of 107.92 million deaths.
- Buddhist civilization comes in fourth place with 87.95 million deaths.
- Primal-Indigenous civilization comes in fifth with a median of 45.56 million deaths.
- Sixth is Islamic civilization, which has a median of 31.94 million deaths.
- Seventh is Indic civilization, with a median of 2.39 million deaths.

According to the study, the distribution of human losses between the seven civilizations is as follows: Antitheist civilization makes up for 21.64% of total deaths during the period covered by the study, Buddhist civilization makes up for 15.19%, and among all the civilizations, Christian civilization has caused the largest percentage of deaths, standing at 30.73% of total war victims during the past 2,000 years. Indic society makes up 0.41%, making it the least violent civilization. As for Islamic civilization, it makes up a percentage of 5.52%, Primal-Indigenous civilization makes up 7.86%, and Sinic civilization makes up 18.64%.

Out of the 30 genocides covered by the study, Christian civilization has committed the largest amount. Out of a total of 50.75 million deaths, it has caused 33 million, spanning all 30 genocides, out of which it has carried out 14. Out of the approximately 50 million total losses, Christian civilization has led to the death of 2/3, or two-thirds, of all genocide victims.

Meanwhile, the number of losses caused by Islamic civilization through genocide is less than four million. This number is exceeded by Antitheist civilization, which has led to the death of 8.25 million people, and Sinic, which has led to five million genocide deaths. The Antitheist and Sinic civilizations rank, respectively, second and third. Fifth place is held by Buddhist society, and Islamic society comes in fourth.

Mockery and Distortion Campaigns

Even though most Muslims, myself included, have our minds made up about ISIS – which I will discuss later in this book – my intention in not to defend the Islamic State. My point here is that as a result of ISIS's dangerous and unaccounted for actions, the mockery and distortion campaigns have transcended ISIS to affect both Islam and the Islamic culture. What I have found to be frustrating is that to any intelligent person, these distortion campaigns are laughable.

The belittling information that fills these campaigns is apparent in what is written by prominent Western newspapers and echoed by major news networks. They claim that ISIS punishes ice sales in Iraq's hellish summers, and has executed children for the crime of watching a football game on satellite. The newspapers claimed that after a professor of medicine was caught alone in his office with a female student, correcting her schoolwork, ISIS, which considered this a forbidden meeting, gave him the choice of marrying the student, or being punished through lashing. When the professor refused the marriage, he had to receive the punishment. The newspapers have written that ISIS forbids women from sitting on chairs, and that those found committing this heinous crime would be punished. They have also written that ISIS will cut off a taxi driver's limbs for not following directions, and that it has crucified children for not fasting during Ramadan. Obviously, the foreigner that fabricated this lie lacks both cleverness and astuteness.

Some people may consider the fact that ISIS has banned smoking a good thing, since even Western states have been trying to do so for quite some time. They have, however, failed miserably due to the influence of tobacco company lobbies. At the end of the 1920s, America prohibited alcohol. As a result, Al Capone's gang and other mafia gangs turned the country into a crime-filled hell, leaving the American government with no choice but to yield to the criminal gangs and nullify prohibition law. Similar efforts have also failed in the United Kingdom. Western countries know that alcohol is harmful, but out of jealousy, will not accept others succeeding where they have failed. The fact that I don't believe ISIS adequately represents Islam is not the issue. The issue is that selfish insolence is not new to Western civilization, which had called its colonial campaigns against the peoples of Asia, Africa, and others, "campaigns of enlightenment and civilization." They claimed that colonization was construction! And as Jomo Kenyatta said, "When the Missionaries (Westerners) arrived, the Africans had the land and the Missionaries had the Bible. They taught how to pray with our eyes closed. When we opened them, they had the land and we had the Bible."

Ayaan Hirsi Ali

The Somali Ayaan Hirsi Ali and the doors that have opened for her is an unfortunate example of the mockery and distortion campaigns that harm Muslims. Considering Ayaan an attack on their highest values, Muslims believe that her advancement, despite a lack of academic and scholarly qualifications or credibility to talk about Islam, is an attack on their religion.

In September 2014, the famous American University, Yale, brought Ayaan Hirsi Ali to give a lecture, and the hall was filled to the brim with audience members and security personnel. Police and FBI members, whose presence on the university campus drew attention, surrounded Ayaan, because it was said that anywhere she went she received death threats. The Muslim Student Association at Yale University opposed Hirsi speaking about Islam due to her lack of scholarly qualifications. However, when their request to ban her was denied, they asked the organizing body if a Muslim could also speak, but that request was likewise denied.

Ayaan Hirsi Ali now works at the American Enterprise Institute, a right-wing institution run by neoconservatives and filled with supporters of the American invasion of Iraq. After a well-known controversy that we will discuss below, Ayaan came – or fled – to America from the Netherlands, where she was a member of parliament.

Ayaan has spoken about Brandeis University's cancellation of both her invitation to speak and the honorary degree they were supposed to give her – the result of Brandeis professors and students highlighting her shameful history and expressing concern at her statements about Muslims. One of these statements was: "Islam is a destructive religion, and a nihilistic cult of death." Ayaan's response to the Muslim students in Yale University was that their stance highlights Islam's behavior towards critics, whom they call "infidels" and "heretics." Hirsi declared her atheism and left Islam for oppressing and despising women, locking them in the home, and forcing them to sacrifice everything. It forces women to bow in complete obedience to fathers, grandfathers, and husbands, to the extent of absolute control and discrimination. Ayaan Hirsi concluded her lecture by asking the audience, "Will you submit passively or actively, or will you finally stand up to Allah?"

On the Thursday before March 18, 2015, Ayaan Hirsi spoke at the Israeli Consul General Ido Aharoni's "Intellectual Salon" in his New York apartment.

On that day, according to a report published by *Jewish Week,* Ayaan announced that she wanted to – and one day would – convert to Judaism, but has yet to do so. Hirsi added that there is a need to defeat, and not reconcile, with Islam. She described President Obama as "naïve" for failing to understand that in the minds of Islamic fundamentalists, understanding, equality, and moderate solutions are equivalent to shame, dishonor, and disgrace. She said that their stubborn minds are still in the Middle Ages, and that in Islam, only infidels can facilitate change.

The Jewish newspaper wrote that Ayaan Hirsi introduces herself as, "a woman, an apostate, a lover of Israel, and a lover of Zion." Ayaan implored the audience in the Israeli consul general's apartment that, if the Muslims killed her, not to submit to them.

As a Muslim, I have no doubts that the Quran promotes justice, and its fairness is revealed in interpersonal interactions. Regarding the People of the Book, the Quran says: {Not all of them are alike: Of the People of the Book are a portion that stand (For the right): They rehearse the Signs of Allah all night long, and they prostrate themselves in adoration (113). They believe in Allah and the Last Day; they enjoin what is right, and forbid what is wrong; and they hasten (in emulation) in (all) good works: They are in the ranks of the righteous (114). Of the good that they do, nothing will be rejected of them; for Allah knoweth well those that do right (115)} (chapter 3. The Children of Imran).

I believe that there are people who forbid what is wrong and enjoin what is right. For example, the renowned writer Max Blumenthal forbid the wrongs of Ayaan Hirsi Ali and enjoined what is right by calling her out on her lies, her evil, and her destructive impact. Max Blumenthal understood that Ayaan Hirsi Ali belongs to the group of sellouts that make money by selling trivial goods that feed the masses' desires, and are thus sold at a trivial price to be consumed by the sheep. Ayaan Hirsi Ali is an example of a person that sells obscenities at a time when there are people to buy them. These obscenities fulfill the masses' delusion of despising Muslims, despite their knowledge of Ayaan's past and present, which are bursting with shame, disgrace, and dishonor.

On the *Daily Show*, Hirsi Ali was marketing her book *Infidel* when she stated that Muslims are responsible for 70% of the violence in the world today. She did not present any sources for her statistics, and it seems to have fallen on the show host's deaf ears. Three days before this claim, Hirsi Ali had written the following in a *Wall Street Journal* article (March 20, 2015): "According to the International Institute for Strategic Studies, at least 70% of all the fatalities in armed conflicts around the world last year were in wars involving Muslims."

Blumenthal stated that he had called the center Hirsi Ali mentioned to inquire about the truthfulness of her claim, but was met with a response that the center did not provide the information Hirsi Ali used in her research. He claimed to have spoken with a number of experts in the field, who said that they did not know the source from which Ayaan got this percentage. The experts seemed worried that her numbers may have been deceptive. When the writer called Hirsi Ali's organization, no one responded, and neither did Ayaan when he wrote to her online. He said that a day after his repeated inquiries, Ayaan went back on her claims regarding the responsibility of Muslims for most of the violence in the world. When Blumenthal went over research conducted by the Center for Strategic Studies, he did not find anything incriminating Muslims for the violence.

The writer says that Hirsi Ali's organization, instead of answering him, referred his inquiries to the *Washington Free Beacon*, an institution with a history of Islamophobia well known for fabricating deceptions to frighten people of Islam. Yet Max was shocked when the organization, instead of replying, wrote an article about his request in which it accused him of anti-Semitism.

Hirsi Ali's History of Fraud

According to Max Blumenthal, the fabricated statistics were only the latest of Hirsi Ali's many lies. Her well-known opposition of Islam has made Hirsi the darling of the American media.

Hirsi Ali's ignorance and shallow grasp of Western cultural norms and inner workings, known only to those with a deep understanding of the society, were revealed when she called for a Martin Luther-like reformer to appear and reform Islam inside out. The poor woman did not know that both Catholics and Jews despise Martin Luther, and even if we claim that Catholics are a minority in the United States, no one can refute the strength and control of the Jews in the West and their overwhelming influence on the media.

Catholics dislike Martin Luther for leading one of the greatest Christian schisms since the coming of Christ. Jews despise him because he called for the burning of their synagogues, comparing them to a "gangrenous disease" that eats away at the body. Both Catholics and Jews see Martin Luther as a tyrannical fanatic, and out of ignorance, Ayaan Hirsi Ali thought that she had done well and brought herself closer to all Americans.

The Western media received Hirsi Ali's book *Infidel* with open arms. Major newspapers and channels including the *BBC, CNN,* and *ABC* hosted her, and the *New York Times* interviewed her. According to Blumenthal, "Hirsi Ali has marketed herself as an expert native informant who has emerged out of the dark heart of radical Islam and into the light of Western civilization. Her tale is an uplifting, comforting one that tells many Westerners what they want to hear about themselves and their perceived enemies." In a context where anti-Muslim sentiment has reached its peak in Europe and America, Hirsi Ali's criticism and assault on Islam, and her description of the religion as a doctrine endemic of violence, extremism, and murder, has received widespread acceptance.

According to Blumenthal, "like her writings on Islam, much of what she has told the public about herself is questionable." He supported that statement by bringing up the Dutch television program that in May 2006 told the story Hirsi Ali had invented to advance her status and position in the Netherlands. The program finished by summarizing her life as "a story full of obscurities."

Hirsi was born in Somalia with the name Ayaan Hirsi Magan. She immigrated to the Netherlands in 1992, where she changed her name to Hirsi Ali. She "lied" to the Dutch authorities about her past, having come to the

Netherlands from Kenya, not "war-torn Somalia." In Kenya, she had been living in a safe environment under the protection of the United Nations, who funded her education in a highly respected girls school. However, in the Dutch media, Hirsi Ali told authorities that she had fled from civil war in Somalia, despite the fact that she had left before the war broke out. She had not lived through a war, anywhere. Thanks to her "fabrications," Hirsi Ali received asylum in the Netherlands after only five weeks.

On a talk show in the Netherlands, Hirsi Ali stated that her religious family had tried to force her to marry a draconian Muslim man, but she did not attend her wedding ceremony. This supposedly led to death threats from her family for offending their "religious honor." However, the Dutch television program Zembla aired a completely different story than the one she had told. On the program, her brother, aunt, and former husband testified that she had in fact been present at her wedding. Since arriving to the Netherlands, Hirsi Ali has tried to ban Islamic schools in the Netherlands. She worked with the Dutch director Theo van Gogh to produce a documentary called *Submission* that targeted Islam, focusing on showing what it claimed to be violence against women in Muslim societies as a logical result of the Islamic belief. The film portrayed actresses wearing the niqab, and others half naked with Quranic verses written on their bodies.

Van Gogh became famous for calling Muslims "goat fuckers." He was gunned down and stabbed to death by a Dutch Muslim who was labeled a "radical." Before fleeing the crime scene, the murderer taped a note to van Gogh's body threatening to kill Hirsi Ali. The fact that Hirsi decided to persist in her work despite the threats helped her earn hero status in Western Europe and the United States after September 11th. In the U.S, *Time* magazine named her one of its 100 most influential people.

Blumenthal believes that Zembla's revelation of Hirsi Ali's "lie" in May 2006 brought her rise to a halt and threw the Dutch government into chaos. Her friend and ally, the immigration minister Rita Verdonk, suffered the most from her "lies." Well-known for her xenophobia, Verdonk was so ashamed that she threatened to strip Hirsi Ali of her citizenship.

A few days after Zembla aired its program on Hirsi Ali, she announced her plan to leave Parliament and begin working with the American Enterprise Institute. A few days after the furor Hirsi Ali's scandal had caused, the Dutch government collapsed.

When Hirsi Ali arrived in the United States, she was embraced by a coalition of liberal interventionists, neoconservatives, and "new atheists." She was awarded numerous opportunities to appear on the extremist, anti-Muslim pastor Pat Robertson's channel, known for blaming September 11th on homosexuality, thus winning her many fans among Christians. According to Blumenthal, the famous Harvard University awarded Hirsi Ali a fellowship for her stance on Islam.

As Hirsi Ali's fame grew, American media platforms ate up her persistent attacks on Islam. The media forgot about both the shameful acts that made her flee the Netherlands, and her concoctions that had overthrown a government. In 2007, her book *Infidel* became a bestseller in the United States. Her complete loss of credibility in the Netherlands was no longer mentioned, and thus, her history of "lies" was suddenly erased. She continued to seize every opportunity to curse and condemn Islam, at one point saying that: "There comes a moment when you crush your enemy."

Hirsi Ali has and continues to try and appear more royal than a king. She criticized the multiculturalism in Europe that the Parliament supports and defends, blaming it for the wave of murders committed by the extremist Norweigian Anders Breivik. Breivik had killed 77 people out of fear that Europe would become Islamic. Hirsi Ali continues to seize all opportunities to reinforce the rhetoric of hatred against Islam. After the Charlie Hebdo incident that ridiculed Islam, she published her book *Infidel*, which brought her back into the media spotlight to reinforce her dark predictions. American media networks remain hungry for everything that opposes Islam, having intentionally forgotten about Ayaan's truly embarrassing history. This piece on Ayyan Hirsi is adapted from Blumenthal's narrative.

The Western Response

Before the stunning seizure of Mosul in mid 2014, the West failed to take the Islamic State seriously. Its opinion of ISIS instead veered on the side of disregard and underestimation, only changing suddenly when it realized that ISIS was expanding and eliminating and crossing borders. It was only then that ISIS became seen as a threat that exceeded geographical borders. The West's frustration escalated after "it was described as the dominant force in the world today," and thousands of young men surged from the West and other countries, filled with excitement and zeal and ready to sacrifice the comfortable living conditions of certain Western countries. The West's frustration increased even further when it realized that ISIS had obtained modern communications technologies, thus launching a propaganda campaign that even the West admitted was one of acumen and skill – exceeding its own capabilities and ability to keep up.

The West was stunned by ISIS's astonishing victories, but due to a lack of preparation, its response was crudely immature, naïve, shallow, and conventional, dealing with ISIS in the same way it had dealt with al-Qaeda. Its response thus failed to eradicate ISIS or stop its media expansion. In contrast to ISIS's powerful media and propaganda message to Muslim youth, the Western message was weak because it depended on simplified explanations that failed to respect the intelligence of their audience, some examples of which will be listed below.

President Obama announced that "ISIL is not Islamic, and ISIL is certainly not a state." Mr. Ban Ki-moon, the United Nations Secretary General, the British Interior Minister Theresa May, and many others in the fields of politics and media echoed his sentiment.

The truth is that ISIS is a state with a government, a leader, territory where its flag hangs, and a bureaucracy that is responsible for safety, security, services, and borders. The truth is also that ISIS is Islamic! Its actions and decisions are based on texts from the Quran and the Sunnah. By saying this, I am not defending ISIS – of which I am not a member – and my words are not meant to cover up its flaws and wrongdoings, which we will discuss below.

It is not natural, customary, or easy for 100,000 boys, men, and women to expose themselves to death, destruction, and discomfort: thus, how can ISIS not be taken seriously, and written off as a sect of fools and lunatics? A person that volunteers for potentially deadly discomfort and hardship must be seriously and deeply studied. Likewise, the reasons behind someone's decision to volunteer for a suicide mission should be investigated, especially when the sacrifice is made out of conviction and contentment, his participation free from pressure, compulsion, and enticement, and his peers happy for him, wishing themselves for the same fate.

We will not use ISIS's actions to accuse it of apostasy and of not being Islamic; however, we will admit that it is both selective and literal in quoting Quranic and Sunnah texts. While ISIS does have roots in Islamic judicial sources, its selectiveness and literalness will be the source of its demise. ISIS's revival of slavery does come with a legal basis, and their burning with fire has a basis in the sources. They claim that their killing of anyone who does not repent has evidence to support it, and destroying what it considers to be idols is supported by a faint trace of religious knowledge. The Prophet (PBUH) and his companions all had slaves, which was the cultural norm during that period of time. However, in the Sunnah, the prophet did not promote this practice. He instead promoted freeing slaves. The Prophet destroyed the idols around the Kaaba, and since some Islamic scholars called for obliterating crosses, ISIS removed them from church towers in Mosul and other cities, and burned with fire as they claim Abu Bakr and Ali had done.

Does ISIS not take into consideration the implications of their actions on the interests of the religion? The religion it claims to have come to preserve? Where is the Prophet's guidance of: "What I have ordered you [to do], do as much of it as you can," and the application of: "He who hurts a dhimmi (any non-Muslim in Muslims country) hurts me" in ISIS's behavior of harassing and terrifying the Christians of Mosul? Are the ISIS scholars more knowledgeable of the religion than the Companions of the Prophet, who knew of the ancient ruins in Iraq, Syria, and Egypt, but did nothing to harm them?

It is shameful for ISIS to implement religious texts without flexibility and with extremism and brutality, without considering the modern context or effect of its actions on Islam's image. The modern media leans towards the West, which is apprehensive of all religions but particularly wary of Islam. ISIS's religious actions have thus provided the media with rich material for antagonistic propaganda that utilizes these actions to defame and ridicule Islam.

When I brought up my aforementioned arguments about the damage ISIS does to Islam's image to the al-Qaeda sympathizer, he said I was dreaming, secretly sympathizing with the West, or was affected by its propaganda. The man got worked up as he asked me, what image remains of Islam, when the West mocks its Prophet! What image, when Israel kills Muslims daily with Western support! The West is oppressing Islam and has defaced its image, while you and those like you want to continue the appeasement that has led to the disrespect of Islam. Did the West not use "shock and awe" against us in Iraq, killing millions of us? For how long will we submit? He concluded with, "shock for shock, and awe for awe, but we have not reached even a tenth of what the West has done to the Muslims." The nonsense in such talk is clear, because the actions of others, regardless of how evil they may be, do not justify killing of innocent souls.

The Western Response (Military Operations)

As we stated earlier, ISIS's control over Mosul worried and concerned all parties. Western forces began thinking seriously about how to face it, becoming even more distressed at its expansion to Iraqi Kurdistan. Once it began posing a threat to the Peshmerga that the US trained, fostered, and armed, the Americans began airstrikes on ISIS locations.

Like its hostility towards those it calls "infidels," ISIS is openly hostile to the United States. Regarding this point and that of reinstating the Caliphate, ISIS and al-Qaeda are in agreement. Yet the two parties differ in terms of tactics, methods, and timing. Al-Qaeda believes that an Islamic state cannot stabilize before it has exhausted the "infidel" countries, and thus made them despair of defeating God's religion, and cease the targeting of Muslims. Thus, the priority in jihad is targeting the "distant enemy," and only after exhausting it and making it despair can the Caliphate be declared. On the other hand, ISIS sees no excuse for waiting, and believes the Caliphate should be declared immediately in all Muslim lands. This would act as a starting point for the "remaining and expanding" Islamic state. ISIS does not want to be another Caliphate that was satisfied with abstaining from jihad. It is convinced that after the United States' latest experience in Iraq – at a cost of two trillion dollars, thousands of losses and injuries, and soldiers suffering from mental illness – the United States has already lost hope. ISIS has also been enticed by its success in fighting the inefficient Iraqi army. In certain cases, the Iraqi army fled without fighting, its soldiers submitting – or fleeing – by the thousands, leaving behind American weapons that have come to make up the majority of ISIS's weaponry. A third factor that encouraged ISIS is the support, or at least acceptance, of Sunni tribes because it saved them from the yoke of al-Maliki's forces and Shiite militias, as some Sunni Iraqis have explained.

In mentioning the support of the Sunni tribes, we would like to point to an Iraqi opinion poll that revealed that no less than 20% of Iraqi Sunni fighters support ISIS. I do not believe that this result is honest or accurate, and the idea that it is backed by a political agenda cannot be ruled out.

However, ground military intervention by the Americans and their allies is faced with obstacles and constraints.

America has been afflicted with what can be called the "specter of Iraq," similar to the specter of Vietnam. Military withdrawal from Iraq was one of the election topics that won Obama the presidency, after which he withdrew 185,000 soldiers from Iraq. Even now, and even after Mosul, he remains hesitant to send ground forces. He did however send 3,000 soldiers to serve as military instructors.

As for the remainder of America's allies in the anti-ISIS coalition, they are all hesitant and unwilling to send ground forces. This coalition is composed of 60 countries, all of which have not sent a single soldier to fight ISIS on the ground, for reasons other than a fear of human losses. Some of these countries do not view fighting ISIS a priority at the moment. Instead, they believe the priority to be weakening the Shiite government in Baghdad and curtailing the Iranian presence and influence in Iraq. Even if they consider ISIS an enemy, some countries believe the priority is weakening the Kurdish forces. Thus, the conflict of agendas is a major factor that has prevented sending ground forces.

The United States and some of its allied countries have found airstrikes to be sufficient in limiting the military expansion of ISIS. It can now no longer send convoys of military cars filled with soldiers to attack multiple new locations. Aerial surveillance through satellites and airplanes have made moving as a group highly dangerous for ISIS, which has led it to resort to guerilla warfare methods, such as sending numerous small-sized regiments to attack Iraqi military spots and its related Shiite militias. However, even these airstrikes have not been as effective as desired. There need to be soldiers that act as spotters and spies in order to pinpoint targeted locations and send coordinates. In ISIS territory, this is highly doubtful, especially at the necessary extent, and with the proper communications and transmission equipment.

The Americans have become more sensitive about direct military intervention for domestic reasons, as well as out of a fear of increasing hostile feelings towards America, especially among the Sunni majority that accuses them of targeting Islam. According to Dr. Michael Connell, senior researcher at the American Center for Naval Analyses, Americans are wary of direct interference by deploying only their forces, because the Muslims will react with the statement: "We built the Caliphate and the Americans destroyed it." So far, military leaders prefer using Special Forces due to the high likelihood of their success, in addition to laser-guided bombs because of their high rate of precision. However, political leaders, especially the president, do not support military operations that require deploying large forces. They contradict what

President Obama had continuously proclaimed since his first election campaign, and would thus ruin his legacy, an important aspect of which was withdrawing the troops from Iraq.

The United States is trying to repeat their experience with the Sunni Awakening Movement, which until 2011 was successful in weakening al-Qaeda. It later failed when the Americans withdrew from Iraq and al-Maliki's government did not uphold their promise to the Sunnis. The United States recommended creating an Iraqi "national guard" that would be mainly comprised and led by the Sunnis. It would be in charge of fighting the Islamic State; however, this endeavor has so far not been successful.

On the other hand, the history of every military involvement in Muslim countries has proved that it is the quickest and most effective way of attracting and mobilizing Jihadist groups in the country invaded. Men volunteer to fight the invading forces, and invasion becomes the magnet that attracts them. The Americans have themselves witnessed that during confrontations they fight with savagery and professionalism – the type of fighting attributed to well-trained forces. With that said, increasing American forces means an increase in Jihadists, to the point that it has even been said that the United States is the best recruiter for Jihadist groups.

It does not appear that observers of the situation are very optimistic that the methods currently being used to fight ISIS will eventually lead to its defeat. Their argument is that weakening al-Qaeda from 2006 until 2011 required a large presence of forces that eventually reached 185,000 American soldiers, not counting the Iraqi forces.

To fight and destroy ISIS, President Obama announced that the United States would use aerial bombardment, the same method that succeeded in both Yemen and Somalia. But the truth is that aerial bombardment did not achieve the desired results in either of those two countries. In Yemen, al-Qaeda is now stronger than ever before. The al-Shabaab jihadist movement in Somalia has weakened, but not as a result of airstrikes alone. It has weakened because African forces, negotiated by the African Union and funded by Western states, accompanied the airstrikes.

It is noteworthy that the United States began its airstrikes in August, that is, approximately two months after the occupation of Mosul. If not for the presence of American citizens working in U.S companies in Iraqi Kurdistan, as well as military personnel that were training and arming the Peshmerga, the U.S probably would not have kept up with the strikes. At the time, specifically on September 8, 2014, the editorial board of the *New York Times* doubted the military coalition's ability to achieve the desired results against ISIS.

Using the Peshmerga under an air cover proved successful in both the Ayn al-Arab and Tell Abyad battles, in which ISIS lost more than 3,000 fighters. This number was equivalent to ISIS's losses across all of its battles during that year. In Ayn al-Arab, its persistence in fighting down to the last man surprised observers, because ISIS had become known for using the tactic of retreating from any battle that was not an undeniable victory.

An American military expert told Atwan that the ISIS fighters know the military topography and terrain of the land on which they fight, as well as how to utilize population dynamics. He believes that ISIS's military plans reflect a complete military understanding, including deception, expansion, dispersal, and timing as governing strategic characteristics.

ISIS fighters have become known for the severity of their discipline, and their respect for hierarchy. These are unprecedented traits in armed movement operations, and do not resemble the work of terrorist organizations. They instead resemble the methods of regular armies.

According to Abdel Bari Atwan, specialists say that the organizations that resemble ISIS's performance and discipline are the Irish Republican Army, the Shining Path in Peru, and Lebanon's Hezbollah.

The Western states that are spearheading the fight on ISIS are working hard to deprive ISIS of weapons, but one of their main obstacles in doing so is the cooperation of similar organizations with the jihadists in Iraq and Syria. The al-Qaeda sympathizer I met in Istanbul for the purposes of this book told me that while he was a member of the jihadist group in Syria, the Ansar al-Sharia group in Libya provided them with 60 tons of ammunition from Gaddafi's stockpiles. He revealed to me that all of the communications and arrangements were made over the Internet, and it is likely that Ansar al-Sharia's reinforcements to the jihadists will continue. He also said that states cooperated in preparing the airplane that landed in Benghazi and smuggled the shipments.

The al-Qaeda sympathizer, who has a deep understanding of the course of jihadist affairs in Syria and Iraq, told me that ISIS now has five war planes. It obtained them from the airbases it captured, and two Iraqi pilots are now training the jihadists to fly them. However, the problem is that the hostile aerial surveillance does not allow them enough training hours to perfect how to fly them. He also told me that the jihadist groups moved the planes, hiding them underground after having built well-equipped shelters. He complained of the lack of sophisticated anti-aircraft missiles, a factor that has weakened the jihadists' execution of missions in both Iraq and Syria.

Western military forces are facing the obstacle of going up against the flexibility of ISIS's field commanders in the battleground. ISIS authorizes them to act in accordance with field circumstances, without waiting for instructions from above, as is the case in regular armies. As a result of the independence the leadership grants its men in the field, ISIS is able to adjust and maneuver itself in accordance with continuously changing circumstances. A result of this has been a greater efficiency of ISIS's forces. This flexibility, independence and delegation of command has made it difficult for Western intelligence agencies to obtain certain facts, due to the forces' continuous movement and changes in military tactics.

Western military circles have found the fact that ISIS forces are trained to fight traditional, urban, and mountainous warfare quite disabling. ISIS is able to rapidly disperse and formulate small and connected yet simultaneously scattered units, which gives it the chance to prevail over traditional forces. This is the strategy ISIS implemented in the Fallujah battle against the American forces.

Military strategy experts say that, "An army marches on its stomach," and because ISIS has senior soldiers from Saddam's old regime among their ranks, they have worked to implement a plan to secure food supply for their fighters and citizens. Specifically, they have seized flour mills, monitored the production of bread ovens, and gained control over river dams. The reservoirs have become a deterrent weapon since they have threatened to destroy the Mosul dam and drown Baghdad.

Policy of Containment

It is no longer a secret that military operations alone will not defeat ISIS. Assassinating its leadership will also not restrain it, the same way it was unable to restrain one of its progenitors, al-Qaeda. It is also true that ISIS is no longer an organization promoting an idea. It now controls an extensive piece of land that it governs as a state. If we make the argument that it is not a state, then it is at the very least a proto-state. Thus, framing and dealing with ISIS using anti-terrorism strategies will not defeat it, because these strategies have been created for something ISIS has surpassed. ISIS has developed and fortified itself against limited measures, so the unchanged methods espoused by the United States and its allies have not gone beyond deterrence.

Until now, ISIS, as a movement, has not posed a threat to the territories of Western countries, but it has posed a threat to the interests of these countries in the Middle East. After ISIS seized territories in two countries, doing away with borders between them and implementing operations outside of its territorial authority, it became an ever-present threat. However, defeating it with the same methods currently being utilized will not be easy. The American Institute for the Study of War wrote that developing a strategy for defeating ISIS "will, in fact, be very difficult." Yet ISIS may be in danger if its enemies are able to understand the exact sources of its strength, its plans, its intentions, and its vulnerabilities. Aggregating this information, or what Jessica Lewis calls "an analysis of its center of gravity," in order to understand its sources of strength and weakness, will enable the formation of a strategy that poses a real threat.

ISIS gains control over land through military force. It then establishes bureaucratic institutions to govern its citizens' affairs. ISIS's strength stems from its ability to transform military control into political control over its territory. If it is stripped of this capability, it will be hit in its most vulnerable spot.

President Obama has acknowledge that military operations alone are not enough to defeat ISIS. Thus, the United States has developed a three-pronged strategy to confront the Islamic State. The first prong is composed of airstrikes in order to weaken and exhaust the Islamic State; however, according to experts, airstrikes are completely unable to defeat the state on their own. The second prong is composed of training and arming the United States' partners that will be in charge of waging direct warfare without the intensive (boots) involvement of the United States. The third prong recognizes the fact that ISIS is not the cause but a symptom of political problems and failures in the countries in which it has expanded. It acknowledges that any long-term solution must be political, according to Professor Thomas Juneau on the website of Columbia University's Gary Sick, or more exactly, the Gulf/2000 project.

Muslim Grievances against the West

It is important to point out how flawed it is to believe that the West is just an evil solid bloc. Likewise, it is wrong to assume that the West, as a whole, targets Islam and Muslims with the intention of eliminating Islam and annihilating Muslims. In the West, there are kind, virtuous, and humane institutions and people that respect and honor different cultures – people that appreciate and enjoy human diversity. In the West, there are diverse sides that oppose injustice in any place. They go above and beyond to respect and defend human rights, and even sacrifice what they have in order to eliminate injustice – all injustice.

For example, politicians, writers, journalists, public figures, intellectuals, and organizations have all taken stances against the war in Iraq. They have exerted similar efforts to oppose Israeli injustice towards the Palestinians. These people have given billions of dollars to fund endless Western organizations that do humanitarian work in areas struggling with wars, catastrophes, and disasters. All of these good parties and people uphold noble principles and values with practical examples. These honorable positions must be appreciated and commended, and most importantly, their virtue must be acknowledged and paid back to its people.

It is possible that the problem Muslims have with the West is confined mainly to the Western establishment. It is completely unjust to generalize and forget the ways in which the West has benefited societies. It is wrong to classify all Westerners as evil beings. Without a doubt, intelligent critics of the West point fingers at the Western establishment, which itself is not pure evil. It contains bright sides, and its humanitarian policies serve as an example, having sheltered millions of people that are persecuted, homeless, refugees, or fleeing from calamities in their countries. It has opened up numerous chances for them to live a dignified life.

When I say the establishment, I do not only mean the state. The establishment is comprised of its allies in the media, major companies, religious organizations, research and scientific institutions, and influential individuals. The establishment's main fault is confined to its foreign policies in the region. Despite the existing tension between Muslims and the West, they are in dire need of normalized relations. It is important for sensible people to work on strengthening these relations and creating an environment that leads to growth and development. Those working at the present moment must work on achieving this.

Nonetheless, the following must be taken into account.

In the Muslim collective memory sits the year 1798, when Napoleon invaded Egypt, and said the following in a speech in Alexandria: "Peoples of Egypt, you will be told that I have come to destroy your religion; do not believe it! Answer that I have come to restore your rights and punish the usurpers, and that, more than the Mamluks. I respect God, his prophet and the Koran. We have been through the centuries the friends of the Sultan (may God grant his desires)." To solidify his authority, he turned to religion. Composed of nine sheikhs from al-Azhar, Napoleon created a divan to govern the capital of Cairo. He worked earnestly to have an al-Azhar imam issue a ruling that would make the Muslims declare their allegiance to Napoleon.

At the time, the Muslims did not have political Islam, Islamic extremists, terrorists, or Wahhabis. Despite this, on October 21, 1798, al-Azhar spearheaded a revolution against the French occupation. Egyptian civilians armed with rocks, spears, and knives attacked the French forces, leading Napoleon to order the shelling of Cairo from atop the Citadel. The fire was pointed towards al-Azhar, and led to the death of 3,000 Egyptians. Six scholars from al-Azhar were killed after the invading forces held mock trials, and others were imprisoned. The French forces killed every Egyptian they found carrying a cold weapon. In his book *Wa Dakhalat al-Khail al-Azhar*, Muhammad Jalal Kishk wrote that the French beheaded the Egyptians – like ISIS and al-Zarqawi have done – and entered the al-Azhar Mosque on horseback, intentionally desecrating this spot so revered by the Muslims. They tied up their horses in the mihrab, and walked inside the mosque with their shoes on, wielding their weapons, destroying the students' housing and offices, and throwing holy books on the ground. In March of 1800, when an al-Azhar student killed the French General Kléber, Napoleon closed al-Azhar.

Also in the Muslim collective memory is the British overthrow of the Ottoman sultan, and the incitement – or rather the enticement – and deception of Hussein bin Ali, Sharif of Mecca, until the Arabs revolted against Islamic unity, as represented by the Ottoman Caliphate. Through this conspiracy, they put an end to a Caliphate that had lasted over 1,000 years. In the end, the promises made to the Sharif were not upheld and with the Sykes-Picot Agreement of 1916, the Muslim states were divided.

The Islamic memory then recorded a memo written by T. E. Lawrence, famous as Lawrence of Arabic (who was known for being a homosexual, and is said to have had a questionable relationship with someone named Salim

Ali). He was a British intelligence agent in charge of tricking the Sharif and his son Faisal, and in a memo written to the presidency of the British intelligence, he revealed the British agenda behind inciting the Arabs to revolt against the Islamic Caliphate: "The Arabs are even less stable than the Turks. *If properly handled they would remain in a state of political mosaic, a tissue of small jealous principalities incapable of cohesion* [emphasis in original]." In a second official correspondence that followed the previous one, Lawrence said: "When war broke out an urgent need to divide Islam was added...Hussein was ultimately chosen because of the rift he would create in Islam. In other words, divide and rule." Lawrence had malignantly distorted the image of this Arab leader, a descendent of the Prophet.

In 1917, a year after the Sykes-Picot agreement, the Balfour declaration promised the Jews the land of Palestine. The British government presented it to Rothschild, the eldest of a Jewish family that is rumored to control the price of gold even today. Britain then gave Palestine over to the Jews, while the Islamic memory took note.

Prior to that, France occupied Algeria and massacred the Algerians – slaughtering, butchering, discarding, and torturing them. Moreover, France buried atomic waste there, and those left from the 1.5 million murdered Algerians continue to suffer, until today, from the waste's remains.

Western armies invaded Muslim countries, colonizing them and pillaging their wealth and resources, in addition to targeting them with cultural invasion.

A laughable aspect of Western policy towards Muslim countries is how it uses and takes advantage of the Muslims' religious sentiments to achieve its hegemonic purposes. Just as Napoleon had done during his speech in Alexandria, Egypt when he played on the religious sentiments, claiming the exaltation of God, His Prophet, and His Quran, Henry McMahon wrote to the Sharif of Mecca promising him that, "Great Britain will guarantee the Holy Places against all external aggression." He announced to the Sharif the United Kingdom's willingness to defend his Caliphate once he ascends the throne with their swords, their horses, and their legs – A statement that resemble what the West now says in its campaign called the "War on Terror."

It is also strange that Great Britain was an ally of the Ottoman Sultan and had fought on his side during the Crimean War in 1854-1856. However, this British support of the Ottoman Caliphate was not for the sake of higher values, but as is the case today, is sparked by interests. The lands of the Caliphate formed protection for the British trade routes with its colonies in India. Similarly, its alliance was to weaken its other adversaries, including Russia and France.

The Algerian war resulted in 1.5 million martyrs. The occupation of Palestine resulted in thousands of martyrs, and millions of displaced persons and refugees. The outpouring still continues today, devouring anyone who goes to the extreme – anyone whose feelings of injustice lead to a development of a desire to revolt and seek revenge. Yet the largest blow came with what happened in Afghanistan and Iraq. In Afghanistan, the United States, the leader of the West, saw that what happened on September 11 resembled a hellish terror that called for a response just as big. It thus employed its developed military tactic to bomb a country that barely had anything to bomb, so most of the victims were civilians. Bagram prison witnessed events that are a disgrace to human dignity, and sorrows occurred that fed the desire for jihad in Muslims throughout the entire world.

In Iraq, Muslims knew that excuses made for invasion were fabrications with no proof, and the idea that Iraq possessed weapons of mass destruction, and that there was coordination between al-Qaeda and Saddam, were false claims. Before the war and the invasion, the economic sanctions killed hundreds of thousands of Iraqi children, destroying the society. Then the invasion came, followed by the death and displacement of millions, destroying the Iraqi state. Thus, Iraq suffered two destructions: the destruction of the society, and of the state, as an Iraqi stated.

People all over the world, Muslims and others, shared the photographs of the American barbarity that had manifested in Bagram, Guantanamo, and Abu Ghraib, bringing an end to claims of respect for human rights and humanity. Claims of rumored fundamental freedoms and democracy also came to an end, due to the West's support of regimes whose political actions the Islamist actors believed went against the foundations of these values. They classified these regimes as dictatorial and oppressive regimes that crush, marginalize, and oppress them, and confiscate their freedoms. They sought refuge in organizations that worked underground, finding what they had been looking for in jihadist and extremist organizations.

This distrust did not come only from religious Muslims, but also included even the nationalist streams that resented the West's targeting of Nasser's regime, the Baathist party in Syria and Iraq, and the Palestine Liberation Organization. They condemned the West for targeting and having a greedy desire to seize Arab oil resources, as well as for hold back their advanced technologies from the Muslim world while making them available for their enemy, Israel, which occupied their lands and oppressed the Palestinians. To both the Arabs and the Muslims, Israel was a Western country planted in its side that espoused the same hegemonic methods.

Both the jihadist and non-jihadist streams of Islamists resented what they saw as a Western plot to overthrew Islamists in countries where they had come to power democratically. As Islamophobic trends grew in the West, the divide deepened. We must point to the fact that the lack of trust did not come only from the Muslim side. After September 11th, every Muslim became a possible extremist and terrorist, the stories of which are endless. My ambassador colleague sent his 75-year old mother to visit his relative working in the United States. In the American airport, the old woman was subjected to a thorough personal inspection. A number of pictures, as well as her fingerprints, were taken. A girl then proceeded to take off some of her clothing, persisting in the humiliation. When her Sudanese escort asked for the reasons for subjecting a woman of this age to this kind of harsh procedures, and if a woman of this age truly posed a threat to national American security, the security officer responded: "Yeah, you have something called Shahada." (Shahada is the Arabic for martyrdom)

When the United States wanted to destroy the Soviet Union through its policy of containment – the vision of George Kennan, the U.S ambassador in Moscow during 1946 – it wanted to use this policy's military dimension against the Russians in Afghanistan, and so it turned to the Muslims to wage their anti-Soviet war for them. When the war had come to an end with the defeat of the Soviet Union and its retreat from Afghanistan in 1989, 100,000 mujahedeen had received military training. Yet when these men returned to their countries, some of them were thrown into the obscurity of prisons, others were kicked out, and others were harassed. This gave birth to feelings of betrayal by both their countries and America, thus intensifying their anger from both sides. Some of these men were radicalized, and others carried out terrorist attacks. There were also those who lived in seclusion, but something from this experience had stayed in them.

In some cases, the radicalism led to targeting moderate Islamic streams such as the Muslim Brotherhood, whom they accused of obstructing the religious duty of jihad. They were accused of being *Mu'attila*, *Murji'ah* and *Jahmiyya*. In ISIS's writings, they call the Muslim Brotherhood the "Corrupt Brotherhood," who supported the apostates, and acted cowardly and ignorantly when they did not heed the lessons about what was in store for them at the hands of the apostates and infidels.

No one knew what the mujahedeen had in store. For them, Afghanistan was not merely a military training camp, but an education on Jihadist texts and jurisprudence. It was an incubator in which numerous Jihadist schools were developed, yet they did not reveal what they kept inside. According to what Abdel Bari Atwan wrote in his book on the Islamic State, the former Pakistani president Pervez Musharraf stated in his autobiography that: "Neither Pakistan nor the US realized what Osama bin Laden would do with the organization we had all allowed him to establish."

The West's frustration with the Jihadists increased when it saw them flock to Eastern Europe in multitudes to fight with the Bosnian Muslims in 1992, bomb the World Trade Center in New York for the first time in 1993, and plant – al-Qaeda and the Armed Islamic Group of Algeria – bombs in the Paris metro in 1995.

The Arab Spring confused and complicated matters. Because of the security grip on and exclusion of Jihadists from Muslim countries, they became more secluded, radicalized, and ever-present. The chaos that struck some Arab Spring countries, such as Libya and Yemen, also created an environment that opened up for them freedom of movement, training, arming, circulation, and money, thus strengthening their relentlessness.

The middle of this century's first decade witnessed calls to engage with the moderate Islamist current from well-renowned, effective Western centers, such as Tony Blair in 2006 and a study conducted for the British Department of Defense in 2004 by the British ambassador in Damascus, Basil Eastwood, as well as the US secretary of state's assistant, Richard Murphy. Despite these calls, action on the ground has been the complete opposite. The paper stated that: "In the Arab Middle East the awkward truth is that the most significant such movements which enjoy popular support are those associated with political Islam," dividing political Islamist streams into two trends: one that seeks to change regimes peacefully, and another, the jihadist trend, that calls for violence to change regimes. Obviously, the West – theoretically – approves of the first trend, but because this is a theoretical preference, the West is not happy with what it has seen.

Social media has broken down the Western governments' monopoly on media; thus, it has opened up the opportunity for the public to express their views and opinions, and has broadened awareness of all issues. Among those who have implemented and benefited from social media are the activists, writers, and Muslims, by exposing Western positions on issues of freedoms, human rights, and the slandering of Islam.

Westerners strongly oppose the application of Islamic Sharia law on principle. They especially oppose the legal punishments that they call barbaric, savage, and punishments of the dark ages that disrespect human dignity. On the other side, this generally angers Muslims. They consider it a lack of respect and wrongdoing to their doctrines. Even non-religious Muslims resent this description of the Islamic punishments, considering it a failure to recognize different cultures. They thus doubt the West's claim of respecting cultural diversity. The Muslim jihadists, however, view it as a mockery of God and His message on the part of infidels, who must therefore be beheaded.

Generally, Muslims reject the Western way of life, which permits homosexual and extramarital relations, and the consumption of alcohol. They reproach Westerners for the weakness in family ties and putting elderly parents into retirement homes. They also criticize the looseness of the youth, despite their appreciation of the technological development, political stability, and care for human rights inside the Western states.

Most Muslim grievances with the West are especially concentrated amongst the Sunni Muslims. For example, they have noticed that Western states do not criminalize or arrest Westerners that join the Israelis in fighting battles against the Arabs, while they criminalize and punish any one of its citizens that joins or contacts the Islamic State. It punishes them with verdicts that can reach 20 years in prison, or preventing them from returning to their Western homelands. It confiscates the passports of those who initiate travel procedures, or those who are heard speaking of their desire to join ISIS.

I have heard from Western officials that they believe the largest threat is that coming from the Sunnis. Thus, they will focus their plans on confronting the Sunni challenge. A diplomat colleague of mine told me that he had heard Western officials in a Western country saying just that.

Muslims even view the coalition strikes as targeting the Sunnis, considering it in part a way of targeting Islam, given that they are the Muslim majority. Many of them have accused the West of this targeting, and of having double standards in comparison with how they deal with Shiite militias who commit barbaric acts no less than those of ISIS. It has been noticed that with every increase in Western and American interference, the number of ISIS sympathizers also increases. Perhaps what confirmed this is that when America started bombing ISIS in August 2014, 6,300 new fighters migrated to its territory over the course of two weeks.

In the Middle East, many people think that, with their support of counterrevolutionary forces that toppled the dreams of the Arab Spring, the West has plotted against freedom, democracy, and all of the values it claims to uphold. They see the West as contradicting its sayings with its actions. While it talks about rights, freedoms, and democracy, it actually supports regimes that contradict the values that it theoretically calls for. They accuse it of prioritizing their personal interests first at the expense of higher values. They also accuse its military adventures of not having brought them democracy or freedom, while having led to their loss of freedom. For example, Sunni Iraqis say that Saddam Hussein did not allow them to enjoy freedoms and democracy, but he did provide them with an undeniable level of security.

Muslims believe that the West deals with them with arrogance, insolence and seniority, imposing on them the guidance of a knowledgeable advisor to an ignorant minor. It speaks to them in a way that does not seem to respect their humanity, their minds, or their intelligence. Robert Fisk has mentioned that the British General Angus Maude spoke to the people of Baghdad when he entered it in 1917, saying that he has brought with him civilization, and that: "Since the days of Hulagu, your citizens have been subject to the tyranny of strangers, your palaces have fallen into ruins, your gardens have sunken in desolation and your forefathers and yourselves have groaned in bondage." Robert Fisk ridicules the British Prime Minister David Cameron that "raves on about 'British' values — and at the same time worships the...immensely wealthy and dangerous men who have helped to inspire ISIS." He proceeds with mocking Cameron, who repeats the words "civilization" and "British values," while at the same time supporting uncivilized powers, says Fisk.

General Maude's speech to the people of Baghdad is reminiscent of Napoleon's speech to the people of Alexandria, and McMahon's letters to Sharif Hussein. In a region that celebrates and lives in history, preserving pieces of writing as old as 3,000 years – a region that is still moved by the seven *mu'allaqat* – what was said remains ever-present in its memory, participating in shaping its emotions and helping to catalyze events.

Just War

There are Western campaigns that aim to differentiate the wars it wages – in which it commits all kinds of terrorism – from the terrorism of freedom fighters and extremists. The West claims moral supremacy in its "just wars" waged because of "necessity," and according to Talal Asad, classifies the actions of terrorists, especially suicide bombers, as "pure evil."

Meanwhile, the West kills thousands more civilians and innocents than the terrorists. It destroys civilian lives in a way that cannot be compared to what the terrorists do. In the wars waged by the West, water purification facilities are destroyed, along with food supply storages, electricity plants, pharmaceutical warehouses, roads, and bridges. It has transformed civilian lives into hell, while claiming that it wages "just wars" and that what is done to civilians is out of "necessity." The murder of thousands of civilians is collateral damage, announced every time as unintentional and accidental. Despite this monstrosity, they claim their wars are "civilized."

According to some Muslims, it appears that the civilian victims mean nothing in these "just wars" because they are Muslims. In regard to the death of 500,000 Iraqi children after the first Gulf war as a result of United States actions, Madeleine Albright, the former American Secretary of State, stated that, "we think the price is worth it." 500,000 children and the price is worth it! Oh God! It appears as though the rift between Islam and the West – which fights "morally" – is increasing day by day. They see the torture in the prisons as well as what is referred to as "ghost prisoners," who America hides in other countries where they are tortured. The exposure of all of these practices has begotten terrorism.

Without making excuses for jihadist violence, I would like to mention that, in the past, the most modern states and empires were built on carnage and bloodshed. It cannot be denied that Athens was built on slavery, bloodshed, and the oppression of women. Likewise, the United States was build on the extinction of native peoples and enslavement of millions of Africans, whose blood continues to flow until today.

The United States has signed bilateral agreements with 90 countries throughout the world preventing the legal referral of its fighters or civilians to the International Criminal Court. American military leaders usually avoid condemning their soldiers that have committed heinous crimes, so as "not to weaken the troops' morale." All of these facts are known and exposed and help terrorism expand, because Muslims see that the strong states protect their citizens, while caring not about what they do to the world's weak.

CHAPTER SIX

THE PRESENT AND THE FUTURE

ISIS and Religious Scholars

Research on the opinions of religious scholars regarding ISIS's practices and their usage of religious references has shown that the majority of senior Sunni scholars have negative opinions on ISIS, both those whom ISIS calls "court" scholars, and those scholars who enjoy independence from the rulers.

Scholars consider that ISIS is fastidious, radical, and exceeding proper bounds. It has not limited its excess and radicalism to itself alone, but forces it on others through violence and force in complete ignorance of the Prophetic hadith, "Make things easy and do not make them difficult, cheer the people up by conveying glad tidings to them and do not repulse (them)," and, in the scholars' opinions, it is not acting in accordance with the moderateness encouraged by the Quran.

Most scholars believe that ISIS is committing wrongdoings by carelessly declaring so many Muslims to be infidels, while killing them and regarding their blood permissible to shed.

Scholars condemn ISIS's low opinion of the great majority of Muslims, its arrogance regarding its own members, and its reference to its supporters as the party of truth. This henceforth means that the great majority of Muslims are the party of falsehood.

We are aware of ISIS's ignorance of the Islamic jurisprudence that takes consequences into account, and its carelessness about the implications of its actions. Scholars claim that most of its actions depend on "the young people," who lack scholarly experience and do not take knowledge from its sources and from clerics. Thus, its legal opinion on grave matters is given without knowledge. As an example of the weakness of ISIS's Islamic knowledge, scholars mention its revival of slavery. This has led some scholars to say that they resemble the Kharijites, who condemned Ali for "fighting but not enslaving women." Scholars believe that Islamic knowledge should come before words and actions in Islam, to which they quote Imam al-Bukhari's saying that: "It is essential to know a thing first before saying or acting upon it," which is based on God's word: {Know that there is no deity worthy of worship except Allah.} Scholars do not accept ISIS's fatwas on most matters, nor do they acknowledge it putting forward opinions as if it has a monopoly on absolute truth.

ISIS is hostile to different opinions, and refuses to accept legal analysis from any scholars other than its own. Its excuse is that its scholars are mujahedeen, and that "A non-Mujahed does not impose fatwas on a Mujahed." This is an old statement attributed to Zayd ibn Ali, may God be pleased with him, and it has been said that the Imam Abu Hanifa al-Numan allowed and supported such a saying. However, ISIS does not take into consideration the contexts or circumstances that surrounded such a saying, or that taking sayings out of context usually leads to error. ISIS, with this rule, wants to insulate its actions from criticism and repel opposition.

Islamic scholars disapprove of ISIS's treatment of the Christians of Mosul, having frightened them until it led some of them to flee the city. The Prophet (PBUH) has stated that, "He who hurts a dhimmi hurts me"; for this reason, scholars were shocked to see unjust treatment of the Christians, because they had not committed anything that called for such treatment. Moreover, ISIS's actions have a negative effect on the image of Islam and Muslims throughout the world.

Scholars do not accept ISIS's claims that all Shiites are infidels, nor do they accept identity-based killings.

ISIS clings to the literal meanings of partial texts without taking into consideration the complete Sharia meanings. It acts rashly on disconnected parts without placing them into historical contexts and circumstances, and takes texts apart without joining them to others. Sometimes, ISIS makes decisions based on a single text while completely ignoring others that may explain the situation or shed light on some of its differing aspects; thus, its vision is fragmented. It appears that its scholars, due to their youth and lack of experience, do not distinguish between the absolute text and the unrestricted, the specific that applies over the general, or the Prophet's particularities, according to the professor and sheikh, Essam Ahmed al-Bashir.

ISIS lawmakers are accused of paying little attention to the principles of Islamic jurisprudence, which reveal the provisions of the Sharia from top to bottom. ISIS has disregarded gradualism in implementing the Sharia, in the same way that it lacks knowledge of the jurisprudence of stages and the jurisprudence of outcomes. Here, we would like to quote the professor and sheikh, Essam al-Bashir, who said that, "The fatwa is composed of three elements: the legal text and its intention, then the current state and its outcomes, and finally the connection between the current state and the legal text." The text must be understood and explained, and efforts must be made to implement it well in a particular context. ISIS scholars barely understand anything about the importance of implementing the text in a particular context so as to ensure positive outcomes. According to researchers, proof of that is its revival of slavery in the 21st century, with implications that were a curse on Islam's international image.

Some scholars, including Yusuf al-Qaradawi, believe that Sayyid Qutb exaggerated in his view that society has reverted to the Jahiliyya state of ignorance. Because ISIS scholars care not for true scholarship and lack knowledge, they have failed to distinguish between which of Qutb's views were and which were not a transgression, taking them literally without grasping their goals. They have failed to grasp the overwhelming circumstances under which Qutb wrote some of his books. They have even come to consider him a legal authority, likewise taking the writings of Ibn Taymiyyah out of context.

ISIS scholars have been accused of accepting Sayyid Qutb and Abul A'la Maududi's sayings on *Hakimiyya, and their sayings,* are not widely accepted by most prominent scholars.

Today, Islamic legal matters and rulings released centuries ago must be reviewed in a way that acknowledges the developments in people's political lives. However, ISIS wants to preserve the way life was in the first centuries of Islam, which has led them to commit grave errors.

ISIS takes accusing people of apostasy too far, making it too easy. It calls anyone who opposes the Caliphate, or criticizes its policies, an apostate. For example, its scholars do not differentiate between those who do or do not agree with Sharia law; thus, there are two different kinds of apostasy. ISIS refers to all leaders as apostates, without differentiating between those who openly oppose Islam and those who agree that Islam is the state religion with

Sharia as the legal basis; but they have somehow erred or been lazy in applying Sharia. (Dr. Essam al-Bashir).

To support this idea, ISIS has depended on Sayyid Qutb's excesses in his interpretation of *hakimiyya* and accusing societies of infidelity, which has been condemned by prominent scholars. It has ignored the Prophet's hadith, "If anyone says to his brother, 'O misbeliever! Then surely, one of them such."

ISIS considers itself a representation of "the Muslim community," not "a Muslim community." Without undergoing the Islamic process of consultation, it has chosen a Caliph to govern all Muslims. The Caliph rules all Muslims in a domineering and oppressive way. Implementing the controversial "Sent by the Sword" hadith, it implements Islamic punishments mercilessly on all, whereas God's Messenger had been sent as a mercy to all the worlds. ISIS has led many astray, because it has made Islam appear to be a religion of war, harm, swords and severity, whereas it had been characterized by flexibility to the extent that implementing certain punishments would be paused in emergency situations, including famines and wars.

When violating major rules in Islam, ISIS does not differentiate between covenantee, protégé and peaceful Westerners. Their fault is that they are from the West, and thus it holds them responsible for the governments with which they likely disagree regarding policies in Muslim countries. This failure to differentiate has defamed Islam and made it appear to be a barbaric and savage religion that does not respect agreements or pacts.

ISIS: A Revolutionary Movement

If we exclude the religious aspect of ISIS, then – aside from having revived slavery – it is no different than revolutionary movements that have preceded it. Regarding the use of violence to control territory and adopting lofty ambitions, ISIS, according to Stephen Walt, is no different than the French, Bolshevik, Iranian, or Chinese revolutions. Scott Atran has recently also referred to ISIS as a revolution.

All of these revolutions were hostile to prevailing international norms, and all of them used ruthless violence to eliminate or blackmail their enemies and opponents. All of them displayed their power to the world.

Revolutions pose a danger when they involve great powers. For the Bolshevik and Chinese revolutions, involving states with large populations and many resources provided them with the opportunity to spread their ideas throughout the world.

On that basis, it does not appear that ISIS, as a revolutionary movement, is able to expand and spread its beliefs internationally, for reasons including a low population and limited resources. Let alone the negative image it created for itself worldwide.

According to Walt, the similarities between ISIS and previous revolutions are that they all "portray their opponents as evil, hostile, and incapable of reform." The Bolshevik revolution argued that capitalism was incapable of reform and would fall as a result of its innate contradictions. Yet the revolution cannot wait for it to collapse on its own like a ripe fruit.

Mao Zedong believed that while imperialism was a tiger, it was a "paper tiger." He would say that, "the imperialists will never lay down their butcher knives" against the revolution. Khomeini would instruct his followers to "squeeze the Shah's neck until he is strangled." Similarly, the French revolution viewed Europe's monarchies as corrupt, unjust, and incapable of reform. ISIS believes that Islamic and non-Islamic governments are no different, all of them infidels or apostates.

Another similarity, Walt continues, between ISIS as a revolutionary movement and other revolutions is that they all view their model as universally applicable, able to liberate the world, and able to establish a perfect world. The French revolution called for a "crusade for universal liberty." Marxism-Leninism viewed that its revolution would produce a classless world, and Khomeini believed that his revolution was the first step towards bringing down the nationalist, un-Islamic states, and creating a global Islamic community on its ashes. ISIS believes that its message applies to the entire world, which is the general opinion of Muslims regarding Islam's appropriateness, even if the ISIS model differs from that of the main current of Islamism.

Another similarity is that all revolutions inspire foreigners to join them. Thousands of anti-monarchical elements swarmed from across Europe to Paris during the French revolution, and people from around the world went to Russia to support the Bolshevik revolution. Stephen Walt states that the most prominent Westerner to have gone to Russia at the time was the social activist and Harvard graduate, John Reed. Similarly, thousands have joined ISIS from around the world.

Revolutions usually terrify existing regimes. In Great Britain and Russia, the French revolution worried the ruling monarchies. Similarly, the West, especially the United States, was disturbed by the Communist revolution, trying to confine it using McCarthyism. Similarly, all states throughout the world today have expressed their worry about the spread of ISIS.

Revolutions generate a flood of refugees that usually paint a largely unrealistic picture of the situation. Heeding the advice of refugees regarding the governments against which revolutions were started has usually resulted in the adoption of incorrect policies. We are still quoting Walt.

If the ruling power that gained control as a result of a revolution endures, then the revolution eventually "cools off" years after the revolutionaries' rule, slowly becoming moderate.

This happened in the Soviet Union's last ten years, and in China starting with the early 1970s. It also happened in Iran this year when Iran made amends with "the great Satan," as it used to call the United States. Thus, the same will happen to ISIS in the rare case that it endures.

Revolutions usually market and sell a "basket of ideas" that contains illusions, dreams, hopes, myths, and facts, all mixed together. However, revolutionary zeal blurs the revolutionaries' vision, making it difficult for them to distinguish between what is and is not true. In the name of these ideas, the revolutionaries kill people. The Bolshevik revolution killed millions, the French revolution killed thousands, and ISIS continues to kill today. These are the facts, but no matter how many people previous revolutions killed, it does not excuse the killing of a single person for opposing the revolution's ideals, regardless of which revolution it may be.

Ideas on the Present and the Future

Jihad is a complex phenomenon whose rise is the result of various interwoven factors. Some of these factors are political, some religious, and some can be attributed to the development of the international jihadist movement and its achievements. Some of these factors are shared Muslim desires to reinstate the Caliphate that connected the Muslim community for over a thousand years. The least prominent factor is undoubtedly the social one, since the people that join jihadist movements come from varying social classes. If we assume factors of social frustration – such as unemployment – are the main push factor, joining such a movement is basically suicide. It is unlikely that an unemployed person will seek to get closer to a movement that chucks him into the throes of battle, likely leading to his death, only because he cannot find a job. Among the jihadists are those that held respected positions in their countries, those that come from countries that find work for the unemployed, and those who were exceptional in their universities.

Explaining why people join such movements with the economic factor alone is to employ the single factor theories that have been proved wrong (Communism). Claims that people join because of religious or legal texts alone only skirts the truth, for global jihad is new, while the text is old. However, it is true that the text interacts with a complex reality, influenced heavily by textual factors; thus, a reality must exist with which the text can interact.

The different schools in the jihadist movement – including ISIS – all long to "apply the law of God and revive the Caliphate," though they differ in the methods and timing. They all believe that secularism, democracy, patriotism and nationalism are incorrect paths with varying levels of wrongness. ISIS disagrees with al-Qaeda regarding the necessity of pledging allegiance to the Caliph, considering anyone who does not do so to be a tyrant. The tyrannical group of Muslims should be fought in accordance with ISIS's jurisprudence. ISIS also disagrees with al-Qaeda regarding timing the announcement of the Caliphate, which it sees as an end to the conflicts and divisions among Muslims. However, the disagreement has grown into permitting the spilling of blood. Al-Qaeda believes that ISIS transformed the notion of jihad into feuds and revenge, and has warned it of taking liberties in bloodletting and declaring someone's apostasy. It condemns ISIS's extremism and excess, as well as its lack of flexibility in absorbing reality's transformations. Legalists that are a part of the jihadist current have condemned

ISIS for disassociating itself from the restrictions decided upon by jihadist leadership, such as Ayman al-Zawahiri. They believe that this will lead to the rise of those who lack knowledge and understanding of the jurisprudence of jihad. In their fighting, they will thus equate piety with debauchery. This departure from the legal constraints of jihad may lead to the appearance of numerous schools, thus facilitating fragmentation and separation.

The contradictions are noticeable in the Islamic State's actions when it fights those with whom it shares ideological beliefs, while accepting allegiance from those with whom it does not share ideological beliefs – some of whom are criminals – under the pretense that they have repented "before the coming of their judgment."

Before we move to subsidiary matters of debate between al-Qaeda and the Islamic State, we would like to point to the Arab Spring revolutions. They formed a major challenge for al-Qaeda because they struck at its main argument – that change in any way but jihad is impossible. The Arab Spring proved that change through peaceful methods – the democratic method – is in fact possible.

It has been noticed that al-Qaeda's response came late and was marked with confusion, even if it was, in quite a generalized way, blessed by al-Zawahiri.

The Arab Spring revolutions pushed the trend of peaceful change forward. This was especially true after Islamists such as the Muslim Brotherhood and some of their Salafist allies rose to power through polls in some Arab Spring countries.

Chafic Choucair, specialist in jihadist movements, believes that "al-Qaeda and others were definitely at one point shocked by the rapid success of the revolutions in overthrowing the regimes," and that when it tried to answer the questions posed by the revolutions' success – as appeared to be the case at the beginning — "it tried to place the peaceful revolution in the context of mechanisms that it accepts and does not reject, considering the fact that it is a step towards complete change." When the debate between al-Qaeda and ISIS intensified and a war of words broke out, some of ISIS's claims against al-Qaeda were that it "accepted appealing to the taghut," by which they mean democracy, and that it did not accuse prominent Muslim Brotherhood members of apostasy despite them being "more evil than the secularists," according to ISIS's official spokesperson, Abu Mohammad al-Adnani. It condemned al-Zawahiri for accepting democracy because he did not condemn Morsi's election, which they viewed as a clear sign of apostasy.

ISIS believes that al-Zawahiri contradicted himself when he agreed with the Arab revolutions and peaceful change. It believes that he followed the Muslim Brotherhood method, which al-Qaeda had previously opposed and for which it presented itself as a replacement.

ISIS went as far as to accuse al-Qaeda of following the Murji'a and Jahmi methods, thereby referring to a sect that Imam Malik ibn Anas and al-Shafi'i's sheikh, Waki' ibn al-Jarrah, had deemed infidels. The Jahmiyya do not believe in almighty God's elevation over his throne, and they do not denounce the major sins. They postpone all reprehensible actions to the afterlife, and do not believe that any Muslim is responsible – whether he is the Caliph or emir of the Muslims – for punishing any sin or crime that is committed. They deny the attributes of Almighty God.

Chafic Choucair believes that the Islamic State deduced the most extreme meanings from the al-Qaeda rules. By announcing the Caliphate, it hopes to legitimize the laws it exaggerated in deducing as well as its selection of a Caliph, which has been criticized by al-Qaeda jurists. Al-Qaeda accuses Islamic State jurists of lacking legal experience, overdoing their labeling of people as infidels, disrespecting people's souls, and contesting the legitimacy of al-Baghdadi's Caliphate.

Al-Qaeda's stance on the Islamic State may expose its inner rifts, especially due to the fact that al-Qaeda has a legacy and historical legitimacy amongst the jihadists. This is despite the fact that someone less charismatic than Bin Laden is now heading it. Al-Qaeda has supporters that attack the Islamic State's actions, including Abu Qatada al-Filistini and Abu Muhammad al-Maqdisi.

Al-Zawahiri used to oppose classifying all Shiites as infidels. His advice was to avoid targeting Iran, due to the fact that it had detained dozens of al-Qaeda members, some of which were senior leadership, including al-Qaeda's first security official, Seif el-Yazal. It is strange that, until now, ISIS has heeded the second piece of al-Zawahiri's advice by not targeting Iran. However, it has not heeded the first piece related to Shiites. It thus appears to be flexible and attendant to political considerations externally, yet severe, ruthless, and barbaric with those inside of its territories, according to a number of experts.

Al-Zawahiri opposes ISIS's killing and slaughtering because of its negative effect on jihad's international image, and the image of the jihadist movement among Muslims ,that it is keen to win them over. ISIS applies – literally – the theories of Abu Abdullah al Muhajir (Abdul Rahman al Ali) and Abu Bakr Naji, author of *The Management of Savagery*. Al Muhajir believes that Islam does not distinguish between civilians and military personnel, stating that, "the brutality of beheading is intended, even delightful to God and His Prophet." Naji on the other hand, whose book we discussed earlier, believes that, "Today we are in a situation similar to that of early apostasy and the beginnings of jihad, therefore, we need massacre and to do just as has been done to Banu Qurayza [massacring their men, the taking their women and children as spoils, and taking their possessions]," which entails enslaving women and children, and seizing finances. (Banu Qurayza were a Jewish tribe during the time of Prophet Muhamad.)

Undoubtedly, the focus of most Iraqi fighters factions was on defeating the British-U.S occupation and liberating their country. They did not consider the blatant dogmatic commitment to be a priority. However, the political and security vacuum that followed the fighters' operations is what provided al-Qaeda the opportunity to expand and reach its peak under the umbrella of the Islamic State. It is certain that the militarization of protest in Syria, and the control of Syrian factions on areas of land in northern and eastern Syria, led to a security vacuum that simplified ISIS's expansion to this territory. According to ISIS, they were not the most religious of factions.

ISIS has continued to not acknowledge the Sykes-Picot agreement, which created borders between the states of the Greater Syria region. It also refuses to acknowledge the United Nations, the paper currency system, or systems of nationality. Al-Baghdadi announced that Syria and Iraq are not for the Syrians and Iraqis alone, but that the state is for all Muslims. Thus, he has called for "migration" in the religious sense of the word.

The jihadists base their rulings on Sharia, which to them is synonymous with jurisprudence. Meanwhile, the widespread understanding among Muslim scholars is that Sharia represents definitive guiding rulings as revealed in the Quran and Sunnah. On the other hand, jurisprudence is the human interpretation of these sacred texts, which may be correct or incorrect. Dr. Motaz al-Khateeb has a solid opinion against those who explain the emergence of jihadist currents by attributing the phenomenon to texts said by jurists. According to al-Khateeb, this line of thinking is incorrect because jurisprudence also led to the moderate Muslim Brotherhood current. Thus, those who ascribe these currents to jurisprudence are, in his opinion, falling captive to the jihadists' rhetoric. Al-Khateeb believes that, "The very same possibilities enabled by that Islamic doctrine are the ones used by the Muslim Brotherhood, which is the diametrical opposite of groups like ISIS. In other words, ancient religious texts, in and of themselves, cannot explain the new emergence of phenomena like the Islamic State." Many Western experts have also supported the idea of the antiquity of the text in comparison with the newness of the jihadist phenomena, which thus means that there is no link between them.

Researchers believe that ISIS jihadists will certainly make reforms because they have, on one hand, "reached the utmost level of saturation with the idea of jihad," and on the other, due to the increase of international pressures. Undoubtedly, ISIS jihadists are set on continuing the jihadist state of affairs; thus, these two factors (that of satiation and of the pressures) will force ISIS to works towards saving the jihadist state of affairs from collapsing or weakening.

It is true that ISIS agrees with al-Qaeda ideologically, even if they disagree in terms of implementing rulings and timing, as well as in the level of severity, which has led al-Qaeda to appear relatively moderate. However, ISIS has taken al-Qaeda's idea of jihad to the state level. This requires legal approaches that operate on the same level, which poses a legal problem and requires an understanding of international political contexts and a level of flexibility. However, the fact that ISIS does not recognize international contexts, and the international community is not prepared to recognize ISIS poses an existential threat to ISIS and has complicated matters.

The jihadist currents grew out of the seeds spread by the experience in Afghanistan. They grew out of an environment where the constricting authoritarian approach was the norm, dealing with the public with confiscation, exclusion, marginalization, and even contempt and guardianship. Decades ago, this approach could have continued. It would have been supported by international conditions and the lack of modern technologies that have made people interconnected, giving citizens the ability to comprehend the state of affairs throughout the world, and leading to an increase in ambitions, demands, and desires. There is another factor – Western hegemony – that has served as the fuel for the engine in moving jihadists from their countries over to distant horizons. The perseverance of these two factors will lead to the growth of jihad. It is certain that every foreign involvement in Muslim countries will give birth to new currents, and help existing ones develop. Muslims consider Israel equivalent to Western interference, viewing it a Western body implanted forcibly inside of them. Thus, even without new Western involvement, there will be instability as long as this implanted Western body is present, forming a reason for new jihadist currents to be born in order to fight against it. The resistance against Israel or foreign interference in Muslim countries will not be restricted to only religious Muslims.

With that said, security and military solutions will not stop the phenomenon of jihad. These solutions do not address the ideas that make up the issue's core, nor do they address the political conditions that are at its root. Addressing political beliefs and ideas must be accompanied by policies of integration that put an end to exclusion, increase participation, and respond to aspects of the Islamic religious and cultural component. This last component is of the utmost importance, because the dissimilarity of ruling policies and cultural component, and its leaning towards Western culture, represents one of the strongest causes of rebellion against the regimes that are accused of depending on the West – and the West has quite a bad reputation among Muslims.

Even though military solutions may achieve a temporary calm, they will not achieve enduring peace and stability because they will not address the roots of the problem and the sources of its eruption and growth.

It is sad that, because of the use and abuse of certain words in the American war campaigns against Iraq and Afghanistan, these terms have completely lost their meaning and nullify. The repetition of these words now draws sarcasm. For example, the Pentagon indicated eight goals for its war in Iraq, which included: "To end sanctions and immediately deliver humanitarian relief, food and medicine to the displaced and to the many needy Iraqi citizens." In the book *Violence, Politics, and Humanitarian Action*, Rony Brauman and Pierre Salignon remind the reader that the United States called the operation of invading Afghanistan "Operation Enduring Freedom," and the Iraqi invasion "Operation Iraqi Freedom." In both countries, the president stated that his goal was to actualize democracy, invigorate progress, and develop the country. This nullification led to the abuse and misuse of the words democracy, freedom, humanitarianism, progress, and development by the West regarding any Islamic country, rousing sarcasm every time they are used.

The al-Qaeda sympathizer I had met in Istanbul mocked such discourse, erupting in laughter and joking that, "this type of freedom is made in America." This is perhaps the first time in the history of humanity when freedom has lead to destruction – the destruction of two countries.

When American forces were bombing Afghanistan, bombs were dropped with pamphlets that commanded Afghanis to, "stay where you are and we will take care of your food situation!" Ready meals did in fact drop down to the people, but they were not enough. During his speech on October 7, 2001, Bush described the meals as a call to "the oppressed people of Afghanistan … to know the American generosity … as we strike military targets, we will also drop food, medicine and supplies to the starving and suffering men and women and children of Afghanistan." The al-Qaeda sympathizer commented on this statement, saying, "How great is the humanitarianism accompanied by explosions and children's corpses … yet again America comes up with a new invention called the humanization of war … and condemning war is not permitted!"

In 33 countries, laws were passed criminalizing joining terrorist groups and supporting them in any way, punishable in different ways. The Security Council released a resolution requiring each country to criminalize terrorist organizations. It was noticed that the United Nations' resolution was broad and loose, lacking precision in its definition and description of what was meant by "terrorism" or a "terrorist act," and does not take some aspects of " the international conventions on human rights in to consideration. Thus, the Security Council released a resolution concerning "foreign terrorist fighters" allowing states to define whomever they pleased as a terrorist. Such a resolution allows states to take repressive measures, which stirs the contempt, anger, and bitterness of Muslims, and encourages them to join terrorist organizations. Instead of making the world more peaceful, this resolution will lead to the exact opposite – making it tenser. As an example of the oppressive policies and decisions this decree allowed states to implement, a state to whom this applied advised its citizens under the age of 35 years to not travel to holy places for the purposes of performing the pilgrimage; thus, it restricted their religious rights. Because of this resolution, many states began increasingly bothering their citizens by passing laws that limited their rights.

Given the prevailing notion that terrorist organizations are Islamic, this resolution, and laws passed as a result of it across a number of countries, will restrict the freedoms and rights of Muslims. In its right, this will increase Muslims' feelings of marginalization, being targeted, and the increase of Islamophobia. As a result, it will make them easy prey for jihadist organizations.

This resolution and laws passed as a result will add to the endless laws that many countries have passed, including countries considered democratic, that transform citizens' lives into what it would be like to live in a police state because of surveillance procedures on their communications, movements, and relationships, which still have not led to a decrease in terrorist activity. Human rights organizations have criticized these laws, giving the example of the German law that allowed the state to confiscate passports of people it deemed threats to security, replacing them with identification cards that have written on them: "Not permitted to travel outside of Germany." The organizations have stated that this card will be a stigma that makes all aspects of life in Germany difficult for the carrier. The organizations also gave the example of a state that jails its citizens on the account of potentially having connections to "terrorist" jihadist organizations for long periods of time without trial. A third state passed a legally vague law that used general phrases such as causing damage to the state's reputation, or seeding discord in the society. Such decisions and laws strengthen ISIS by increasing the number of people willing to join.

The Islamic State uses a black flag as its banner. This is a symbol of a banner that is attractive to all Muslims, because it is one of the banners of the Prophet (PBUH); thus, this is a symbol that implores people to join the Islamic State. It also points to the banner of the Abbasid dynasty, which represents the golden age of Islamic civilization, and ruled the area from North Africa and all of the Middle East until Central Asia. It is noteworthy that the Jews historically considered the black banner to be a warning sign, but Muslims saw it as a positive inspiration.

The jihadist theorist Abu Bakr Naji, who wrote *Management of Savagery* may have influenced ISIS. He wrote that the Abbasid state was built, strengthened, and expanded because it used extremism and ruthlessness. Thus, the jihadists must follow their example and not show any mercy on their opponents. However, jihadist theorists selectively apply this by taking parts of the entire picture and neglecting the majority. The Abbasid Caliphate was cosmopolitan. It built relationships with states, and its rulers exchanged gifts with kings and emperors. The Abbasid Caliph gave a watch as a gift to Emperor Charlemagne. In the Abbasid Caliphate, sects of Jews, Christians, Persians, and Turks lived in safety. The Caliphate was filled with diversity. The al-Qaeda sympathizer I had met in Istanbul tried to make excuses for ISIS by telling me that the Abbasid Caliphate had not got this far in one day, and that ISIS is still in the establishment or formation phase.

Undoubtedly, the kind reader has noticed that, as a rule backed by history, major military defeats pave the way for the rejection of and grievance toward the regime that led to the defeat. This rejection and grievance leads to thoughts of establishing an alternative regime to rival the defeated one. This may explain the establishment of the Muslim Brotherhood movement, which accused the Khedive regime of weakness in facing the colonial powers. This may also explain the rise of the Islamic Party of Liberation after the defeat of 1948 – the loss of Palestine – as well as the emergence of Hamas, furious with how the Fatah organization was administering the Palestinian situation, and the defeat of the Arabs in their wars against Israel.

This rejection has been applied to every nation state in the Middle East and its half secular model. Islamists accuse it of weakness and dependence and of opposing established cultural norms. They accuse it of failing in modernization as well as in integrating the varying racial and sectarian parts of the state; thus, it has remained weak. The Islamists presented the Islamic alternative in varying degrees on the Islamist spectrum. However, the jihadists chose the violent current due to their disappointment with the effectiveness of peaceful alternatives, and their conviction that many internal and external powers would not allow the continuation of a peaceful Islamic alternative, even if it was the decision of the masses.

The jihadist stance led to the rejection of the democratic option as a political model without proposing an alternative to political participation that would include all other political powers and currents. This will eventually create a challenge and spread seeds of dissent inside the Islamic State, if a miracle occurs and its existence persists.

The public will not accept remaining under the control of the one model enforced by the Islamic State. If it finds that methods of political expression are closed off to it, then it may turn to external powers to support it against ISIS, which would be relatively simple considering that the Islamic State has spared no state without declaring its hostility towards it, since it categorizes anyone that opposes it as an infidel or an apostate. On the other hand, this polarization made by the Islamic State will make it impossible for al-Baghdadi to actualize his "general authority" over all Muslims.

Democracy went through many stages before reaching its current state as in the West. During its initial stages, the English required the ability to read and write in order for an English citizen to be permitted to vote. The excuse was that the political process required the voter to know the programs offered by competing candidates, which is not possible if a person is illiterate. At one point, they required voters to meet a financial minimum under the pretense that anyone who did not have money could not vote responsibly because his vote may be bought. Even women were not allowed to vote, leading to the suffragette movement and the law that became known as the "Cat and Mouse

Act" during the time of protests by women demanding the right to vote, which theygained in 1928. Democracy did not reach its current state until national consensus was achieved, as was the acceptance of national fundamentals and principals to guide the democratic system.

I thus believe that the success of the democratic system in countries where social cohesion has yet to be achieved is difficult. Similarly, these countries are rife with illiteracy and poverty, and its people are not in agreement regarding national fundamentals concerning political work. This does not mean that the matter should be left to a dictator, but that a participatory design must be reached, taking into consideration historical effects and economic, cultural, and social assumptions.

When the Americans invaded Iraq, they imposed on the Iraqis a democratic system without paying any mind to the social, sectarian, and historical factors that were reacting within Iraqi society. Precursors to an explosion were at work in the depths of Iraqi society, but Saddam had silenced them with force. The Americans imposed a system that would protect individual rights, but ignored the sectarian identities in a country where they play a highly significant role.

I once read that a leader of the Iraqi Islamic Call Party said after the invasion that, "Iraq was nothing more than a donkey and rider." The Sunnis were the rider, and the Shiites were the donkey. Now, the time has come for the Shiites to be the rider. The Shiite leader's concern was not to spread democracy or ensure rights but to merely ensure that his people became the riders. When the Shiites tried to implement this theory, the Sunnis revolted, creating resistance factions and embracing al-Qaeda until it was weakened by the Sunni Awakening movement. But the American formula was not to be successful, and the the entire country failed to achieve the required political stability.

From 1991 until today, America, the United Kingdom, and their allies have waged three wars in Iraq. After America withdrew forces in 2011, the rise of ISIS forced them to enter a third war, even if it was without ground forces. My belief is that the jihadists will be thrilled if America sends ground forces because they will see it as an opportunity to rub its nose in the ground, as they say. Their main thinker, Abu Bakr Naji, has instructed them to try and get America to fight them directly, instead of what he calls through their proxy war. He believes that weakening America's prestige is crucial for defeating the regimes that depend on and are supported by the United States. Thus, it is expected that ISIS will continue to harass America until they come with their horses and their men to the ISIS region: ISIS will then cry out "this is what we wanted!"

The Sunnis believe that air strikes against ISIS are supporting the ethnic groups and sects that oppose them, mainly the Kurds and the Shiites. The American forces have bombed ISIS over 3,000 times, intensifying strikes after ISIS began fighting the Peshmerga in Ayn al-Arab and Tell Abyad. America bombs ISIS but not the Shiite militias, whom they believe to be worse than ISIS. The Kurds and the Arabs – particularly the Sunnis – are not in agreement and their misunderstanding increased after the Peshmerga seized the oil city of Kirkuk and implemented a program of demographic change by moving Kurds from different areas to the city, according to Iraqi testimonies. To the Sunnis, ISIS, despite its savagery, is their protector against the Shiites. Thus, they believe that weakening it through warfare will mean that they will be subjected to a new wave of oppression, which is precisely what creates new jihadists. Unfortunately, the violent conditions in the region have transformed "religious identities" into extremist ethnic groups. This is clearly visible in the relationship between the Sunnis and the Shiites, and the Sunnis and the Alawites. This ferocious fighting has the possibility to lead to "ethnic cleansing," or "religious cleansing," when fighting is based on identity.

We previously mentioned that the Montevideo Convention, a part of international law, makes ISIS a state since recognition is not one of the conditions of statehood. There is no body commissioned with releasing recognition documents. We also mentioned that ISIS is Islamic, despite its selectiveness in the Quran and Sunnah texts it depends on, and its literalness in understanding and implementing these texts, and this is what will harm it. Graham Fuller has described ISIS's method in choosing from the texts as being selective in order to achieve its political strategy of establishing an Islamic Caliphate. This idea has been created and shaped by political circumstances that have been described as pressure, frustration, the closing off of all horizons, and the difficulty of expressing oneself verbally or organizationally, thus leading to extremism. The high-pressure environment that dictatorship creates usually leads to extremism because it closes off all horizons and leads people to rebel and radicalize. There is a correlation between dictatorship (and injustice) and extremism. An extremist can become a dictator if he is given the opportunity, and a dictator creates the extremist with his injustice. When an idea gets radicalized, it paves the way for violence out of fear that other methods will fail to get rid of injustice. The more unjust a political regime gets, the more violence and extremism increases.

Getting back to what we had said about the selectiveness and literalness of ISIS, we believe that this literalness will prevent ISIS from absorbing the changes that are happening in the lives of Muslims. Muslims believe that Islam is suitable for any time and place, and some Islamists often raise the slogan of "Islam is the solution." This means that Islam should be able to respond to all social changes that occur in human life.

All extremist ideas developed in environments of failure, injustice, and desperation. You find that Nazism, according to Fuller, would not have developed if it were not for the destruction and vengeful sanctions from the Allies that Germany faced after World War I. Lenin's Communist revolution would not have succeeded if it were not for the hopeless and miserable conditions the Tsardom of Russia experienced at the end of World War I. Thus, if it were not for the American invasion's destruction of the Iraqi state, preceded by the sanctions – imposed after the invasion of Kuwait – that destroyed Iraqi society and created an environment of desperation and feelings of injustice, the idea of jihad would not have found the appropriate context for its development. Those who joined ISIS from the West complain of injustices, including Islamophobia. Similarly, those who came from Muslim countries complain of local and international injustices, and a disbelief that peaceful paths could achieve their goals of getting rid of all injustice.

Proponents of violent methods chose the land of Syria and Iraq. This piece of the world did not choose them voluntarily. Instead it was them who forced themselves upon it. However, the area excused them because it thought that they would be better than their predecessors.

Those who rebuke ISIS's violent method are faced with numerous difficulties. For most Muslims, most clerics are considered to be "court" jurists, and most Muslims do not buy the Western anti-ISIS rhetoric. They accuse the West of losing its moral high ground, referencing its colonial history and near past in Palestine, Iraq, and Afghanistan. With that said, the solution to this dilemma likely lies in a political formula that would integrate even the extremist powers, bringing back political and social balance in order to defuse the tension.

During my time as a diplomat in Washington D.C in 1994, the U.S Department of State hosted the Sudanese ambassador Mr. Ahmed Suleiman. At the time, it expressed its discontent with Bin Laden's presence in Sudan. The ambassador asked the Department of State, after an appropriate introduction, why they did not ask themselves why a millionaire would sacrifice all of the joys he could achieve with his money to instead accept living in poor countries, where he suffers, as is the case in Sudan and Afghanistan? Could he not buy an island and live a life of plenty and opulence instead? The American diplomats fell silent, unable to respond.

Despite the Western media attack on Bin Laden, he remained popular among Muslims, according to opinion polls conducted after September 11th. In comparison with ISIS, bin Laden used to take into consideration the implications of al-Qaeda's actions, especially after September 11th. For this reason, he opposed al-Zarqawi's excesses and the liberties he took in shedding blood.

Al-Qaeda was thus considered "moderate" after the appearance of ISIS. The Muslim public did not doubt ISIS's good intentions and understood that many of the fighters sacrificed pleasant living conditions to come to ISIS territory, suffer unfavorable conditions, and even expose themselves to the possibility of death. However, they do doubt the correctness of their way of expressing their religiosity. They believe that ISIS's religious method does not grant preachers the opportunity to make the claim that Islam is consistent with the spirit of the times, or that it is a religion that is at peace with non-Muslims. The ISIS method does not consider the negative effect its actions have on the image and attractiveness of Islam; thus, it has harmed religion when its goal was to fix it. These Muslims believe that positive intentions themselves do not mean correctness.

Most of ISIS's economy depends on smuggling oil that it sells to middlemen for about half of the global price; its economy thus lacks diversity. In addition, ISIS is exposed to a system of international sanctions and an embargo harsher than what any other country has been exposed to. ISIS cannot process business transactions with the world thus its banks operate locally, nor can it normally process financial transfers, even through financial transfer offices. This is all enough to suffocate ISIS economically, and there is no doubt that its financial situation is now worse than it was a year and a few months ago, as a result of the decrease in oil prices and an increase in the prices of goods. The public cannot withstand these economic pressures, even if the jihadists, who are prepared to live in severe conditions can. The worsening of economic conditions does not bother those who immigrated seeking martyrdom, but it does bother the general public.

ISIS has entered the "Meccan boycott of the Hashemites." It has become like the clan of Banu Hashim and the clan of Abdul-Muttalib, whom "no one should either buy from or sell to," but the world's states do not have an Amr ibn Hisham or Mut'im ibn 'Adi. ISIS itself is not in the position of the clan of Banu Hashim and the clan of Abdul-Muttalib, which would allow it a far greater ability to coerce. In our time, states are not able to live easily in a boycott.

It is now clear that the United States failed in "waging war" on terrorism, just as it failed in "waging peace" (because empires veer towards hegemony, not peacefulness). It continued to cover up its failure with masks, deceiving others and deceiving itself. How can it claim success, when the result is the appearance of ISIS, which is hundreds of times stronger than al-Qaeda, and has reached the level of creating a state in a region far more strategic than Afghanistan? Since the first year of the occupation in Iraq, the danger of its deceptive propaganda has been clear. This is because the occupation forces in Iraq, a year after the invasion, began to control isolated islands, but despite this the propaganda continued to present it as victorious. This is similar to how media propaganda stated that the regime of President Assad was about to fall in 2012. It has been proven that assassinating leadership will not bring down the jihadist movements, but it does offer the deception of reassurance. Bin Laden was killed, along with the great majority of his assistants. In Yemen, al-Awlaki and al-Wuhayshi were killed, and America claims to have killed half of the ISIS leadership with air strikes that started in August of 2014. Prior to that, that, when it fought al-Zarqawi, it killed or captures 34 out of 42 of his leaders. Nevertheless, all of this did not lead to achieving the desired results.

The simplification of the media narrative and the inflating of roles in portraying an unrealistic picture of the situation has a damaging effect. The American media finds pleasure in broadcasting scenes of fighting, in order to ensure greater viewership, following its rule of "if it bleeds, it leads." Simplification, or magnification, is the beginning, but it is followed by deception through journalists that work with military forces, otherwise known as embedded journalists. They cannot reflect anything aside from the official narrative. If they were to deviate from it, they would lose their opportunity to provide coverage for the military forces.

The magnification and exaggeration through the media narrative is not restricted to the West. ISIS uses the same method to try and paint a rosy picture of the reality of living conditions in its territories. It is impossible that the living conditions are easy and pleasant, due to the fact that they are in a period of war and embargo. It is confirmed that prices, especially bread prices, have increased, and that electricity fluctuates, even in the ISIS capital of

Raqqah. In addition, the bombardment creates danger, fear, and alarm that prevent a normal flow of life.

The jihadist movements control the flow of events in Syria because they are the strongest and most dangerous. Thus, the American vice president, along with the journalist Patrick Cockburn and many others have stated that that there are no "moderates" in the Syrian opposition. It seems that "moderation" only means secular or non-Islamic in the Western thinking, a conclusion very difficult for the majority of Muslims to understand. Generally speaking, the West ascribes "radicalization" to the Wahhabi doctrine, claiming that it is the intellectual origin that created radicalization and then terrorism. Cockburn has mentioned that, "The 'Wahhabisation' of mainstream Sunni Islam is one of the most dangerous developments of our era." He said that the war on terrorism did not achieve its goals because the West did not target Pakistan and Saudi Arabia. On September 2, 2015, the famous journalist Thomas Friedman wrote in the *New York Times* that, "The fact remains that Saudi Arabia's export of Wahhabi puritanical Islam has been one of the worst things to happen to Muslim and Arab pluralism — pluralism of religious thought, gender and education — in the last century."

Saudi Arabia and the Wahhabi doctrine have remained in the Western sights since September 11th. The Americans and the English lean towards forgetting their wrongdoings against others, and that these wrongdoings create extremism. According to many intelligent Westerners, are al-Qaeda, ISIS, and all other extremist organizations anything but a reaction to the heinous Western mistakes? Not all of the thousands that joined extremist groups belong to the Wahhabi sect, which in fact has not been known for using violence. The only time Wahhabis used violence was for a clear goal, which was uniting the Kingdom of Saudi Arabian, which was completed in 1934.

My close following of the relationship between the West and Saudi Arabia shows an intensity in Western media attacks against the Kingdom. Since mid-2015 I have counted more than 63 articles and reports against Saudi Arabia in prominent periodicals, newspapers and magazines. This negative campaign is paving the way and preparing the public opinion against Saudi Arabia. This in light of the IMF's report that states that Saudi Arabia's foreign reserves will amount to Zero by 2020 as a result of the drop in oil prices and high local expenditure within the Kingdom.

The campaign against the Kingdom of Saudi Arabia included even Hilary Clinton, who in 2010 claimed that Saudi Arabia was the largest funder of terrorism. In a 2013 study, the European Union echoed similar sentiments. They all reached for the easy explanations that lean towards denial – denial of their mistakes that have had extremist reactions.

ISIS is a radical reaction to these mistakes. I am certain that this radical reaction would have happened even if the Wahhabi doctrine did not exist. I believe it would have happened even if Islam did not exist, as long as there was injustice. Muhammad Ahmad al-Mahdi, a member of a Sufi order, re-belled, as did Abdelhamid Ben Badis, who was a follower of the al-Maliki sect in the Arabic Maghreb. Omar Mukhtar also rebelled, and not a single one of them was of the Wahhabi doctrine. Yasser Arafat and Khaled Mashal rebelled, and they were not Wahhabis. Mandela, Gandhi, Castro, Hugo Chávez, and Ho Chi Minh all rebelled, along with others, and not a single one of them was Muslim. Thus, the rule is that injustice begets radicalism, and hegemony is the biggest helper of radicalism.

Another simple and naïve analysis is the claims of some Islamists that ISIS was established by the American and Israeli intelligences. The illogical nature of this claim lies in the fact that America has killed and continues to seize any opportunity it gets to kill anyone associated with ISIS. The United States says that it has killed, until now, half of ISIS's leadership; thus, how can it kill and chase its own agents?

Some of the most dangerous effects and repercussions of the invasion of Iraq was the sectarian differentiation that came as a result of the invading Amer-ican forces' preference for the Shiite sect, while it marginalized and excluded the Sunnis. It is certain that the radicalization of al-Zarqawi, then al-Muhajir, and after them al-Baghdadi worsened the situation. The Sunnis rebelled, for-mulating militant factions and their tribes embraced al-Qaeda at the beginning of the invasion, thus leading to the widening of the rift between the two sects.

The rift between the Sunnis and the Shiites expanded from Afghanistan and Pakistan to include all Arab countries. With the arrival of Shiite militants from Afghanistan, Lebanon, and Iraq to participate in the fighting in Syria and Iraq, the sensitivities became more complex and widened. Sudan, Mo-rocco and Malaysia made decisions to close down *hussainiyat* and ban pro-motion of the Shiite doctrine. They learned their lesson from what happened in Yemen and other places, and took the decisions out of fear for the societal safety that was threatened by the Shiites that belonged to the Twelver branch.

It is unlikely that the two sides will eventually get closer, especially after the Iranian nuclear deal with prominent states, which will provide it with financial resources that the Sunnis fear will strengthen Iran with Western support aimed against them. The separation between the two sides may have reached the level of separation between the Catholics and Protestants during the religious reform movement in Europe during the 16th century. However, it is unlikely that the situation will end with Shiite victory, since they are the majority in only four out of 57 Muslim countries.

Sunni Muslims lean towards conspiracy theories, which is the lazy explanation for the situation. They repeat what was said by the American president Harry Truman during the Second World War, when he stated that, "If we see that Germany is winning the war, we ought to help Russia; and if that Russia is winning, we ought to help Germany, and in that way let them kill as many as possible." It is true that the United States did help both sides during the Iran-Iraq war (1980-1988). In the current tense environment between the Sunnis and the Shiites, and between Iran and most of the Arab states, attacking and eliminating ISIS without eliminating the Shiite militias will arouse bitter feelings from the Sunni public, despite ISIS's extremism. In this way, eliminating ISIS will remain a problem. It will remain, boiling underneath the surface, and will eventually explode, bringing back the cycle of violence once again.

The jihad phenomenon is complex and multi-faceted, and the "digital revolution" has enabled it to expand and spread. The digital revolution undid the monopoly of governments on media production, and undid the larger Western monopoly on the international media outpout, even if only slightly. This digital revolution allowed jihadist groups to produce films and media products at a low price, through which it has expanded its propaganda and battlefield beyond its geographical borders, leading to an increase in its influence.

As an example, when al-Qaeda released its film about the killing of the American journalist Daniel Pearl in 2002, few people saw it. Five years later, al-Zarqawi released his terror films, and hundreds of thousands saw it. Now, millions of people watch the ISIS films. According to the Daily Express, by the beginning of July of 2015, 42 million people supported ISIS. It has now been proved that propaganda through the media, or through words, has the same effect as actions. When it was rumored that al-Qaeda would spread Ricin poison in the London subway in 2002, a wave of fear spread over the people. When the rumor spread that al-Qaeda would spread cyanide gas in the New York subway in 2003, a wave of terror spread over the people. The danger of terrorism is that it obviously commits its terrifying act, but then anyone that hears of it, or watches a video about a terrorist act, begins to feel as if he is the victim. Thus, its indirect effect is its most effective.

President Obama has stated that the war against the jihadist movements will take a long time. According to Leon Panetta, former U.S Secretary of Defense, the war against terrorist groups will take 30 years. I am certain that this war will continue for generations, as long as we do not address the objective conditions that prepare the environment for the eruption of jihadist groups, and provides an impetus for them. I am certain that eliminating the jihadist or terrorist movements (whatever you wish to call them) is impossible. It is not good policy to bury our heads in the sand, and call them gangs, mafias, or criminals. The goal of gang members is living and receiving financial gain; thus, they are keen on protecting their lives and avoid death as much as possible. The jihadists, on the other hand, desire death as one of the best possible options. Third, I am certain that the jihadist movements will not be killed. It is easy to kill a person, but it is very difficult to kill an idea, regardless of my or your opinion of it.

ISIS is truly radical, for it accuses even those with whom it shares similar principles, such as Abu Mohammad al-Julani, of being infidels. It knows nothing of flexibility and smoothness, and takes liberties in killing and severity. As an example, we would like to mention that it published, in its magazine *Dabiq*, a call for women to divorce their husbands who opposed the Caliph al-Baghdadi, under the pretense that they are apostates.

On the other hand, it appears as though al-Qaeda has become more clever, experienced, and pragmatic. It also appears, from al-Julani's statements and actions, that he is cooperating with other Syrian factions, and that al-Nusra respects the Christians in Syria. Its leader states, referring to the members of Syrian factions, that "they are Muslims no different from us." In Yemen, al-Qaeda seized Al Mukalla, thus building relationships with the local community. When they saw that the locals were not excited about the implementation of Sharia law, they decided not to impose it, instead taking upon themselves not to administer the area, and were content with a police station to break up conflicts. Al-Julani also did not enforce Sharia over the places al-Nusra gained control, and was content with preaching.

A rebellion movement must flow through its environment smoothly, to live and integrate in its society like a fish lives in water, according to Mao. Thus, doomsday will be upon ISIS as the water turns against the fish! As of today, attempts are being made to repeat the Sunni Awakening movement to turn Sunni society – which has embraced ISIS – upside down. These efforts are facing numerous difficulties, but their success will be possible if it achieves the integration and absorption of the Sunnis politically. This would provide them with the guarantees necessary to reassure them, which would overpower the bitter reality of the previous decades.

When some states saw al-Julani's flexibility and moderateness, they co-operated with him. They supported him with money and weapons to the same extent as they had supported the other Syrian factions, indirectly, but while still ensuring that their assistance was reaching him. Some countries formed a sort of alliance with al-Qaeda in the Arabian Peninsula, especially in its Yemeni branch, which it battling the Houthis. Al-Nusra announced that it would not target the West, and that it implemented a "national jihad" instead of an international jihad. The *New York Review of Books* drew upon these de-velopments in its June 15, 2015 article entitled, "Why We Need Al-Qaeda." It concluded the article by stating, "In the months ahead, we should not be surprised if formal talks between al-Qaeda and these Arab states begin."

Yaroslav Trofimov wrote a similar report in the *Wall Street Journal* on June 11, 2015 entitled, "To U.S. Allies, Al Qaeda Affiliate in Syria Becomes the Lesser Evil." In the article, he stated that calls for the U.S and its allies to move closer to al-Nusra are increasing. He added that some of the United State's allies, as well as Western political figures, believe that the Syrian branch of al-Qaeda should be wooed and not bombed, and that moving closer to al-Nusra is more pragmatic and thus the only logical choice for the interna-tional community.

Supporters of this method believe that proof of the plan's pragmatism is that al-Nusra does not target Israel, despite the fact that it controls villages on its borders, along with other reasons they believe reflect its practical method.

On the other hand, attributed to General James G. Stavridis, fleet com-mander of the U.S Navy, the United States would not object if it's allies work with al-Nusra. This is because the United States had previously allied with those it strongly opposes, such as Stalin during the Second World War.

It may be that the trend heading towards assimilating these jihadists through a well-studied plan is better and more effective than fighting them.

In conclusion, yes, the jihadist movements have become a "congregation of the desperate." They are despairing of all of us, and if we do not assimilate them, they will become more desperate, and will then be filled with more contempt and hatred towards us. The more their desperation increases, the more their radicalism grows. The matter will lead them to do what they wish, and what rids them of all of us, including those who love Islam, and those who hate it. It is better to search for a perfect way to assimilate them. And if you were to ask me what this perfect way was, I will answer to you disappointedly, that I simply do not know!

I do not think that the Islamic State will remain or be able to achieve its slogan of "remaining and expanding." However, I think that eliminating it will not achieve security, peace, and stability. Yes, perhaps the Islamic State in Iraq and Syria will be brought down, but then where will these thousands of fighters go, and what will we do with them? Will we kill hundreds of thousands? After Tora Bora, Bin Laden was accompanied by about 1,000 mujahideen. Now, al-Baghdadi is supported by hundreds of thousands, and the rule states that each mujahed creates 100 mujaheds over the course of ten years. This means that the next wave will include millions of jihadists!

CPSIA information can be obtained
at www.ICGtesting.com
Printed in the USA
LVOW10s1606060417
529881LV00022B/456/P